EFFECTIVE CLASSROOM TEAMWORK

New teams are emerging in classrooms: remedial teachers are now called support teachers, and they now work alongside classteachers; parents are working in classrooms; welfare assistants are helping children with special educational needs in class. It has been assumed that these teams must be for the good, but this book, the product of a decade of research, shows that this attitude is at best simplistic, and at worst damaging to effective classroom practice. When extra adults move into the private domain of the classteacher, all kinds of stresses and tensions emerge – individuals have different ideas of what they should be doing, and of what education is about. Ambiguity and ambivalence can destroy working relationships, and instead of helping, these 'supporting' adults may be hindering effective teaching and learning.

Gary Thomas looks in detail at these new teams and offers advice on how they may be helped to work more effectively. He draws on lessons learned from teamwork in other situations, such as industry, and from his own experiences as a support teacher. He also reports on interviews with team participants in which they talk candidly about their difficulties. Picking out key areas for concern, including inadequate role definition, poor communication and status barriers, he outlines strategies for dealing with these stresses and tensions in teamwork. The book will be of interest to all who work in classroom teams, all who are involved in classroom support, and those who are interested in the dynamics of groups and management in education.

Gary Thomas is a Senior Lecturer at Oxford Polytechnic and has taught in primary and secondary schools. He has worked as an educational psychologist in Manchester, and, from University College London, as a staff tutor to two psychological services. He has jointly edited two other books, *Planning for Special Needs* and *Tackling Learning Difficulties*.

EFFECTIVE CLASSROOM TEAMWORK

Support or Intrusion?

Gary Thomas

London and New York

First published in 1992
by Routledge
11 New Fetter Lane, London EC4P 4EE

Simultaneously published in the USA and Canada
by Routledge
a division of Routledge, Chapman and Hall, Inc.
29 West 35th Street, New York, NY 10001

© 1992 Gary Thomas

Typeset in Baskerville by
NWL Editorial Services, Langport, Somerset

Printed in Great Britain by
Biddles Ltd, Guildford and King's Lynn

British Library Cataloguing in Publication Data
A catalogue record for this book is available from the British Library.
ISBN 0–415–08048–7
ISBN 0–415–08049–5

Library of Congress Cataloging in Publication Data
Thomas, Gary, 1950–
Effective classroom teamwork: support or intrusion? / Gary Thomas.
p. cm.
Includes bibliographical references and index.
ISBN 0-415-08048-7. – ISBN 0-415-08049-5 (pbk.)
1. Teaching teams – United States. 2. Master teachers – United states
I. Title.
LB1029.T4T48 1992   91–45960
371.1é48 – dc20   CIP

For Kate and Emily

CONTENTS

FIGURES

TABLES

PREFACE

I became interested in classroom teams when I realised that although these teams were springing up all over the place, no one seemed to be paying much attention to them as groups of people. People behave very differently when they are in a group, even a small group. It seemed to me that the great benefits being claimed for parental involvement or classroom support could be neutralised by the tensions which might arise in these groups.

All sorts of trends encouraged schools to welcome extra adults into classrooms, but no one seemed to have given very much thought to the changes which might occur when extra people move into the domain of the teacher. There seems to have been the assumption that these people would effortlessly and seamlessly slide into the classroom to work alongside the classteacher; that simply to provide 'help' for the teacher would automatically be a Good Thing. Unfortunately, it isn't: often it can be a burden rather than a help. Teachers have enough battles to fight without additional burdens. It seemed to me that the question of classroom teams was one which was worthy of research, if by researching it those burdens could in any way be lightened.

This book represents a summary of my attempts over the last few years to look into classroom teams. But the more I have looked at the question, the more complex it has seemed to become. In trying to make sense of this complexity, I have used some ideas and theories which readers who are looking simply for practical advice may find unfamiliar and initially off-putting. (For this reason I have given what I hope is a user-friendly glossary of some of the terms I use which may seem particularly foreign.) My reason for using these theories is that they have helped me to understand what is going on in these teams. I hope that by doing this my reflections are the more keen and my conclusions are all the more practical.

Throughout, I have concentrated on the team rather than the individuals who comprise it. However, I realise that some readers will be more interested in what I have to say about those individuals – support teachers, parents, ancillaries, welfare assistants – than about the team as such. I hope that for these readers the book will prove to contain much that is of interest. For instance, those who are interested in support teachers may be particularly interested in the diary of my experiences as a support teacher (chapter 10) and in my interviews with support teachers (chapter 9).

The general message of the book, though, is that there is nothing peculiar about the tensions which particular groups of people feel in any kind of classroom team. Those tensions, whether they be felt by the host teacher, by a visiting peripatetic teacher, by parents or welfare assistants, are general to classroom teams. More than this, they are general to teams of whatever kind. I hope that I have been able to come to conclusions which are of relevance to all who find themselves in teams.

One last apology: non-sexist language. I've tried to use it but at times it can be rather cumbersome. I hope I will be forgiven for occasionally presuming that the classroom team member is female. This is for no better reason than the fact that the great majority of those whom I have met have been female. (Some 97 per cent of the parents working in classrooms are mothers.)

ACKNOWLEDGEMENTS

I should like to thank Sarah Tann and Stephen Fearnley for looking through drafts of this work and for their many invaluable comments and ideas and for their encouragement.

Thanks are due to the large numbers of teachers and headteachers who gave their time to assist the research, in particular those anonymous individuals who partook in interviews and suffered my presence in their classes.

I am indebted to the editor of *Educational Research* for permission to reprint parts of chapters 7, 8 and 13, which first appeared in that journal.

I would also like to thank Helen Fairlie and her colleagues at Routledge for all their support and encouragement.

1

THE NEW CLASSROOM TEAMS

Good teamwork is notoriously difficult to achieve. In industry, an enormous research effort on the workings of teams attests to the truth of this fact.

In education, also, the difficulty in making teams effective is conspicuous. The demise of team teaching provides ample evidence of the problems of teamwork. Team teaching began in the late 1960s with high hopes of success. It has, however, failed. Many studies, both in the UK and in the United States, have shown that only a fragment of the original team teaching edifice remains. It appears that teamwork in classrooms is more difficult to achieve than many had anticipated.

Indeed, looking at the history of teams in classrooms one could quite justifiably claim that classrooms provide an especially uncongenial environment for teamwork. Despite this, classroom teams have formed the subject of surprisingly little research.

The issue of effective teamwork in classrooms is more important now than it has ever been. Although team teaching may have had its heyday, a new kind of classroom team is emerging. The new teams are more widespread and more varied than those which arose from the move to team teaching. The new teams are generated principally from two main trends: the trend to integration of children with special needs, and the trend to parental involvement. The former results in personnel formerly associated with special settings (special schools, withdrawal rooms, etc.), moving to the mainstream classroom to work alongside the classteacher. The latter results in far greater numbers of parents working in the classroom than would ever have been the case previously.

Team teaching meant, of course, teams of teachers, and was often in response to a coordinated programme of introduction. But the new teams are emerging not in response to an ideal about teamworking. Instead, their emergence is in response to unrelated trends which in themselves are unconcerned with teamwork. Unlike team teaching teams they will comprise participants from very different backgrounds, with different ideologies, skills and interests.

The very diversity and instability of these classroom teams make them and their members especially vulnerable to the tensions and stresses which threaten the effectiveness of groups elsewhere.

The people comprising these new groups probably fail to recognise themselves as teams. Their reasons for existing have nothing to do with the benefits which are brought by working as a team. They are none the less teams, and as such they are characterised by the same stresses that mark teamwork in any other kind of setting.

The fact that the 'teamness' of these new teams is unrecognised – or at least unremarked upon – means that they stand even less chance of surviving than did the team teaching teams of the 1960s and the 1970s. The latter at least had the dynamics of the team as a central question to be addressed. It would be a pity if the new teams atrophied in the way that team teaching atrophied due to inadequate attention to the working of the team. If that happened, it would mean that the ideals behind the new developments – parental participation and the integration of children with special needs – would be rejected, and worse, rejected for the wrong reasons. Teams can be made to work, but team members need first, to recognise that they are part of a team, and second, to employ strategies which will maximise their chances of success.

In order to devise those strategies, it is necessary to examine the dynamics which so often seem to be responsible for the attrition of teamwork.

This book will argue the case that the new collections of people in classrooms are, in every sense, teams. It will provide documentary evidence for the existence of the new teams. It will examine the dynamics of teams generally. It will provide case study data about the kinds of tensions which exist in the new teams. It will provide a model for analysing 'team personalities', and it will provide guidelines for the effective working of classroom teams.

CHANGES IN THINKING WHICH GIVE RISE TO THE NEW TEAMS

Over the decade 1980–90, many adults moved into the classroom to work alongside the classteacher. The new teams have emerged by stealth, almost unnoticed. There was no fanfare, no top-down initiative which inspired the creation of these new teams, as there had been for team teaching.

Rather, there were a number of discrete and separate changes in educational thinking which gave rise to the new teams. Two have been of overriding importance:

1 the idea that children with special needs should be integrated into mainstream schools; and

2

2 the idea that parents have a central place in their children's education – including full involvement in their children's schools.

Both of these trends have, as I shall show, brought extra adults into classrooms. The picture of classrooms containing two, three or even more adults working together, represents a major departure from the stereotype of the classroom (one adult to one class) which the public probably holds.

The effects of these trends are exaggerated by other wider social developments to result in an unprecedented influx of additional people to many classrooms. However, the ways in which this influx alters the working environment of the classroom have remained unexamined. As I indicate in the remainder of this chapter, there is widespread recognition among researchers, observers and commentators that analysis of this alteration is necessary.

EXTRA PEOPLE DUE TO INTEGRATION

Fundamental changes have taken place in schools due to the move to integration over the last ten years or so. Calls for the integration of disabled people into society generally have been responded to in education and have been legitimised in this country by the report of the Warnock Committee (Department of Education and Science 1978) and by the 1981 Education Act. While integration has not occurred to the extent that some would have wished, calls for integration have given rise to a number of changes in the way in which services for those children who are experiencing difficulty are organised.

There are a number of trends within the integration movement, all of which result in the movement of additional adults into the classroom:

1 *Peripatetic teachers* are beginning to provide help for these children by working alongside the classteacher in the classroom, rather than by withdrawing children, a practice which may isolate and stigmatise the children who are withdrawn.
2 It is becoming increasingly common to find that local education authorities are, rather than placing children with special needs in special schools, seeking to make special arrangements for those children in ordinary schools; in practice, these arrangements often include the allocation of an *ancillary helper* to work with a child in his/her classroom for a set period of time in a week. Allied to this is the developing practice in some LEAs of providing *welfare assistant* time for children whose special needs are 'statemented' under the 1981 Education Act and who are attending ordinary schools. This looks set to increase with the 1988 Education Act and its provisions for exclusion from the National Curriculum.
3 A resource-based approach to special needs in secondary and middle

schools has seen a transfer of resources and personnel from remedial departments to the mainstream of the school. In practice, this has resulted in a change from systems of withdrawal to a range of new team teaching arrangements; in these new arrangements, *remedial teachers* are working alongside mainstream colleagues and are now often designated *support teachers*.

4 In some LEAs, 'outreach' schemes are enabling the devolution of the skills of special school teachers (who remain on the special school staff) to mainstream classrooms.

5 Similar kinds of developments, with teachers seeking to work collaboratively, are occurring in other, related areas. For instance, in the teaching of children for whom English is a second language, the Bullock Report comments:

> We are wholly in favour of a move away from E2L provision being made on a withdrawal basis (p. 392) [and] in secondary schools we believe that pupils with E2L needs should be regarded as the responsibility of all teachers.
>
> (Department of Education and Science 1975: 394)

The move to integrate children with special needs from special to ordinary schools means, therefore, that many of the staff who had been working with children in special schools, special units or other special settings within the ordinary school may now be deployed to work in the mainstream class alongside the classteacher. Many of those practices, which lay at the backbone of special needs provision in ordinary schools (e.g. withdrawal for remedial work) and which were also segregating in their effects, are being replaced by practices which involve specialist staff going into the mainstream classroom to work alongside the classteacher.

Despite the general accord with which this move has been received, there have been suggestions that without proper organisation integration may not result in the benefits which were envisaged (e.g. Hodgson, Clunies-Ross and Hegarty 1984 in research conducted by the NFER; Strain and Kerr 1981 in a large-scale American review of the effects of integration). The success of integration hinges on the effective assimilation into mainstream education of special sector personnel and resources: in some cases it may be possible to meet special needs through the provision of equipment or through adaptation of the physical environment. By contrast, the assimilation of *human resources* from special settings is infinitely more complex and more problematic.

EXTRA PEOPLE DUE TO PARENTAL INVOLVEMENT

Running parallel with moves due to integration is another major trend which results in additional people moving into the classroom to work alongside the classteacher. The parental involvement movement has gained increasing momentum over recent years and has been accompanied by a vigorous debate over the role of parents in the school. The concern of teachers' unions, for instance, centres on the implications for the teacher's status and on effects on staffing levels, with parents perhaps supplanting paid ancillary help; surveys by trade unions show that in some areas of the country as many as fifty parents a week have been working in some schools (Caudrey 1985). It appears that the debate is being won by those who favour involvement, and teachers' unions seem to have re-examined their policies on the issue.

Despite the enthusiasm for parental involvement, research is beginning to support the notion that in its own right such involvement may not provide the unqualified benefits which some presume for it: Atkin and Bastiani (1985), for example, examining the effects of the very rapid movement of parents into primary schools, feel that teachers need special training to work effectively with other adults in the classroom – training which, they say, is conspicuously lacking from the curricula of most teacher-training establishments. Stierer (1985) finds that to make parental involvement a success may involve the teacher in substantially more work.

OTHER TRENDS TENDING TO INCREASE ADULT PARTICIPATION

Wider social trends may exaggerate the effects of these changes and the problems that accompany them. The influence of technology on the economy and ultimately on the school is a case in point. At its simplest level this might find its translation into practice through young people on training schemes being placed to work in a school.

Some argue (for example Cohen, Meyer, Scott and Deal 1979; Miskel, McDonald and Bloom 1983) that the activities of people in school become more complex as the technological environment surrounding them becomes more complex. They argue that technology facilitates the appropriation of complex skills from professionals; they assert that this enables a loosening of professional constraints in such a way that potential participants in the classroom may be able to participate with fewer inhibitions than they would have experienced ten or even five years ago.

GENERAL ISSUES CONCERNING THE INFLUX OF ADDITIONAL ADULTS

The developments concerned with integration (and the integration of 'special' personnel), with parental involvement and with other moves result in radically altered classroom dynamics. If Doyle (1977) is correct in seeing the classroom as a fragile ecosystem in which the alteration of even minor variables may have profound effects, the effect of introducing another adult participant is, of itself, worthy of study.

However, little attention has been paid in this country to the means by which additional people in the classroom may work together to the best possible effect. By contrast, in the USA, where the enactment of Public Law 94–142 (the Education for all Handicapped Children Act) pre-dated the 1981 Education Act by some six years, studies noting the effects of moves to integration in terms of the transfer of personnel from specialised settings to mainstream settings have been commissioned. DeVault, Harnischfeger and Wiley (1977), for instance, looked into the effects of personnel allocations to the various Project Follow-Through curricula. They make the observation that little if any attention has been paid to the question of how best to deploy additional personnel. They state:

> It is high time to investigate this question. If we staff typical-sized classrooms with up to four full time instructional adults then we [had] better find out how to use them most effectively, as the educational costs are surely high.
>
> (DeVault, Harnischfeger and Wiley 1977: 47)

Despite such clearly articulated recognition of the need for analysis in this area, little systematic investigation has been undertaken. Neither has there been any examination of the extent of the trends as a whole or the issues which arise from their introduction, despite the manifest coherence of a set of problems which appear to exist irrespective of the nature of professional groupings of the individuals concerned.

One of the assumptions of this book is that the influx of very varied groups of people is accompanied by problems which are general to the teams thus constituted, irrespective of the nature of the participants. The uncertainties engendered by these moves carry with them a host of questions which none of those groups has had the chance to formulate coherently, let alone address or resolve. An assumption throughout will be that despite the diversity of the groups of people moving into classrooms, they are homogeneous at least to the extent that such questions exist for them.

Although these questions have not been addressed in education, substantial amounts of work have been done in other areas, notably in industry, on the working of task-oriented groups. While much of this work is relevant here, classrooms – in contrast to factories – present an environment populated with diverse inhabitants and governed by loosely formulated rules. These make the setting and the interpersonal connections more complex than those found in industry. In terms of the definition of the task to be done in the classroom, and of the nature of the rules in the environment, markedly different expectations exist between schools and the environments in which most work on group dynamics has been undertaken. These classroom teams therefore offer unique dynamics for study.

In the chapter that follows I shall look at the dynamics of teams and the special dynamics of classroom teams.

2

THE DYNAMICS OF TEAMS

In this chapter I shall look at teamwork research which has its origins in all kinds of different environments – the factory shop-floor, the hospital, the management group. In delving through this research, I shall be seeking insights into the working of classroom teams. What are the stresses which characteristically afflict teams? How do these teams overcome these stresses and manage to work more effectively? And how relevant for the classroom team are the findings made in these other kinds of team environment?

Teamwork research identifies a number of factors which determine the success or failure of teamwork: quality of leadership; role definition and role ambiguity; the nature of the task to be undertaken; the mix of team members; the ease with which team members can communicate.

But the problems of teams seem to be centrally located in not knowing (or agreeing about) what you are supposed to be doing, or having conflicting demands on your effort, time or loyalty. Individuals' uncertainties about their roles in teams have formed a central position in small group and organisational research. With this in mind, classroom teams are off to a bad start: they are – for the best of reasons – loosely formulated with tacitly held pedagogic or humanistic aims rather than tightly formulated goals. The culture of schools, and particularly primary schools, does not lend itself to clear role definition, seemingly so important for good teamwork.

I shall look at some of the explanations that have been proposed for the success or failure of teamwork in different kinds of settings, having in mind all the time the relevance of these explanations for the classroom setting. I intend to look at the dynamics of teams and especially at the notion of *role*, which forms a central place in teamwork research. Various models for making groups more effective – such as quality circles and semi-autonomous work groups – will also be examined for their relevance to the classroom.

INQUIRY INTO THE PHENOMENON OF
ADULT TEAMS IN CLASSROOMS

Although schools conspicuously operate as social institutions, very little attention has been paid to the working of adults together in those institutions. Partly, this is because schools have traditionally operated as a collection of working units (namely, classrooms) which have functioned strictly as the working domain of one person. This very isolation has led to the concerns of educational research and evaluation being centred on the solitary teacher and her class of children.

If social psychology has ever concerned itself with classrooms its interest has been among the children and the ways that groups of children work and interrelate with the teacher. If management and teaming issues have been examined it has customarily happened at the school level, for it is only here that several adults exist working together as a unit. Since the received wisdom has been that teachers work on their own with their classes, analysis has ostensibly needed to go no further.

Even where people have begun to work together in the classroom, as for instance in the case of team teaching, it has been assumed that the 'team' in question is too small a phenomenon to be worthy of interest in itself. Alternatively, the functioning of the people working together was taken to be a matter subordinate in importance to certain pedagogic matters, and generally unworthy of concern. There may also have been the feeling that professionals working together would be unfettered by the kinds of unwelcome baggage that appeared to accompany teamwork in other settings.

The literature, however, to be examined in this and the next chapter indicates that such simplistic assumptions are unfounded. Teamwork in classrooms experiences as many problems as it does anywhere else. Indeed, the very diversity and instability of these classroom teams make them and their members particularly susceptible to the kinds of tensions and stresses that threaten the effectiveness of groups elsewhere.

There are other important reasons for the fact that education has disregarded the topic of adults working together in the classroom. The dearth of research into this area stems partly from the research tradition of education and the research tools which education uses. The legacy that psychology has made to education, as I have suggested elsewhere (Thomas 1985), has been one of singularity. Events are stripped of their contexts and examined in isolation, as they would be in a laboratory. The wider whole has tended to remain unexamined.

The place of teamwork in mainstreaming is a good case in point. The trend to integrate children with special needs into ordinary schools has been accompanied, as will be discussed fully in the following chapter, by a move of personnel and expertise from special classes to mainstream classes. Rather than examining this latter move in such a way that help can be effectively delivered to such children in the new settings, concern has tended to remain on methods of teaching the individual child in the integrated setting.

Psychologists have perhaps felt less comfortable researching the interpersonal variables of the team of adults delivering help than investigating the individual learning difficulties of those who are most manifestly their clients – the children. Particularly where children with special needs are concerned the analysis of the workings of the classroom has typically been seen by traditional educational psychology as peripheral to an understanding – or diagnosis – of the individual child's problem and a remediation programme – or treatment – for it. The focus in defining need has been individual-centred rather than situation-centred. Classrooms have been viewed as inert modules whose constituent parts, if they do interrelate, do so only in order irritatingly to occlude the mechanism of programmes of help which psychologists have so carefully worked out.

A FRAMEWORK FOR ANALYSING GROUPS: THE KRECH MODEL

A number of recurring themes dominate literature on the effectiveness of people working together in groups. A useful framework for describing the variables influencing such effectiveness was attempted by Krech, Crutchfield and Ballachey (1962). They note that there are first of all a number of situational features which exist when a group is established. Calling these the independent variables of group effectiveness, they go on to suggest that these can further be subdivided into: structural variables, such as the size of the group, the status hierarchy, members' skills and the heterogeneity of members; task variables such as the nature of the task and its difficulty; and contextual variables such as the physical setting, the group's place in the larger organisation and relations with other groups.

The effectiveness of the group is not determined solely by these variables however, but rather by a set of 'emergent group processes' which in turn are dependent upon the interrelation of these 'givens'. Thus, whatever the original status hierarchy, an actual hierarchy will evolve; however the formal communications are organised, an actual pattern will emerge. These emergent processes will involve variations in roles, motivation and group cohesiveness to determine the group's mode of operation and its effectiveness. The model is shown in Figure 2.1.

This model (henceforth called the Krech model) succinctly encapsulates some of the most important features of group effectiveness. Its relevance to classroom groups (as well as industrial or commercial groups, about which it was primarily framed) is manifest.

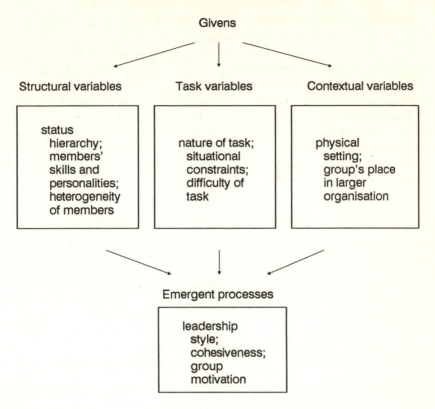

Figure 2.1 The Krech model

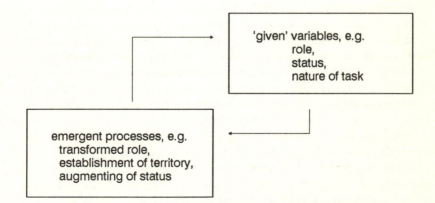

Figure 2.2 The underpinning framework derived from
the Krech model

11

The Krech model suggests a particular kind of team dynamic. It suggests that a team's behaviour *develops* – it is not simply laid out at the outset, forever after to remain unchanged. This seems a particularly appropriate model for viewing the behaviour of classroom teams: in these teams, as I shall show, nothing very much is 'given' at the outset anyway. Roles have to develop, but they may develop in helpful or unhelpful ways.

The model suggests ideas which lay the foundation of the work in this book. I look at the ways in which people form their roles in classroom teams and I pay particular attention to the developmental nature of that process. Thus, the framework underpinning this exploration might be drawn as in figure 2.2.

ROLE – A KEY NOTION IN TEAMWORK

Turner makes explicit what is only implied in the Krech model:

> Role 'exists' in varying degrees of concreteness and consistency, while the individual confidently frames his behaviour as if they had unequivocal existence and clarity. The result is that in attempting from time to time to make aspects of the role explicit he is creating and modifying roles as well as merely bringing them to light; the process is not only role-taking but role-making.
> (Turner 1952, cited by Olesen and Whittaker 1970: 383)

Role is the key notion to be explored in this book. The concept of role has been called the building block of the understanding of social systems (Kahn, Wolfe, Quinn, Snoeck and Rosenthal 1964). As I shall show, the notion has been widely used in a variety of situations and it has achieved some currency as a useful concept in understanding social systems. However, in classroom teams it is at best problematic and at worst downright impossible to discover how roles are formulated.

Role is viewed here both as a 'given' and as an emergent process. The tensions and dynamics that structure it will be examined. In the literature it is discussed frequently in terms of *definition* or *clarity*, and *ambiguity*. Lack of definition or presence of ambiguity is often reported to result in *stress*. These ideas and their contribution to the development of notions about classroom teams will be discussed here.

Although Linton (1945), in a classic account, used the term 'role' to mean the *required* behaviour of someone in a given position (placing it firmly as a 'given'), it has now come to be used in a rather broader way. For instance, Hargreaves (1972) used it to mean the *expected* response of persons occupying a particular position. Often roles are loosely defined, and this will be particularly so in the informal teams of classrooms. People may be able to choose among various elements of a role and fashion it to their own inclinations.

12

Individuals' uncertainties about their roles and the effects these have on their behaviour have formed a central position in small group and organisational research. Looking at role in education, Hargreaves (1972) identifies six basic varieties of role conflict or strain:

1 *Occupancy of two or more positions whose roles are incompatible.* The union representative who has to maintain loyalties both to the union and the management, is an example.
2 *Disagreement among occupants of a position about the content of a role.* Personal and social objectives may be valued by one teacher, while another values academic achievement; these conflicting roles will lead to different ideas about the role to be fulfilled.
3 *Disagreement among occupants of a complementary position B about the content of position A's role.* Working-class parents, for instance, may differ from middle-class parents in their expectations of teachers.
4 *Disagreement between role partners about the definition of one or other role.* A parent may have a different view from the teacher about what constitutes a teacher's responsibility.
5 *Different role partners have conflicting expectations of a third party.* A teacher operating in a team provides a good example here. She may have to satisfy a parent that she is meeting the parent's expectations; to satisfy an ancillary helper that she is not undermining the paid assistant's role; and the headteacher and the rest of the staff that their expectations in terms of educational goals are being met.
6 *A single role partner has conflicting expectations of another.* A parent, for instance, may expect that a teacher be both gentle and strict.

These are all examples of conflict arising from different sets of expectations. Stress may also arise simply because roles are not well defined, or because an individual is unsure about appropriate behaviour (role definition; role ambiguity).

However, the conflicts arising from differing expectations are clearly more problematic and will form a central focus of the qualitative aspects of the studies comprising the latter part of this book. I shall attempt to show how, because of differences in various kinds of expectation, those originally defined roles undergo a process of transformation in such a way that conflict is diminished.

Insufficient work has been undertaken on the ways in which individuals go about managing such role conflict. Making an overview of the topic, Stephenson (1978) reports that personality differences seem to be significant: some individuals may give way to those who seem to yield most power, or to those whose pressures seem most legitimate. There may thus be transformations in interpretations of individuals' own roles or about the status of self or others in relation to these.

Role conflict and role ambiguity and their influence in producing stress have been much discussed in areas outside education (e.g. Kahn *et al.* 1964). Communication and its dependence on organisational structure and climate (e.g. Bate 1984; Likert 1961), and notions such as job enrichment (e.g. Paul, Robertson and Herzberg 1969) have proved to be important avenues for research into the effectiveness of groups. Knight (1983) identifies a number of contemporary management issues: who takes responsibility for what decisions (role conflict)? How far does personal discretion go in the interpretation of one's role (role ambiguity), and should work become more specialised or more general (job enrichment)?

Firth (1983) in reviewing case studies from her own experience as an occupational psychologist, suggests that it is a combination of these various constructs which contribute to the experience of uncertainty. She suggests that stress at work is caused by a number of types of ambiguity which include role ambiguity, inadequate feedback and uncertainty in relationships. Drucker (1985) adds another dimension relevant to the classroom: he says that the success of a team depends on the successful matching of person to task with an understanding of the requirements of the task to be done and the strengths and weaknesses of the person.

Clearly in the *ad hoc* arrangements which often develop in the classroom, such matching is missing. The arrangements that emerge do so as much out of expediency as any other reason: Ferguson and Adams (1982) showed that invariably there is no analysis of the task to be done in support teaching, and were the task to be analysed, the support teacher would not be the person to be doing it.

Interestingly, Adair (1986) adds to the discussion with the notion of 'role underload' that may occur when individuals are given roles that fall far short of their self-concept. This may be particularly relevant for support teachers, where the new role may involve them in much work which is subsidiary to that of the mainstream teacher.

Despite the impression given by Knight (above) that not very much has changed in research on work groups, there have recently been some critical accounts of the traditional perspective. Van Sell, Brief and Schuler (1981), for instance, in reviewing a wide range of research on these topics, reveal that there are numerous omissions in the role conflict and role ambiguity research as well as numerous conflicting and unresolved findings. They criticise research in the area as adopting designs that do not allow for causal relationships to be established: 'quasiexperimental, longitudinal and experimental designs are scarce'. They might have added qualitative designs to this list.

Furthermore, research designs in the area were insufficiently sophisticated to offer insight into the antecedents and outcomes associated with these concepts. Examining more complex relationships would require, these authors say, multivariate and longitudinal designs. They suggest that very few conclusions can be drawn from the research.

Of the conclusions that can be drawn, the most important are that first, role conflict and role ambiguity appear to cause tension, dissatisfaction and distancing from the work group, and second, that they are a function of an interaction between job content, leader behaviour and organisational structure. I shall explore this notion of interaction as a key 'emergent process' in the rest of this chapter and the presentation of notions such as 'leader behaviour' as unproblematic. Qualitative research appears to show that notions such as 'leader behaviour' and 'support' *are* problematic: they inhere in that 'interaction' and are not separable from it.

Making a more general review of the status of the area of role conflict and role ambiguity, Glowinkowsi and Cooper (1985) set the concepts within the larger context of 'organisational stress research'. They conclude that there are five main sources of organisational stress, banding together role ambiguity, role conflict and responsibility for others as one of the major sources of stress and calling this 'role-based stress'. Other sources identified are: factors intrinsic to the job such as overload and time pressures; relationships with colleagues and superiors; organisational structure and climate. Support from team colleagues can reduce stress, they say, and this is more important than support from superiors or family.

Looking at this suggestion through the 'overlay' of the Krech model, the nature of this support is embedded in the quality of the 'emergent processes' which arise from the mixing of variables. I do not view 'support' as a property that people give depending upon their generosity (which is an implication which might be drawn from Glowinkowski and Cooper's account) but rather as a process that emerges from an interplay of forces.

Clearly such support is less likely in the loose, informal, constantly varying groups found in classrooms than in the more stable groups associated with industrial processes. The very instability of the former may account for the problems which will be noted and analysed in the following chapter.

Trendall (1989), in looking at stress in teachers, repeats many of these findings, and reiterates the issues and arguments. He sees stress in teachers as centrally related to role conflict and role overload. Teachers are often uncertain about an appropriate course of action because of the many roles in which they are cast.

Trendall suggests that stress can be reduced through organisational changes, by improving relationships or by clarifying goals. In order to avoid stress, Trendall finds a need for full staff involvement in decision making, and that 'many teachers feel inadequate or inexperienced in "people management"'.

Disappointingly, these last findings are not discussed further. They appear to reveal that no simple associations can be made between stress and the independent variables of Krech's model. Rather, stress is linked

15

with opportunity to talk. But Trendall seems to construe resolution of stress via the latter almost in terms of availability and good fortune, rather than in terms of a complex toing-and-froing among participants which depends upon factors such as their ideological similarity and shared understandings about the difficulties which are faced. In short, this and other research in the same mould view the parameters within which the classroom team situation is framed as fairly rigid 'givens'. There is rarely the suggestion that meaning among the participants is generated from the very social interaction of the team, from the quality of the emergent process.

THE EMERGENT PROCESS: GROUP CULTURE

It is in this interaction – in the toing-and-froing to which I relate in the last paragraph – that Krech's emergent process is located. Explorations of such interactive processes are perhaps best achieved through qualitative research, and this is attempted by Bate (1984) in his examination of group culture.

Bate sees many of the problems of teaming as related to the organisational culture within which teams operate. He believes that through their own shared beliefs and consensual understandings, people create their own culture (or emergent process, in the Krech model), which is receptive to new practice or antagonistic to it. While conventional wisdom says that people can adapt to new situations if the conditions are right, Bate's interactionist perspective takes him to the position that people actually collude in a process which removes all possibility of a resolution to their problems:

> people in organisations evolve in their daily interactions with one another a system of shared perspectives or collectively held and sanctioned definitions of the situation which make up the culture of these organisations. The culture, once established, prescribes for its creators and inheritors certain ways of believing, thinking and acting which in some circumstances can prevent meaningful interaction and induce a condition of 'learned helplessness'.
>
> (Bate 1984: 44)

I take issue with Bate's inference that this process removes all possibility of the resolution of problems. The view I take is that such processes indeed exist but take different forms, at times resulting in the learned helplessness of which Bate writes, but at other times resulting in the kind of synergy hoped for in teamwork. In whatever way these emergent processes take form, though, they always serve the purpose of reducing uncertainty. If the process results in this kind of learned helplessness, such a condition nevertheless serves the purpose of enabling group members to externalise in some way the reasons for their difficulties and thus reduce their own tension.

Bate's conclusions come from being a participant observer in three large industrial concerns where he made extensive tape recordings of individual interviews and of work meetings. From these he identified aspects of each culture that had a strong impact on organisational problem-solving. One of these 'root constructs', as he calls them, *unemotionality*, throws some light on the difficulty of groups openly to discuss the ways in which they will work on the problems they confront. Differences between people, he says, tend to be repressed, to smoulder on, or are dealt with unsatisfactorily at a distance. Different ideas on ways of working are played down out of a sense that it would be impolite, embarrassing or just 'plain useless' to do otherwise.

If the inhibitions to which Bate refers are common to work-teams it would be unlikely if similar inhibitions were not to arise in classroom work-teams, though in the latter such issues have received scant attention, if any. The problems in communicating ideas and resolving differences are clearly formidable; in industry the acknowledgment of the problem is manifested in the development of ideas such as the semi-autonomous work group, or quality circles, which will be examined later in this chapter.

Bate acknowledges the need to seek resolution of some of these problems, though he clearly views roles existing not so much as pre-existing variables, in the way that Krech *et al.* have done, but arising out of shared understandings.

Goffman's (1969) position is similar; the process of coming to terms with a set of different understandings is central to his analysis and is perhaps analogous with Krech's emergent process stage. For Goffman, what is laid down at the outset is far less important than this emerging consensus. Indeed, actors may seek to detach themselves from roles by using certain strategies. Goffman says that they may try to disqualify some of the 'expressive features of the situation as sources of definition of themselves' by explanations, apologies and joking. He calls this 'role-distancing'.

In this book, I shall attempt to discover the ways in which 'actors' in classroom teams, faced with these conflicts, attempt a variety of strategies, including such distancing, to resolve conflict.

PEOPLE WORKING IN GROUPS

Teams are groups of people who share a purpose. It may be valuable therefore to look briefly at research into groups to see how the dynamics of groups may be harnessed.

The functioning of various kinds of small work groups which maintain high participant motivation has been examined in detail after the stimulus

17

of the work of Likert (1961) and others in the early 1960s. Relating the success of groups far more than Goffman to the Krech model's 'givens', Likert suggested that

> the form of organisation which will make the greatest use of human capacity consists of highly effective work groups linked together in an overlapping pattern by other similarly effective groups.
>
> (Likert 1961)

He asserted that the nature of highly effective groups rests on factors such as leadership skill, interpersonal relations, shared goals and problem-solving occurring in a sharing, supporting atmosphere. In saying that 'there is nothing implicitly good or bad, weak or strong, about a group', Likert seems to be saying that given the right conditions and the right stimulus, teams can be made to work effectively.

In noting that there is great variation in the ways in which groups perform, Hackman and Oldham make the same point. They note that an individual may well do a task better than a group (a fact which is discussed in chapter 3); a group is only likely to be better if the task and the team are 'well designed'. Furthermore, it has to be feasible to create well-designed work groups given the nature of the work and its organisation and where it is to be done. Success also depends on whether the group is well supported and well managed. Again, the notion that these variables exist separately and in an unproblematic relationship with 'support' and 'management' is evident here.

My contention is that through consensual understandings participants in the team define for themselves the nature of the support. The variables of which Likert writes provide only the larger frame within which these definitions are made.

Small work groups would seem to have a direct bearing on the educational domain and the area under study here. These groups have variously been called 'autonomous work groups' (Bucklow 1972), 'self regulating work groups' (Cummings 1978) and 'self-managing work groups' (Hackman and Oldham 1980). They are defined by Hackman and Oldham as:

> intact (if small) social systems whose members have the authority to handle internal processes as they see fit in order to generate a specific group product, service or decision.
>
> (Hackman and Oldham 1980)

Recently the literature has seen an emergence of papers on 'semi-autonomous work groups' where the interpretation of 'authority to handle internal processes' is looser; it is probably here that the closest analogy to the classroom with participating adults from a mixture of backgrounds is to be found.

It is necessary to think about teaming and the work group as these additional adults come into the classroom because whatever the specific nature of the work group, there is the question of whether a task is better fulfilled by an individual or a group. In the case of the classroom this would mean exploring whether

1 the teacher's task would be an appropriate subject for differentiation, with the expectation that teaming would follow (perhaps involving role specialisation), or
2 classroom activities were to be seen as a series of discrete functions to be fulfilled by a number of individuals working in parallel.

Hackman and Oldham, in taking a systems perspective in reviewing a range of literature usually based on in-depth studies of the introduction of small group working in large industrial organisations, note that there is great variation in how groups perform and that given the choice between a group performing a task seen as a Gestalt, or a set of individuals performing a series of unitary tasks the choice will depend on whether it is feasible to create well designed work groups given the nature of the work and the organisation; it also depends on whether the group is appropriately supported and managed.

They thus point strongly to the importance of Krech's 'givens' for the success of teamwork, implicitly suggesting that an inauspicious admixture of these at the outset will lead to role conflict. This position contrasts with that of Bate and Goffman (above) who suggest that definition of roles and the resolution of the conflicts which arise happen almost simultaneously and that the 'givens' are not definable in the way that observers such as Hackman and Oldham aver. Such a back-and-forth process of definition, reworking and simultaneous resolution of diffi- culties would certainly seem to be a more likely scenario for the classroom, where a far looser set of constraints operates than is the case in industry.

IMPLICATIONS FOR CLASSROOMS

Many of the concepts employed in groupwork research have direct relevance to schools, as teaming arrangements become more common. It is to be expected that both teachers and the additional people may feel uncomfortable as they explore unfamiliar territory and negotiate new working practices. It would be expected intuitively that the scope for role ambiguity would be great in these new teams. Where a new role displaces an existing role, one which is perhaps well established (e.g. remedial teacher to support teacher), there is the opportunity for role conflict. Where the consequences of inviting parents into the classroom have not been fully thought through and where parents have almost by default been allocated a series of repetitive, unappealing or menial tasks, the issue of job enrichment arises. Teachers are likely to experience stress by virtue of overload and time pressures which the effective involvement of additional people may ameliorate. The organisational structure of the school may be such that teaming arrangements receive little support, feedback or encouragement and, as a result, atrophy.

Cohen sums up the situation well, following a longitudinal study of teaming arrangements among 496 teachers. She concluded that teaming arrangements are extremely fragile and that 'there is little understanding by team members or administrators of the kinds of support required for its success' (Cohen 1976: 49).

A number of studies can be seen implicitly or explicitly to use the notions already reviewed ('given' role, emergent process, role definition, etc.). Woods and Cullen (1983), for instance, note the ways in which roles change even if they are defined at the outset. They start by pointing to the importance of clear role definition in looking at the effects of the role organisation system known as 'room management' (see chapters 12 and 13 for a full account of room management). They showed that room management had dramatic effects on the engagement of residents in an institution for mentally handicapped adults. But although there was this immediate initial effect, this steadily tailed off over 15 months. Further-more, it was impossible after 15 months for the researchers to determine from watching staff behaviour which of the staff were adopting which of the highly differentiated roles involved in room management procedures. They attribute this tailing off partly to lack of monitoring and support. But an alternative explanation, based on Krech's model, might be that a new set of working practices has emerged – overlaying the room management system – which serves the purpose of resolving the conflicts of the participants.

Hackman and Oldham warn that groups cannot simply be left to 'get on with it', citing evidence of the kind of 'vanishing effects' where the beneficial effects of innovative team designs eroded over time. To avoid these vanishing effects support from management is needed; 'support' includes the need for feedback, for training, for time allocated for the organisation and meeting of the group, and for training and consultative assistance. The acknowledgement that changes – emergent processes – do occur is made here, as is the acknowledgement that the provision of the 'right ingredients' in terms of initial variables is insufficient to ensure the success of the group. Embedded in the notion of 'support' is the acceptance that these transformations do occur and that these need to be monitored and shaped if the group is to work well.

As far as design of the group task is concerned, Hackman and Oldham see one major element as significant: the degree of motivation in the task. This in turn rests on a number of other factors: the variety of skills required in the task; whether the task can clearly be seen as meaningful;

the task's significance (whether it makes 'a difference'); latitude in deciding how the work is to be carried out; and the availability of reliable feedback. All these have clear implications when thinking about the work of extra people in the classroom: many of the activities given to parents and ancillaries to perform may easily become dull after a short time; they may be perceived by parents as token involvement and therefore not meaningful; there might be little discussion about how activities are to be undertaken or about how they were ultimately done.

This also applies to the support teacher, if Ferguson and Adams' view (1982, see chapter 2) is correct. A review by Gill, Menlo and Keel (1984) goes some way towards setting in the context of a framework the sort of anxieties and tensions that support teachers experience. Gill *et al.* review literature on the antecedents to participation in groups, recognising that a prime feature of the person's perception of the usefulness of group experience lies in how much s/he participates. The review identifies a number of factors as being of importance in deciding whether members collaborate effectively in small groups, factors such as how the group is run; whether there is an absence of evaluative or judgemental comments; attitudes towards the task; attitudes of other group members; group atmosphere. Clearly, in the loosely formulated groups of classrooms, these antecedents rarely exist together, if at all.

It may be difficult for such antecedents to be set up even in the more formally organised teams of team teaching schools. It is possible that the variety and diversity of the teams sits uneasily with the seemingly inherent intimacy of teaching as a task. Paisey (1981) in an analysis of questionnaire returns from more than 500 teachers and headteachers, differentiated by their placement in classteaching or team teaching schools, found no evidence for team teaching being a special source of job satisfaction. There are alternative explanations possible for this. The first, not put forward by Paisey, but indicated from the rest of this review, is that only a limited form of teaming is in fact occurring in the team teaching schools. Other studies indicate that better participation ought to occur, but for a variety of reasons does not.

The mismatch between ideal and real may be a source of dissatisfaction, though such dissatisfaction is not indicated from Paisey's research. Rather, teachers in both classteaching and team teaching set-ups desired participation in excess of the actual level, while indicating satisfaction with these actual levels. This accommodation to managerial realities may be interpreted as resignation rather than satisfaction. The manifest resistance to team in spite of the expressed willingness to, strongly suggests the kind of learned helplessness of which Bate spoke. Colleagues appear to be colluding in a process which conveniently submerges the conflicts among them which teaming would bring to the fore.

The value of participation and the role of the leader in facilitating this

21

is further reinforced by a study by Arikado and Musella (1973). They questioned 529 teachers in 134 teams in 71 open-plan schools. Greater satisfaction was reported in those teams which did not have a formal leader. In those teams which were formally led, satisfaction with the set-up is related to the team's rating of the adequacy of the leader. Satisfaction was higher where team members had a say in the selection of fellow team members, and in teams with a balanced status structure and smaller teams (up to four members). The overt focusing on the role of the leader may seem a little simplistic in the context of the earlier discussion about consensual understanding and construction of the group process. According to the Krech model, the adequacy of the leader would be related not just to personality characteristics of the leader but to a range of other variables. The style of leadership would emerge out of an interaction among these.

Returning to Hackman and Oldham's analysis, a feature of major importance for the success of a group is its composition. Three major themes are isolated:

1 Composition should provide for high levels of task relevant expertise.
2 The group should be no larger than necessary. They cite in this latter context particularly the work of Steiner (1972) on the process of diminishing returns when introducing additional people to a task over and above an optimum number; evidence in support of this phenomenon in education is provided by many of the studies in the following chapter – e.g. McBrien and Weightman (1980) found that the introduction of extra people to the classroom proved to be either unrelated or *inversely* related with the engagement of the children.
3 In the composition of the group there should be a balance between heterogeneity and homogeneity – if the group members are too much alike, the special advantages of the team are lost; if they are too different there is insufficient common ground for good communication.

Here again the relevance of these conclusions to the classroom is manifest. Regarding task-relevant expertise and heterogeneity, one of the major advantages of involving parents in the classroom may be in bringing new skills (both practical and interpersonal); indeed, in the survey of 1,401 primary schools conducted by Cyster, Clift and Battle (1979) the involvement of parents 'with specialist knowledge' was ranked the fourth most common type of parental involvement out of ten categories of involvement.

Akin to Hackman and Oldham's ideas on semi-autonomous work groups, at least in terms of the problems and stresses which give rise to the need for alternative ways of making groups work, are ideas on 'quality circles'. A quality circle is defined as 'a small group of workers who meet regularly on a voluntary basis to analyse problems and recommend solutions' (Katzan 1985), or 'a group of four to ten volunteers working for the same supervisor . . . who meet once a week for an hour, under the leadership of the supervisor to identify, analyse and solve their own work-related problems' (Robson 1982). The directness of these definitions conflicts somewhat with the consensus-mindedness of educational literature, and the management-oriented phraseology is alien.

However, there does seem to be recognition here, by groups working in industry, of many of the problems of classroom teams (to be examined in the following chapter), particularly in relation to the need for discussion among team members and the need for time to be allowed for such discussion. There seems here to be an implicit recognition of the need for this process of negotiation to be facilitated. Inside the frameworks proposed by Krech *et al.* and Bate, this might be interpreted as a shaping of the emergent processes of the former, or the consensual under-standings of the latter. Without such shaping, quality circle proponents would say, the processes that emerge may inhibit rather than facilitate the working of the team.

A study of particular interest in relation to work organisation and one which examines many of the points already considered is that of Cohen *et al.* (1979). It is of interest here since while its focus is the testing of an hypothesis within organisation theory, the setting in which it tests that hypothesis is educational. The central hypothesis is that organisation becomes more complex as the activities of an organisation and the environment surrounding it become more complex. The authors take teaming practices as an index of the complexity of the activities of the organisation. A number of factors – broadly congruent with the 'independent variables' outlined by Krech *et al.* – are identified as possibly affecting the degree of teaming on the basis of the hypothesis: complexity of instructional materials; complexity of grouping practices; school size; nature of classroom (e.g. open-plan or closed); involvement of parent or community groups; influence of teacher organisations. The authors test the hypothesis by making an analysis of longitudinal data from 83 schools randomly selected from a number of school districts. Questionnaire and interview data were obtained from principals and teachers within the schools and from the school superintendent (equivalent to the area education officer in the UK) in each of the school districts surveyed. The tenets on which the research is based interestingly have shifted away from constructs rooted in role conflict/role ambiguity continua. Rather, these researchers believe that

> teaching teams seem more often to form as a result of teachers' informal decisions to work together than from any formal school or district organisational decisions.
>
> (Cohen *et al.* 1979: 21)

23

In talking of an emergent social structure in which this emerging pattern takes the place of interest, the authors appear to be finding consonance with the emergent processes of the Krech model and Bate's consensual understandings. Consistent with this, is the finding that teaming appeared to be an unstable feature of school life, coming and going with the conditions within the school:

> The stability terms measuring the continuity of teaming in schools over time were strikingly low. We had expected teaming to be a more highly institutionalised school characteristic, exhibiting considerable stability over the two year period [of the study]. Instead, it appeared to behave more erratically, affected perhaps by such factors as coordination problems experienced by teams.
>
> (Cohen *et al.* 1979: 26)

The main finding of this research was that the factor having the most profound influence on teaming was the architecture and layout of the class: not surprisingly, open-plan classrooms encouraged teaming. However, more surprisingly, the influence of the headteacher was found to be unrelated either to the amount or degree of teaming among teachers. This finding is at variance with those who have pointed to the importance of 'support' and reinforces the contrary view that teams themselves may in some way provide access to the support, or altern- atively, collude in insulating themselves from it. This may be particularly the case in teams of professionals who are able more articulately and forcibly either to encourage or resist 'support'.

This study has greatest interest and appeal as an analysis of the way teams develop, clearly through perceived needs of the participants (rather than through fiat of the head), and the way in which their working practices are negotiated and formulated, given that certain needs are met (such as the provision of appropriate rooms) in the larger organisation of the school. But especially relevant is the fact that teams in schools are frail organisms; of particular interest is the fact that teaming practices decline in complexity over time. The authors conclude that their findings are not confined to teaming among teachers – their findings also apply to the use of aides and volunteers.

They quote further research to show that interdependence among teachers, aides or specialists follows a very similar pattern to that among just teachers. The findings they make about teaming among teachers are therefore applicable also to teaming among other personnel.

CONCLUSIONS

A framework for understanding the difficulties that may arise in classroom teams may now be put forward.

It is in the transformation of initial expectations about the teamwork enterprise into the reality that ultimately develops that those factors associated with stress arise. Thus, role conflict and ambiguity may cause a distancing of the individual from the group – effectively a breaking down of the team process. Role allocation may break down if the nature of the task is poorly understood or rests upon different understandings of the tasks to be accomplished – which may easily occur in the culture of the classroom, where ideological differences may exist between team members.

Work on small groups indicates that effectiveness rests on relationships and shared goals, but in the heterogeneous groups of classrooms these conditions are unlikely to exist for reasons to be examined in the next chapter.

What seems crucial for classroom teams to operate effectively is a common set of understandings about roles and expected outcomes. The latter will prove far more difficult to define in the classroom than in the factory. The need for enabling processes wherein such understandings may be enhanced therefore seems paramount. In the following chapter I shall attempt to disentangle some of the complexities of the classroom as a place for teamwork to occur. I shall relate the notions about role raised here to the thought processes which seem to be employed by participants in either facilitating or inhibiting teamwork.

3

CLASSROOM TEAMS
Teachers working together

In the passage that follows, Hargreaves emphasises the privateness of teaching:

> The most startling feature of teachers in their relations with adults, including colleagues, is their sensitivity to observation whilst teaching. Like sexual activity, teaching is seen as an intimate act which is most effectively and properly conducted when shrouded in privacy. To be watched is to inhibit performance. Most teachers simply prefer to work alone with a class of pupils.
>
> (Hargreaves 1980: 141)

The difficulties to which Hargreaves alludes take a number of forms and change their nature according to the personnel involved. The central themes of this and the following chapter will be the ways in which these difficulties are perceived and defined.

People who are not used to working with others will face strains due to the problems of managing and being managed; they will face personal and interpersonal tensions, differences of opinion, matters concerned with the definition of their tasks. They will have to resolve practical issues such as finding time to plan with colleagues. They may experience conflict due to mismatches between their own ideologies and those of their colleagues, and they may experience alienation due to the essentially marginal nature of the roles in which they find themselves.

This and the next two chapters focus on

1 the extent to which additional people are working in classrooms, and
2 the tensions which are thereby created due to issues associated with status, style of teaching and personal autonomy in such teamwork.

In this chapter I focus on teamwork involving just teachers. In the following chapter the focus is on teams comprising teachers and non-teachers.

WHO ARE THE EXTRA PEOPLE?

The introduction of other adults into the classroom is a relatively recent phenomenon in so far as it has occurred to any significant extent either in terms of number and variety of personnel or in terms of its geographical distribution. I have already indicated that there are two principal trends bringing extra adults into the new classroom teams: the integration of children with special needs, and the parental involvement movement.

However, additional adults were working in classrooms before these trends began. The team teaching movement perhaps marked the first concerted efforts at cooperative work in the classroom. Team teaching began at the end of the 1960s both in the UK and in the USA. Ancillary helpers have for some time played an important role as teachers' aides. But there is no way in which one can chart the growth or decline of classroom teaming.

There have been few, if any, studies of the extent of classroom teaming, important though it undoubtedly is. This is a serious omission in educational research given the problems that inevitably seem to arise when people share a task. The position in education contrasts sharply with that in industry, where research into the kinds of problems and oppor-tunities arising when people work together is represented in an enormous literature, as indicated in chapter 2. There is much support for the theoretical benefits of involving people working together as a team in the classroom, yet the studies I shall review demonstrate that those benefits are difficult to realise.

Such research as there is does little even to distinguish between different categories of adults working alongside teachers. For instance, Stierer's (1985) survey about volunteers who were helping with reading at school distinguished only between parents and 'others': 39 per cent of schools were using parents, 14 per cent just 'others' and 47 per cent parents and 'others'.

Given that reports about the effects of the practice are still therefore somewhat scarce, a useful analogue for predicting possible effects of the practice is found in the small minority of educational environments where the existence of extra people is commonplace.

Team teaching, together with nursery education and the schooling of children with severe learning difficulties, provide possibly the only situations in the UK where additional people have traditionally been consistently available to work with the teacher. In the USA, funding for teacher aides has been rather more generous than in the UK, and there has been some significantly funded research into the effects of teacher aides, particularly as a result of evaluations of Project Follow-Through. Each of these situations – team teaching, nurseries, schools for children with severe learning difficulties, teacher aides – enables me to examine adults working together in the classroom and I shall draw from each in the sub-sections that follow and in the next chapter.

The aim of this book is to document some of the emerging trends to adult collaboration in classrooms and to investigate their associated effects and their implications. Parallel situations (team teaching, teacher aides, etc.), while not completely analogous, can – where investigations have been reported in the literature – provide laboratories for examining the effects of people working together. Many of the issues identified in this chapter and the next chapter do appear to be general to the different situations. The situations to be isolated are:

1 team teaching;
2 special education (special schools and mainstreaming);
3 teacher aides and teacher assistants; and
4 parental involvement.

In examining each of these areas, from team teaching to parental involvement, I shall attempt to isolate the existence or otherwise of each of the likely areas of conflict for the participants. Team teaching and support teaching are the situations examined in this chapter.

TEAM TEACHING

In team teaching, relationships are found which raise many of the issues already outlined: there may be clashes in educational ideology among participants, and/or interpersonal tensions. However, there will also be managerial issues in determining where sets of responsibilities begin and end, and who defines them, as well as practical issues concerning time for negotiation and planning.

Geen (1985), in tracing the history of team teaching in England and Wales, found that there are serious difficulties encountered when teachers are expected to work together in one class. He found, from sending letters to Chief Education Officers of the 104 LEAs of England and Wales, that despite the enthusiasm for team teaching in the 1960s and 1970s, 'it has failed to establish itself as a permanent strategy in many schools'. Out of 49 schools that pioneered team teaching in the 1960s only 7 retained it by 1984.

Among the reasons Geen identifies for schools abandoning team teaching are: the time and energy consumed in planning; the reluctance of some teachers to teach before colleagues; and differences between team members. These relate to the constructs already identified: time and energy in planning is a practical issue; reluctance before colleagues an interpersonal one; differences between team members may be due to clashes in ideology or personality.

Interestingly, very similar results are found in the United States. Cohen (1976) longitudinally analysed questionnaire data from 469 teachers. The data are taken at two points: in 1968 and 1975. She notes, like Geen, that the amount of teaming has dropped substantially over the period; in 1968, teams of five or six teachers were common but by 1975 the most common team size was only two (45 per cent of all teamed teachers were in teams of two; 35 per cent were in teams of three and only 8.5 per cent were in teams of five or more). Suggested reasons for the decline were to do with the amount of coordination and communication needed for the effective functioning of the larger group; teachers do not have the time for it. Associated with successful teaming are attention to team dynamics and the support of school management; teaming was 'not unconditionally associated with teacher satisfaction'. Satisfaction rested in part on the balance achieved in the teaming process with balance in turn being determined by the enabling of participation in all team members. Analysis of respondents' replies led to

> a growing understanding of the fact that when team participation was good it was very good, and when it was bad it was awful.
>
> (Cohen 1976: 58)

She concludes that

> team arrangements are extremely fragile. . . . Teaming appears to be an organisational innovation trying to survive without effective preparation or support.
>
> (ibid.: 61)

Other American research highlights some of the problems noted here and it points to the possibility that teachers (or possibly any adult doing any task) will work to define his or her own territory away from the influence of others.

Interested in the amount of collaboration in which teachers will engage, Nolan (1977) reviews the use of open-space classrooms, drawing a distinction with 'open' classes (the American equivalent of open-plan versus informal). He concludes that collaboration only increased with audibility and that teachers aim to decrease interference with each other by quietening down. It was only noisy activities which would have to be jointly planned. The inherent autonomy of the teaching task again seems to be evident here. Although Nolan does not specifically mention the features which make autonomy desirable for teachers, one can again assume that the concern over personal or ideological tensions make for the desirability of such autonomy.

Bennett, Andrae, Hegarty and Wade (1980), in research funded by the Schools Council into open-plan schools, explore teachers' attitudes to the open-plan environments in which they found themselves. They emerge with similar findings to those already noted, though the report is scrupulously even-handed in its treatment and judgement of the (then) charged issue of open-plan schools, and in this sense it sometimes fails to make unequivocally clear the conclusions which appear to be tacitly emerging from the research.

In their review of the literature, Bennett and his colleagues note that teachers appeared to feel they had more influence in decision-making in the open-plan setting – that they ceased to be isolated and become involved with joint responsibility. But the difficulties encountered in making cooperation work are more frequently mentioned than the advantages of that cooperation. Teachers list the advantages of teaming as the pooling of ideas, and that it is good for specialisation, for probationary teachers and for improved discipline.

However, these advantages were countered by the disadvantages (in order of frequency) of: personality clashes, more preparation time needed, stress – and, interestingly, given that some teachers mentioned these as advantages – not good for probationers or for discipline. The quality of interpersonal relationships seems to be of paramount importance, and incompatibility not uncommon. The latter is cited as probably the most important problem that occurs in open-plan classes. They say that this, together with frequent team changes, can cause low morale. Differences in teaching ideology are not mentioned: such differences are perhaps assumed to be personality differences.

In their questionnaire to their open-plan teachers Bennett *et al.* noted marked discrepancies between what teachers actually did (the practice) and what they said they would like to do (the ideal) in terms of teaching independently or cooperatively. The same discrepancy between real and ideal was noted in the responses from the heads, though here a prestige bias can be noted, with the heads' responses veering more to the ideal than those of their staff.

Interestingly, teachers were doing more than twice as much independent teaching as they think is the ideal, and only two-thirds as much cooperative teaching as they thought ideal. Disappointingly, the reasons for the differences between the actual and the ideal are not discussed. It might be inferred that all the problems already noted to do with lack of proper planning time, ambiguity over role and differences in personality are to blame.

Conclusions congruent with those already noted are made by Hatton (1985) in reviewing recent research on team teaching in the UK, USA and Australia. She concludes that 'teacher culture strongly supports an individual orientation to the work of teaching'. She says that evidence points to the fact that teachers try to maintain privacy, feeling embarrassment and intimidation when others are present and that they try to arrange 'alternative cover' for themselves when the barriers afforded by classroom walls are removed in open-plan classrooms – e.g. by rearranging the furniture.

A strikingly similar picture is drawn by Hargreaves in the quotation used at the beginning of this review:

> The most startling feature of teachers in their relations with adults, including colleagues, is their sensitivity to observation whilst teaching. . . . Most teachers simply prefer to work alone with a class of pupils.
>
> (Hargreaves 1980: 141)

He continues this polemic with an attempt at understanding the teacher's isolated position from an interactionist perspective:

> teachers do not wish merely to be autonomous in freedom from control by 'outsiders': they seek, in the classroom, autonomy *from one another*. The heart of the matter, at the experiential level, is the teacher's fear of being judged and criticised. Any observation will be evaluative of the teacher's competence, and the threat therein becomes the greater because such judgments may remain implicit and unspoken, and therefore incontrovertible. . . . Differences in educational philosophy and pedagogical preference among teachers exacerbate this sensitivity . . .
>
> (ibid.)

Here, then, Hargreaves suggests that the desire for autonomy rests primarily in a fear of judgement. Such fear is simply exacerbated by ideological differences.

The emerging picture is one where it seems that collaboration is not a natural thing for teachers to do in the classroom. The classroom environment does not seem to be congenial to the equal or shared collaboration of two or more adults. Beardsley, Bricker and Murray (1973) introduce the notion of territory to account for these difficulties, in looking at teachers' reactions to open-plan schools, where teachers are constrained to work with and in front of each other. They suggest that absence of personal space defined by walls threatens many teachers' sense of personal territory. They say that teachers may find teaching in open spaces 'personally disastrous' and that many teachers enjoy working in a protected environment in which areas of responsibility are clearly specified. The notion of territory is an interesting one, locating Hargreaves' fear of judgement almost in a psycho-biological need. The interpretation made later in this review is that the resort to territory is strategic rather than inherent, and one of a number of strategies that participants may choose to adopt in the classroom team.

Further evidence for the ideas contained in Hargreaves' entertaining homily again comes from the United States where Miskel, McDonald and

Bloom (1983) examined the amount of collaboration among teachers in the context of certain new 'programs' – notably those involving help for children with special needs – which require high levels of cooperation among staff. They say that the new orthodoxy is that people will get along together fine if the institutional and managerial structure allows them to, that they will be creative and imaginative in collaborating and that this will make for some kind of synergy: 'the emergent view is that schools are not tightly-coupled bureaucracies where firm lines are needed for effective communication; rather, it rests on confidence and good faith'. But inter-dependent activities turn out, even in these programmes which require cooperation, to be relatively infrequent. Questionnaires were completed by 1,697 teachers from 89 schools; respondents were asked how often every month (a number between 0 and 5) they jointly planned ('jointly planning' could comprise simply talking) with the learning difficulties specialist; the most frequent answer was less than once a semester.

These authors suggest that individuals adapt attitudes, behaviour and belief to their social context and go on from here to suggest that 'work dependence for teaching and planning typically occur on an informal and low-frequency basis' because the context for such dependence is not present. However, it seems unlikely that the unpalatability of team working for teachers can be accounted for wholly by the larger social framework within which they work. It may be more valid to suppose, on an interpretation of the research already reviewed, that difficulties are located in the micro-climate of the classroom – in the perceptions of interpersonal difference; in clarity of managerial responsibilities; in perception of philosophical or pedagogical mismatch.

Team teaching involves a grouping of professionals of equal status, working with broadly similar aims. Despite this, team teaching appears to confront serious difficulties and it has declined substantially over the years. There may be different ideas from the team members about what is to happen in the classroom. Desire for autonomy is seen in the notion of territory, with teachers sometimes aiming to maximise time on their own or to minimise contacts with others. There is a dislike of scrutiny from others. However, despite the documentation of these difficulties and the clear recognition of their existence, there is little work on the interpretations made by the participants of their experience, nor on attributions about the success or otherwise of teaming.

MAINSTREAMING THROUGH SUPPORT TEACHING

Mainstreaming provides several kinds of team situation which are analogous to team teaching and I look at these in the remainder of this chapter. I look at teachers working with classroom assistants in the following chapter.

Mainstreaming of children with special needs has occurred for somewhat longer on the other side of the Atlantic than it has in this country. Where it has existed there, and in innovative schools in the UK, it is possible to look at the effects of people working together. However, most research focuses, understandably, not on teamwork, but on the children who have been mainstreamed. Nevertheless, occasionally those outcome measures are directed at providing an analysis of the effects of staff working in a team situation.

For instance, Strain and Kerrs' (1981) review of major findings on the educational effects of mainstreaming in the USA can be interpreted as providing further evidence that improving adult–child ratios does not in itself have beneficial effects for children with special needs. They conclude that in special classes, where assistance has traditionally been available to the teacher on a far more frequent basis than in mainstream classes, children with special needs did not achieve significantly better educationally than matched groups of children in regular classes. Moreover, in mainstream classes where additional help was provided, benefits could not be shown for children with special needs unless special arrangements were made for the working arrangements of the additional personnel.

An important feature of the dynamics of people working together in classrooms is alluded to in Strain and Kerrs' meta-analysis. In identifying a second, general trend from the research as the superiority (in achievement outcome measures) of children who had received more individual teaching, they note that one of the initial arguments in favour of special class placement was the low staff–pupil ratios there. (Special class placements in the United States are characterised by additional aide support, improving the staff–pupil ratio.) But the research reviewed by them finds that little individualisation takes place despite these better ratios. This points again to a possible drop-off in personal effectiveness when people work in classroom teams.

Despite the manifest importance of these findings, it is interesting to note that much commentary accords in-class support a taken-for-granted positive status. For instance, Gartner and Lipsky (1987) in an otherwise thoroughgoing review of the status of mainstreaming since the introduction of Public Law 94–142 in the USA, make no mention of in-class support whatsoever, let alone acknowledge its problematic nature.

However, there has been work which takes this up. A study specifically directed at support teachers, working alongside mainstream colleagues, again from North America, comes from Wilson (1989). This Canadian perspective on support teaching reveals tensions and problems which bear a striking similarity to those already noted in team teaching. Wilson looked at school boards which were deploying colleague consultants to the regular classroom teacher. The problems she identifies in the shift of roles from withdrawal remedial teaching to support in the mainstream are: lack of clear direction in the transition of roles; lack of training programmes to help the teachers adapt to the new role; reluctance of regular teachers to open doors to 'experts'; belief of most classroom teachers that one deals with at-risk children by referring them to a special track. She draws on research by Fisher and Ysseldyke to show that when children are moved from special classrooms to the mainstream the amount of reading they do and the amount of academic engaged time falls to the average for the mainstream class. She asserts that we therefore have to improve the quality of what special children receive in mainstream.

Wilson, drawing on an earlier study (Wilson 1988) which factor-analysed semi-structured interview responses from 54 teachers and which isolated a restorative–preventative belief continuum existing among teachers, feels that the fall-off in engagement is in part due to teacher attitude – with assumptions teachers hold about what she calls *restorative* or *preventative* education. However, a major problem comes in adapting to the new team-working enterprise and in interfacing with a hetero-geneous set of teachers, some of whom are committed to a preventative approach and some of whom are wedded to a restorative philosophy. Here, difficulties similar to those highlighted in team teaching are seen to emerge – the teams are homogeneous with, nevertheless, Wilson is suggesting, a low likelihood that there will be ideological congruence between teacher and co-teacher. There will, then, be an immediate point of friction around which tension may crystallise.

Resource teachers, Wilson says, need consultation skills to help them meet their new role, and to help them challenge the beliefs and assumptions of mainstream teachers. She says that recent research stresses the need for consulting roles, 'but there is little on what these skills are or how to achieve them'. She suggests that as part of this consultative exercise mainstream and resource teachers need to set out what they expect and how far they are prepared to go; that resource teachers need to practise active listening, restating the other's case, goal setting and checking for clients' discomfort. The kinds of gaps in the resource teacher's skills seem to coincide with those gaps which are responsible for the demise of team teaching. She concludes that resource teachers need to have 'respect from colleagues and a desire to give away ideas rather than be an expert'.

Stainback and Stainback (1990) in the USA also see team teaching as the way forward to 'inclusive schooling'. However, they identify the undoubted theoretical advantages of this approach, without indicating that the area might in any way be problematic. In the same volume, and in similar vein, Thousand and Villa (1990) claim to have searched the literature and identified 100 specific, yet overlapping characteristics of effective teams or groups. They categorise these broadly as follows: the distribution of responsibility in the team; frequent face-to-face interactions; a positive sense of interdependence; small group social skills in leadership, communication, decision making; periodic assessments of how the group is functioning and how it might do better; and clear accountability for personal responsibilities. However, they do not identify the tensions created by the interface between these 'team-needs' and the reality of classroom life, nor do they suggest how or why 'frequent face to face interactions' should occur when evidence appears to show that team members may actively avoid such interactions, even if time is available for them. In terms of the analysis in chapter 2, features of the team situation are here simplistically taken as 'givens', and not as emergent processes.

Widlake (1985), in reviewing the move away from withdrawal and toward support, sums up the situation by saying that for some secondary school teachers the arrangements for support teaching seem strange and perhaps threatening. The techniques required for successful teaching in these circumstances, he says, are different from those usually practised and they have not usually been acquired during initial training.

Ferguson and Adams (1982) provide some insights from the Scottish experience of support teaching. In Scotland the move away from remedial withdrawal and towards support antedates the English experience by several years. Interestingly, in this early paper about such a move, support teaching is described as 'team teaching in remedial education'. The authors interviewed 36 remedial teachers, 48 classteachers and 54 pupils from 6 secondary schools. The proportion of time the remedial teachers spent in 'team teaching' varied between 20 per cent in one school and 61 per cent in another. The explication of the variety of activity that occurs under the rubric of team teaching is fascinating. In one school, subject specialists worked together with remedial teachers on themes within an integrated studies context; children would be organised into small working groups which then drew on the resources of the entire teaching team. However, many of the remedial teachers reported that classteachers worked through a syllabus with 'an extraordinarily restricted range of methods and a heavy reliance on work sheets and a prescribed text'. Here, 'remedial teachers believe that their task is to listen while the subject specialist talks to the whole class and then circulate among the children responding to the needs of those who are in difficulties'. Only 5 of the 41 remedial teachers jointly prepared lessons with a subject specialist. The only occasions when teaching with the whole class occurred from the support teacher was when, for instance, the 'teacher had been spirited off somewhere'.

Remedial teachers were not sharing teaching in the way that the term 'team teaching' implies. Only five of the classteachers said that the support teacher had taken the class. Support teachers may have difficulty with the subject being taught and classteachers could be surprised and 'scathing' about this. Preparation for team teaching tended to be very limited, mainly because of pressures of time, and because classteachers were not available to discuss work. Nineteen of the 43 subject specialists said that the remedial teacher's preparation was inadequate. The authors say that 'nearly all remedial teachers are cast in the role of teachers' aides'. Forty-nine of the 54 pupils described the classteacher as 'the real teacher' or 'the proper teacher' or something similar. Remedial teachers were characteristically described as 'the helper'. They go on to say that the general picture is of support teachers passively accepting, and content with, an undemanding role. In turn, classteachers 'jealously guard their right to maintain control of the progress of each lesson'. One classteacher commented 'She seems to have this need to have a whole class. Suddenly she's in the middle directing the class if I go out for a minute.' They comment in concluding that 'Individual attention, even in a classroom with two teachers, is rarely planned in a detailed way and is likely to consist of brief and infrequent encounters with those who require further explanation'.

Bines's interviews with teachers, support and mainstream, working collaboratively support these findings. She says that having another teacher in the classroom could impinge on teachers' autonomy and create anxieties about competence. With a support teacher in class you could not be 'quite yourself':

> There might be inhibitions about 'having a laugh'. . . . Some teachers talked about the feeling . . . of being 'spied upon' . . . young teachers might be particularly 'threatened' by support work since they had not had the chance to 'establish themselves'.
>
> (Bines 1986: 109)

Interesting as far as Ferguson and Adams's view of what is required goes, is their comment that 'an approach is yet to be found which marries the benefits of systematic individual attention to the advantages of awareness in detail of the demands of the regular classroom' (Ferguson and Adams 1982: 29).

An attempt to find an approach which marries such difficult-to-reconcile benefits comes in the use of room management in ordinary classrooms (see chapters 12 and 13 for a full account of room management). Newton (1988), in a case study using structured observations, noted that a support teacher and mainstream teacher were not working effectively to provide an integrated approach in the class-room; rather, the organisation could be described as withdrawal within the classroom. Further, the classteacher and support teacher had not established an effective method of co-working: during an hour-long observation period, teacher and support teacher were recorded talking to *each other* for 40 per cent of the time. With the introduction of room management, the teachers were able usefully to structure their time, and to share the tasks which formerly it would have been the tacitly accepted role of one of them to fulfil. Also, the amount of adult-to-adult interaction decreased under room management, with a corresponding increase in the amount of time both teachers spent with the special needs children. Both adults reported enjoying the room management sessions, though they were found to be time-consuming and impracticable for more than one session per week.

Such a system would seem to offer a framework for the deployment of adults in the classroom. Through the specification of tasks, ambiguities and uncertainties are diminished, and even differences in teaching style neutralised. However, the systematisation of planning for teamwork in this way does seem to return us to the need for time for such planning and the problems in finding that time.

It might be thought from an HMI survey that support teaching arrangements in teaching children for whom English is a second language (E2L) were relatively unproblematic, in comparison with support teaching of children with special needs:

> Evidence of the relatively few examples of in-class support by E2L teachers suggests that, where organisation and collaboration between the E2L and subject teacher are good, pupils are able to engage more effectively than in withdrawal groups.
>
> (HMI 1988: 14)

However, a closer examination than the HMI found possible in their survey of E2L teachers has been undertaken by Williamson (1989) and a pattern of reactions, tensions and uncertainties which is remarkably similar to those of the remedial teachers is noted. Williamson examines the change to support, but in this latter case, in the context of E2L teachers. Here, the client population shares little in common with that of the remedial teachers, yet the ambiguities and stresses felt in the E2L teachers' new role seem to be almost identical. Williamson explored the attitudes and feelings of teachers towards withdrawal and mainstream support as ways of helping bilingual pupils. He undertook six semi-structured interviews, with three teachers from each of two secondary schools. The teachers were aware of the value of support teaching and the arguments evinced for it in reports such as Bullock (Department of Education and Science 1975). But they felt that it was hampered by poor organisation, unhelpful attitudes on the part of mainstream colleagues and lack of status for support teachers. When the teachers were asked how support teaching could be improved, the issue most frequently mentioned was the need for prior consultation with colleagues if support is to be effective – 'Often we don't know what we're going to do so we can't prepare.' 'It's unsatisfactory grabbing 15 minutes at lunchtime.' There was a need to 'identify exactly the role of each teacher in the process'. There was a lack of awareness of the support teacher's role. One said she felt uncomfortable when her presence in the classroom was not acknowledged and commented also on personality differences – some teachers were 'welcoming and friendly, others difficult'. Teaching styles were important; if the teacher talked to the class a lot 'it's very difficult for the support teacher to participate'. The support teacher should have an intimate knowledge of the curriculum so she doesn't 'spend so much time standing around waiting for relevant moments where she can step in and give help'. The support teachers felt they weren't seen as 'proper' teachers. They missed 'not having a classroom and doing what other teachers do'. They felt the sense of sharing someone else's classroom and needing to establish one's position in the room, and having no time to sort this out in advance. 'You have . . . no autonomy . . . you feel you don't belong anywhere in particular . . . you need to make your role clear to the class.' 'It can be hard to assert your discipline level in classes where the class teacher has a different level . . . it can affect your morale when you are never properly in control, never have your own classroom.' As to other teachers, 'some can't function with another adult in the classroom'. On pupils, some were embarrassed by the support teacher's presence – 'no child wants a minder'.

It is clear from this juxtaposition of similar situations – remedial support and E2L support – that personnel with very similar status, despite their different client groups, are experiencing a parallel set of problems. The apprehension here, and in every other adult mixture examined so far, appears to emerge not from the pedagogic tasks undertaken, but rather from the interpersonal strains that ensue from certain misunderstandings and conflicts – of interest, style and approach.

This difference of approach is examined further by O'Hanlon (1988), in taking up again the focus on the special needs teacher. She, like Wilson (above), sees the difficulty in establishing good support teaching as stemming from a tension emerging from the different perspectives of special needs and mainstream teachers. Through an action research report – via analysis of conversations between special needs teachers – she tries to tease out the differing perspectives as a way of accounting for some of the tensions that are felt. The comments made by the teachers are very similar to those already noted in the Williamson and the Ferguson and Adams papers: 'I think it gives you a terrible stigma being a special needs teacher'; 'They [staff and children] don't regard you as a *real* teacher'. She sees these misunderstandings stemming from mainstream teachers being what she calls 'technicist'; i.e. being subject-centred and interested in academic outcomes, in results, while special needs teachers primarily are 'intuitionists', concerned with relationships with pupils. 'Special needs teachers are by nature and role different from ordinary teachers. They differ in focus, practice and clientele.' The more special needs teachers tried to gain favour with mainstream colleagues by changing their styles, the more they experienced tension in their special needs role. They experienced alienation.

O'Hanlon's analysis, in its drawing of a distinction between technicists and intuitionists, is similar to Wilson's, which in a similar way constructs a continuum (restorative–preventative) to account for the differences in style between special needs and mainstream teachers. While these draw us more towards a pedagogic/ideological dimension rather than an interpersonal one, they nevertheless highlight the differences, pedagogic or otherwise, among people which can lay at the root of the frictions noted.

Supply teachers, though they are not working as additional adults in the classteacher's territory, are nevertheless working in that territory and may almost be said to be working under the shadow of the teacher they are temporarily replacing. Clifton and Rambaran (1987) note a number of features about the feelings of supply teachers which parallel those of team teachers and support teachers. After participant observation in supply teachers' classes, and after interviews with them, they say that substitute (supply) teachers experience anxiety; they don't feel competent or satisfied; they have low status and prestige; they don't have authority in the school and don't know the rituals of the classroom. The parallels here are perhaps most apposite with the work and feelings of support teachers. Supply teachers are seen by pupils as being incompetent teachers. They are not familiar with the routine of the lesson. Supervision projects a picture of incompetence. The supply teacher, like the parent, the support teacher or the welfare assistant, is not familiar with the loose rituals of the classroom, and the methods they apply may not match with those of the main teacher.

Clifton and Rambaran conclude with an interesting analysis which does much to illuminate the tensions noted existing in the work of the additional people in the classroom: they draw on Stonequist's notion of marginality (in that they are not integrated; they feel like strangers) and Weber's notions of power in the bureaucracy of the school (not recognised as holding official positions) to explain supply teachers' feelings of uncertainty. Supply teaching is marginal; there is no clearly established set of rules that legitimates the behaviour of supply teachers. This would appear to be at the core of the problem for any additional adult in the classroom.

In this chapter I have looked at teachers working together. In the following, I look at teachers working with non-teachers.

4

CLASSROOM TEAMS
Teachers working with non-teachers

In the previous chapter I looked at teachers working in team teaching arrangements – in other words, teachers working with other teachers. In this chapter I examine teachers working with non-teachers. I shall look at three kinds of situation in which teachers are working with non-teachers in what I shall call heterogeneous teams: first, I shall examine teams in which teacher aides and teacher assistants are found; second, I shall look at the teams that are found in special education; and third, at teams in which parents are working alongside teachers.

TEACHER AIDES AND TEACHER ASSISTANTS

Perhaps the most detailed account yet undertaken of the work of teacher aides is one done as an extension of the comprehensive analyses of the Project Follow-Through curricula. Looking at some of the highly funded projects that comprised the Project Follow-Through curricula, DeVault, Harnischfeger and Wiley (1977) note that the employment of teacher aides (teacher assistants) was often one of the ways in which the money allocated to a project would be spent. Having employed the aides, the question remained as to the best way of using them. They see the answer lying in the analysis of the teacher's role in order that there can be some specialisation in the work undertaken:

> In addition to one or more teachers, aides and volunteers must be co-ordinated, and opportunities, not usually available, exist for *differentiating* [my emphasis] teaching functions. The Project Follow-Through observation data provide a unique perspective on how these decisions are handled. They allow explication of the grouping and individualisation strategies used in the implementation of the several curricula with simultaneous accounting of the personnel resources used.
>
> (DeVault, Harnischfeger and Wiley 1977: 50)

The results of the DeVault study are complex, analysing relationships between and among variables which include curricular selection, personnel resources and grouping strategies. But just looking at the features of the study that are directly relevant for this book, the results may be summarised as follows. More teacher than aide or volunteer time was spent in large (i.e. more than eight pupils) groups. Aides spent considerably more of their time than teachers in activities which did not involve direct contact with children, about the same proportion as teachers in small group (three–eight children) work, but less than teachers in large group work. Volunteers were found to spend most of their time in tutorial (one-to-one or one-to-two) settings. Thus, 'in essence, all personnel are used in all settings with increasing emphasis on smaller-sized groups as levels of training [of the personnel] diminish'. There was most variation in the use of volunteers: in some curricula they were seen as members of the teaching team, while in others, which used volunteers, no mention was even made of their work.

A significant finding, and one already noted in other kinds of group, is that the presence of extra people did not automatically improve the situation: having volunteers and aides in the class did not generally free the teacher for more time with pupils but rather resulted in the teacher spending more of her time *without* pupils. Here is a replication of the finding made in team teaching: having extra people in the classroom does not necessarily result in more 'teacher-time' for the children – perhaps because of the complex set of interpersonal uncertainties already discussed. The focus of the DeVault study, however, is not on these uncertainties, but rather on empirically determined outcome measures of pupil success.

One of the many interesting findings of the study is that curricula which were seen as the most successful in the Follow-Through analysis (e.g. the behavioural Kansas curriculum) prescribed relatively large amounts of small group or tutorial instruction, which in turn depended upon more adults in the classroom. These curricula, requiring higher 'intensity' of schooling, were more likely to be implemented in better resourced school districts. The authors warn that it is therefore necessary in looking at both the reasons for and the consequences of grouping and individualisation to take account of resourcing – which in practical terms in the Follow-Through classrooms translated into number of personnel in the classroom.

The work of aides, then, generally follows the same pattern as that of teachers. It might thus be inferred that in the absence of clear role definition, a form of modelling or apprenticeship is filling the vacuum.

The DeVault study shows that the provision of extra personnel, far from freeing the teacher for more time with the children, in fact usually resulted in the teacher spending more of her teaching time on administrative and non-teaching activities. These researchers conclude that too little thought has been given to the ways in which teacher aides work:

If we staff typical-sized classrooms with up to four full time instructional adults then we better find out how to use them most effectively.

(DeVault, Harnischfeger and Wiley 1977: 47)

While many teachers in this country would consider having four full-time adults in the classroom a luxury about which few questions would need to be asked, this research indicates that the existence of these extra people is far from being an unproblematic issue.

Stallings, Robbins, Presbrey and Scott (1986) touch on the same theme in meta-analyses of the same Follow-Through data. Their hypothesis is that if teachers are taught to be more efficient, then aides will not be needed. Using schools involved in Follow-Through, teachers were trained in classroom management skills, and heads were trained in staff support skills. Comparison was made of provision of either aide support or additional training for teachers in instructional skills. Longitudinal analysis was undertaken over three years with 13 teachers and 208 students. Highly significant improvements in attainment were found for the group whose teachers had undertaken additional training in instructional skills.

The rather odd conclusion that is made from this is that money spent on training teachers in instructional skills may be more productive than money spent on aides. However, no thought is given to how aides could be shaped up in similar ways, or strategies looked at for maximising their performance – perhaps even more cheaply than training in instructional skills for the teachers. The lesson that emerges from the DeVault study – using Stallings' original data – is that aides are used to less than maximum effect. It seems to be an inappropriate comparison to make in this case, given the original aims of the study (i.e. training for teachers versus more aides) to compare teachers with post-experience training with aides who have no training at all. An alternative comparison might have been teachers trained in class management and instructional skills versus teachers trained in managing their support more effectively.

If it may seem impossible to replicate the DeVault study in the UK, given lower levels of staffing and resourcing for compulsory school-age children, the nursery is an environment in the UK which provides situations where the deployment of additional personnel can be studied.

Clift, Cleave and Griffin (1980) studied forty nurseries, looking especially at the nature of the adults' activities there. Discriminant analysis showed teachers and assistants to be differentially deployed by profession, as one would expect. The most significant difference between the professions was found in respect of frequency of change of activity, reflecting in turn differences in how groups spent their time: teachers spent most of their time on children's activities and administration; assistants spent more time on housework (routine activities) and equipment. Teachers were more homogeneous in the way that they behaved, assistants tending to reproduce the pattern of their teachers (perhaps, again, in the absence of role definition, relying on modelling, as in the DeVault study above). 'Others' in the classes most often were students, ancillaries, parents and school pupils.

Interestingly, this research – in line with much already reviewed – indicates that a plateau occurs in the benefits accorded by having extra adults in the classroom: most involvement with children occurred when three adults were present – beyond this, there was no improvement. The extent to which role differentiation occurred varied: where it was low teachers were more often involved in the domestic work of the nursery at the expense of involvement with children. The importance of role allocation and role differentiation is reinforced once again.

Tizard (1981) criticises the research of Clift *et al.* for not adopting a design which would allow the question posed at the outset (i.e. are there clear advantages in employing teachers rather than nursery nurses?) to be answered. A comparative study would be needed for this, she asserts. Neither did the authors address the question 'How can we use volunteers most effectively?' This is almost exactly the same question put by DeVault *et al.* at the conclusion of their research, but one which, in a similar way, seems to have been side-stepped by Stallings *et al.*

LeLaurin and Risley (1972) begin to focus on some of the processes involved in the drop-off in personal effectiveness when two or more people are involved in the classroom in a study of the organisation of day-care environments. They say that it is inevitable that time is lost from planned activities during daily transition from one activity to another and they use time lost as a measure of staff effectiveness in two methods of organisation for staff activity. In the first of these methods (the 'zone' procedure) each adult (teacher or assistant) was assigned responsibility for a particular area in the class, and for all children who passed through that area. In the other method ('man-to-man') each adult was responsible for a particular group of children. The zone procedure was found to be associated with a significantly smaller loss in child participation in planned activities than the man-to-man procedure.

LeLaurin and Risley stress that the structures within which personnel operate have significant effects on children's behaviour. They go on to emphasise that with untrained personnel there is an even greater need for specific guidelines on the ways in which activity is structured and organised.

Johnston (1984), in an analysis of the replies of 291 respondents in a United States national survey, found that teachers in nursery classes reported more problems related to the area of supervision of subordinate staff than in any other area:

They reported problems such as getting staff to follow through on assigned responsibilities, getting staff to be on time for their shifts, and getting staff to recognise and act on children's needs in an appropriate fashion. Prekindergarten teachers want to provide for communication among their staff and report problems in getting staff to work in a cooperative fashion. The teachers report problems in finding time to adequately supervise staff, particularly when the teachers are also responsible for children.

(Johnston 1984: 35)

Some of the problems identified here – such as getting staff to be on time for their shifts – reveal a lack of contiguity between the kind of situation likely to be experienced by the nursery school teacher in the United States and that experienced by the mainstream primary or secondary school teacher in the UK. Nevertheless, the same tensions noted by Clift *et al.* are reported here.

However, not all the issues that arise for these non-teaching personnel are concerned with definitional clarity. Riches (1982) – through case study analysis – looks at what he calls the micropolitics of non-teaching staff, which in this case includes not just ancillaries and welfare assistants, but also technicians. Through trying to establish power, status and improved conditions in situations which are characteristically undervalued and underpaid, non-teaching staff resort to ploys which minimise rather than maximise their effective team involvement with other groups. He says: 'Most female non-teaching staff, especially the part-time ones, would appear to offer minimal criticism of the way they are managed.' However, they can develop power: the controlling caretaker, the gatekeeping secretary. Non-teaching staff are not necessarily passive. Riches draws on a case study where technicians sought to align themselves with teachers through use of the staff room; by 'distancing', i.e. hiding in the preparation room and making themselves available only to the head; by 'leverage', i.e. delaying doing tasks to show that their service was a favour which could not be taken for granted. The micropolitics involved here may have particularly significant effects where there is more than one from a particular non-teaching group involved in a class (see, for example, McBrien and Weightman 1980 p. 45) and may to an extent account for the phenomenon of diminishing returns which I note in that situation.

Ward and Tikunoff (1979) also pick up the issues of micropolitics in a review of the use of non-teachers. They go further than suggesting that the introduction of other adults may not in itself have beneficial effects. They state:

Using nonteachers for instructional purposes may have both desirable *and undesirable* effects.

(Ward and Tikunoff 1979: 300)

In making this claim Ward and Tikunoff point to factors in social organisation, feeling that introducing others into the classroom alters several features of the classroom, a major one of these being the distribution of power and authority. This contrasts with interpretations made of the alterations which emerge from team teaching teams where the emphasis has been on interpersonal and ideological mismatches and the infringement of territory.

SPECIAL SCHOOLS

Special education presents several opportunities for looking at the work of additional people in the classroom. One of these, the use of support teaching, has already been examined as one particular kind of team teaching.

Special education, though, also presents the opportunity to look at the ways in which classroom assistants have been deployed, since in special schools and special units their employment has been commonplace. It is useful to separate the deployment of teaching assistants in this setting from their deployment in mainstream settings for two reasons. First, the dynamics of special and mainstream classes are very different and comparisons are not always valid. Second, in special schools the tradition of employment of extra people in the classroom is a long and stable one. A whole range of people have been present: nursery nurses, ancillary helpers, volunteers and specialist professionals such as physiotherapists and speech therapists. The issue of teaming has therefore been addressed, often with imagination.

An interesting study, which repeats the kind of findings noted already in other settings and tries to suggest answers to those questions and some solutions, comes from McBrien and Weightman (1980). In a school for children with severe learning difficulties they noted that the injection of extra assistants into a class was, without closely structured organisation, unrelated with measures of the children's engagement: the engagement of the children remained at around 30 per cent whether the number of staff in the class was one, two, three, four, five or six. Furthermore, they assert that the quality of the contact that staff make is not always appropriate (e.g. loudly attending to children who were misbehaving): only 48 per cent of assistants' time was spent in activities of which the researchers approved.

They attempted to tackle this problem by directly addressing the issue of definitional clarity. Simply training staff in appropriate activities and dividing up the teachers' role so that there was less room for ambiguity among the team members – a technique they call *room management* – raised the staff's 'on task behaviour' figure from 48 per cent to 74 per cent, and raised the children's engagement from around 30 per cent to 57 per cent.

Conclusions here appear to be very similar to those of Stallings *et al.* in the context of aides in mainstream schools. Similar findings are made by Spangler and Marshall (1983), who report that training for child-care workers (in prompting, circulating and making available appropriate activity) increased the activity level (i.e. engagement) of the children from 10 per cent to 70 per cent.

However, Woods and Cullen (1983) contest the notion that it is the definitional ingredients which are responsible for the success of room management. Like McBrien and Weightman, they were able to show that room management had dramatic effects on engagement – this time of severely handicapped residents of a long-stay hospital (from a mean of 10 per cent to one of 60 per cent) when compared with other small-scale interventions (using toilet training and a token economy). However, their data show that while there was an immediate initial effect this steadily tailed off over 15 months. The authors identify the operant psychology of room management as more important than the definitional ingredients. However, they point to the latter in accounting both for the initial success and subsequent tailing off of the techniques, tacitly suggesting that experimenter effects are particularly strong where the focus is on roles and interpersonal behaviour.

There is an interesting contrast to Woods and Cullen's findings in a more recent study by Ware and Evans (1987) which directly identifies definitional clarity as an important variable in the success of the team. Their research casts doubt on the value of room management as a means of significantly increasing the engagement of multiply-handicapped children. However, it supports the idea that the beneficial findings noted under room management regimes can be attributed to the ingredients of room management that make clear knowledge of responsibilities easier for staff. They looked at two classes which both used room management procedures with multiply-handicapped children and found that room management had the effect of more evenly dividing staff attention among children. However, it did not affect the engagement of the children when they were not being attended to by the staff member. It increases the share of adult attention but not their level of engagement 'very much' (they do not say whether the increase is significant).

Much of what has been said so far relates to ambiguity, uncertainty and lack of definition in the roles people are being asked to play when they work together in the classroom. Escudero and Sears (1982) point to similar problems, again in the context of severely and profoundly handicapped pupils. Questionnaires were sent to teachers of these children and their aides, and using the questionnaire responses their roles were examined. (Seventy-two teachers and 65 teacher aides were questioned.) They discovered a lack of consensus about the roles of the different personnel. Analyses isolated some areas where there was little difference between teachers and aides in their views about their roles but some areas where there was a significant difference.

PARENTAL INVOLVEMENT

Parental involvement represents a trend somewhat removed from the foregoing in terms of the likely relationships among participants. Parents provide their time voluntarily, and their status is therefore very different from that of ancillary helpers. They are far less a part of the 'host culture' than those who have been discussed so far.

In addition, the trend to parental involvement is emergent in nature, and it will be instructive also to look at the changes in ideology behind the move in so far as these affect relationships among participants. Existing studies of its extent will also be examined (since these represent the only documentation of the occurrence of any kind of new team), as well as the problems and implications which emerge.

Research on the trend to parental involvement did not begin in earnest until the late 1970s; it was only then that attitudes were changing about the desirability of involving parents in the class. Discussion at the beginning of the 1980s stressed the desirability of parental involvement: Meighan (1981) and Cullingford (1984) both make the point that parents ought to be seen as having a right to involvement at school. Only their effective exclusion by the professionals for so long has enabled the question of whether they should be in the classroom to be posed at all.

Even when the philosophical and educational credentials of parental involvement had been established, there was still debate about the ethics of involving parents and volunteers, untrained and unpaid, in the classroom, especially if by involving them it was depriving someone – perhaps an ancillary helper, perhaps even a teacher – of a job. The discussion therefore became political as well as educational.

There was a great variety of sometimes strongly held opinion on the theme: as recently as the mid-1980s Stierer (1985), in his survey about volunteers who help with reading in schools, found that the practice was very patchy even within schools due to disagreement among staff about whether to use volunteers. Epstein (1986), from a vantage point gained from some quite detailed research on the place of parents in American schools, also points to two trains of thought about parents in school: one rooted in the sociology of Parsons and Weber, which says that the roles of family and school are incompatible, and another more recently articulated view which suggests that they are complementary and that communication should be encouraged.

The most detailed account of parental help in primary schools is still to be found in the research of Cyster *et al.* (1979). The comprehensiveness of that account has yet to be superseded. Given the extent and intensity of debate about parental involvement, updates and refinements of the work of Cyster *et al.* are long overdue: their national survey in 1979 found that parental involvement in school-based activities most commonly took the form of 'help on school visits and outings' followed by 'sewing . . . and minor repairs to school equipment'. Help alongside the teacher in the classroom formed a relatively insignificant dimension of parental involvement, and was not felt to be worthy of attention in itself.

Given the developments that have occurred more recently – in parental involvement in reading, for instance (e.g. Jackson and Hannon 1981; Tizard, Schofield and Hewison 1982; Macleod 1985) – it is to be expected that activities such as sewing might now be less important (in relation to other activities) than they were in 1979. Research of varying quality, but widely reported in the press, has proclaimed the benefits for academic attainment inherent in parental involvement and it is to be expected that this would have effected some shift away from the traditional parent activities that Cyster *et al.* noted. There is ample research now to document the gains to be made in children's attainments when parents have been systematically involved, though it has to be said that the most thorough research in this area is American.

The British research tends to be single-school or single-local authority-specific – as in the work already mentioned (Jackson and Hannon 1981, at one school, Belfield, in Rochdale; Tizard *et al.* 1982, in Haringey; Macleod 1985, in Coventry).

American research is wider ranging. Olmstead and Rubin (1983) summarise two reviews of parent participation programmes in the United States; in the first (of 35 studies) all the programmes were found to be associated with gains in children's achievement; in the second (of 40 studies) 83 per cent reported such improvement. However, no comments are made on significance of gains in achievement or quality of research design in these studies.

Irrespective of the quality of the research, a wealth of studies points to the benefits of parental involvement for children's attainment. On the basis of this one would have expected to see some shift in the nature of parental involvement at school. One might further expect that shift to be toward parental involvement in more formal areas of the curriculum. This indeed appears to be the case: in Stierer's 1985 survey of 500 schools, 53 per cent of responding schools had unpaid people regularly helping children with reading, a 'core curriculum' subject, and in 86 per cent of these the helpers included parents.

Tizard, Mortimore and Burchell (1981), in looking at the involvement of parents in nursery and infant schools, emerge with a typology of objections to involvement which reveals the ideological tensions existing at the beginning of the 1980s. On the one hand was the idea that parents should be involved and that there should be a freeing-up of institutions and a debunking of the over-professionalism of previous decades. On the other hand was the notion that to involve parents was to play into the hands of the emerging anti-dirigiste political consensus.

In this study Tizard and her colleagues did action research in seven nursery units in London. Their aims were to develop a programme of activities for fostering involvement and to find out why parents did or did not take up opportunities offered. They point to the fact that professionals seemed to be moving to a consensus that parental involvement is beneficial but note that 'Few attempts seem to have been made to seek the views of parents [about involvement], or even to describe their reactions to the attempts to involve them'. After interviews with parents and staff they conclude that participation may be seen by parents as a 'new and extra burden'. Interestingly, six of the 14 staff interviewed thought that parents made no positive contribution to their children's education, reinforcing the fact that at this time (1980) we were at an intersection in ideologies about involvement. All but two of the 14 staff saw potential dangers summarised by the comments 'You must be firm. Otherwise if you give them half a chance they'd take over the place', and 'I feel torn between the parents and the children ... it's hard to know how to distribute my attention'.

This study also points to misunderstandings in aims, underpinned by mismatches in ideology. For example, in the 'Wendy House' (as the home corner was still called in 1980) used by teachers to stimulate imaginative play, 30–50 per cent of parents thought this facility was for early domestic science training (in setting the table, etc.).

The typology of objections to parental involvement in class is very similar to that set out at the beginning of chapter 3:

1 managerial objections – e.g. the need for timetabling help, and coping with 'difficult' parents;
2 professional objections – the fact that teachers and nursery nurses have specialised skills which may be diluted or undermined by the presence of untrained parents; parents gossiping, etc.; trade union-based – unpaid help, unemployed teachers;
3 educational objections – the teacher can educate children adequately without parents;
4 personal objections – the teacher may be embarrassed by the presence of others or may feel they interfere with relationships or authority.

However, the other side of the coin was that parental involvement was seen positively by some of the teachers: 'We see parents not as a cheap alternative to employing more teachers, but an important potential supplement, or resource to the life of the school, which is at present under-utilised.' 'What many parents liked best was to work regularly with the same child, or the same small group of children.' In the seven classes the number of parents willing to work regularly at least once a week varied between 1 and 12 depending mainly on size of family and where the mother worked.

The conclusion at the end of the project was that the aims set at the outset were met only in a limited way – and even this limited success had to be taken in the context of motivated volunteer schools, and an outside project team providing support. Problems had arisen out of a lack of appropriate training for parents and teachers; out of communication difficulties; out of narrow views of professionalism. These points are of particular relevance here, and they form recurrent themes through the remainder of this book.

Similar disjunctions in understanding and communication are found by Goode (1982). In a study of parental perspectives in the process of schooling she found that teachers felt disquiet about home-school projects: parents did not understand the aims of worksheets, etc.; they found difficulty helping children over an obstacle; they handled children inappropriately, by for example telling children off for minor mis-demeanours. She concludes that parents were being used as apprentice teachers without being prepared for the task. Again here, a definitional lacuna is accompanied by mismatches in ideology which are inadequately addressed.

Mortimore and Mortimore (1984) review a range of studies looking at parental involvement at school. They conclude that helping *in class* was one of the least successful of a range of activities for stimulating involve-ment. They say that parents sometimes appear to be hesitant because they are unsure of what is expected of them and because they feel that their presence may be seen as 'interfering'. Tying in their own research with that of others and in particular that of the ILEA junior school study, they note that any success achieved had to be interpreted in the context of special programmes supported by enthusiastic teachers and aided by committed outsiders (as in the Tizard *et al.* study just reviewed). Involvement which did take place *in the classroom* was by a small minority (5 per cent) of the parents of children in the class. Looking at the factors which might have limited successful parental involvement they point to poor *communication* between teacher and parent (too much jargon used) and inability by teachers to *organise* additional help in the class. They note that little attention is given either in initial training of teachers or in INSET to work with parents: 'Work with parents, although paid lip service is rarely given priority in ... training, or in any subsequent assessment of a teacher's work. Hence the teacher may not only feel role conflict but guilt if he or she devotes much time to parents.' They go on to point to the 'opportunity for misunderstandings and tensions' where someone with a clear legal responsibility works alongside others whose *status* is that of unpaid volunteers.

Interestingly, very similar attitudes, results and conclusions are revealed in American research on parental involvement. Epstein (1985) surveyed 3,700 first, third and fifth grade teachers in Maryland, with follow-up interviews with 82 of those teachers. Some 1,200 parents from those 82 classrooms were surveyed and their children's attainments and behaviour assessed. She found that 70 per cent of the parents never did anything at the school, while only 4 per cent (a figure very close to the 5 per cent reported by the Mortimores in the UK) were very active. Despite the rhetoric about involvement, she says, relatively few teachers frequently or systematically involve parents in the classroom. This is related by the author to lack of attention to parental involvement in teacher training.

Other American research points to similar attitudes and similar problems – but similar gains where parental involvement had been handled sensitively. Leyser (1985), in a survey of parents of disabled students, found conflicts between home and school because of differences in goals, philosophy, values and expectations; differences were also found due to differences in opinion on what constitutes appropriate education.

There is a lingering lack of communication between teachers and parents and a lack of consonance over the aims of parental involvement. Stierer's (1985) survey of schools' use of reading volunteers (already reported on p. 47) shows the way in which responding schools were viewing parental involvement. The benefits cited included: 'extra reading practice' (66 per cent of respondents), and 'frees teacher from repetitive tasks to concentrate on more specialised aspects of teaching, e.g. work with less able' (33 per cent). The problems cited were primarily *status-related*. They included 'unsuitable' helpers; parents' gossip; resentment of parents by non-professionals; and enabling authorities to shirk their responsibilities to staff schools properly. These were also the main reasons given by schools who did not use helpers for not doing so – these schools also saw such giving of help with reading going over professional boundaries – helpers should be concerned with non-academic tasks.

Status-related concerns of this kind are likely, in themselves, to lead to definitional uncertainty. Anxieties about the legitimacy of involving or being involved will lead to ambiguity or conflict over the appropriateness of certain classes of activity.

Essentially, these problems are – at least in the form that they are articulated – stemming from the heterogeneous nature of this teaming. The difficulties appear to be principally attributed to managerial and professional concerns, although these often emerge from ideological differences or concern over status.

Thus, caution and diffidence on the part of parents is often matched on the teachers' side by lingering doubts about the validity of parental involvement in the classroom and inability to cope with its consequences in terms of the altered dimensions of classroom management. This is borne out by Jowett and Baginsky (1988), who surveyed all LEAs in England and Wales, enquiring about work with parents. Parental involvement is taken by the authors to mean a broad spectrum of activities: involving parents in the curriculum, e.g. reading; transition (primary to secondary); classroom activities; and providing courses and support for parents. Their interviews show that 'While it may no longer be defensible to say that "parents are not interested" exactly what the focus of their interest is – and should be – is still contested'.

As far as involving parents specifically in the classroom went, there was still, even in the late 1980s, the finding that 'the essential differences between parents and teachers are sometimes viewed as the reason for not promoting these developments'. However, there was also the encouraging development that these very differences were also sometimes cited as the rationale for the existence of parents in the classroom.

There are a host of tacit assumptions and expectations about existing practice which are violated in any change of this kind. Parents are expected to be assimilated smoothly and seamlessly on the twin assumptions that first, having an extra adult in the classroom will automatically be helpful, and second, that parental involvement, of whatever kind, is beneficial. Many studies point to the difference between the rhetoric and the reality of this kind of partnership, highlighting the frictions which emerge out of mismatches in ideology, threat to beliefs about status, and the changed parameters of organisation which such misunderstandings occasion. Discovering how far such factors are responsible for inhibitions about making adequate role definition when parents and others form part of classroom teams will be one of the tasks of the remainder of this book.

A strategy in this task will be to examine the *attributions* of those involved in the classroom teams about the dynamics of the team and the behaviour of their co-team members. The attributions made about team difficulties by teachers are moderated by assumptions made about the backgrounds of those who are helping in the classroom. Indeed, the contrast in the kinds of attributions made about reasons for teamwork succeeding or failing form a fruitful avenue for further discussion and will be discussed further in the following chapter.

5

A MODEL FOR ANALYSING CLASSROOM TEAMS

This book addresses two main questions. The first is about the extent of the new teamwork; the second is about the nature of the problems which people confront in the new teams. I shall be looking in more detail at the extent of the new teamwork in chapter 7. However, the substantial, difficult-to-answer questions concern not so much the extent of teamwork but rather the *nature of the problems* that emerge from the new teamwork; the main part of this book examines these problems. In order to give shape to that examination I shall put forward in this chapter a model for analysing classroom teams. This model is based on the review in the previous chapters and I shall use it in most of the studies that comprise the rest of this book. It is used to organise the ideas that arise from these studies; it is used to generate explanations, and it is used to generate ideas for further research.

THE NATURE OF CLASSROOM TEAMS' PROBLEMS

A summary of the problems noted in chapters 3 and 4 is given in figure 5.1, and a typology proposed to accompany it. It is suggested that there are mismatches or tensions which impede the effectiveness of teams. Those mismatches or tensions may be managerial, interpersonal, ideological, definitional, practical or personal. There are also concerns due to participants' feelings of marginality. Interestingly, the difficulties which are highlighted most prominently and consistently across the typology are in the area of role definition. The isolation of these various concerns will be used as the basis for part of the research which follows in chapters 8 to 11, particularly in organising and grouping interview responses.

More shape may be given to this analysis than that provided by figure 5.1. The various schemata highlighted throughout this review as explanatory or simply descriptive features of teamwork phenomena in classrooms can now be seen to be interrelated. The success of the classroom team is inhibited by a range of real or perceived mismatches between participants.

Nature of problem

Category of person

	Support teachers	Team teachers	Parents	Aides	Supply
Managerial	**Williamson** '89 – host teachers unwelcoming	**Bennett** '80 – personality clashes among colleagues	**Tizard** '80 – teachers' difficulty supervising parents	**Riches** '82 – some aides try to establish power **Johnston** '84 – problems supervising staff	
Interpersonal	**O'Hanlon** '88 – host and support different ideas on need also **Williamson** '89 and **Wilson** '89	**Hargreaves** '80 – different members' philosophies inhibit teaming	**Leyser** '85 – parents' and teachers' different views on what constitutes education also **Goode** '82		
Ideological	**O'Hanlon** '88 – tension as ideas conflict with host's **Williamson** '89 – new role unclear	**Bennett** '80 – team members uncertain about roles	**Mortimore** '84 – teachers feel conflict in helping parents **Epstein** '86 – differing roles family/school	**McBrien** '80 – room management a success because it removed ambiguity **Escudero** '82 – little agreement on roles	
Definitional					**Clifton** '87 – supply feels uncertain in another's territory

Practical

Personal

Marginal

Williamson '89 – no time to negotiate roles also **Ferguson** '82 and **Newton** '88

Geen '85 and **Cohen** '76 – teaming declines due to lack of time **Bennett** '80 – one of concerns noted – time

Johnston '84 – time for supervising

Bines '86 – inhibition about being oneself

Geen '85; **Hatton** '85; **Hargreaves** '80 – teachers reluctant, embarrassed, intimidated, sensitive

Tizard '80 – teachers may be embarrassed in front of others

O'Hanlon '88 – different views alienate support from mainstream

Clifton '87 – supply marginal outside routines of 'resident'

Figure 5.1 A typology of problems faced by classroom team participants, with examples taken from the literature review

These may be on ideological or personal grounds, or they may exist because the ground rules for cooperation have not been clearly set, thus generating a host of ambiguities and mismatches in expectation.

These various mismatches may be either attenuated or exaggerated by organisational strategies, such as the provision of extra time for communication or planning. Depending on the intensity of the original mismatches and depending also on the effects of these attenuators/exaggerators, participants will seek something which many observers have called the autonomy of the teacher. The degree to which autonomy is sought may be placed on a continuum: participants will at one end of the autonomy continuum seek to increase autonomy, through, for instance, more closely defining their territories. However, others may seek to decrease autonomy through taking active steps to increase team working and encouraging fuller participation by all those involved.

At both ends of the continuum there is an attempt to reduce stress. The different characteristics of these attempts to reduce stress at these polar extremes result from completely different ways of viewing the situation. Where attempts are being made to define territory it seems likely that players in the arena will be construing their parts in terms of status, perhaps formalising status relationships to relieve stress; I shall call such attempts at reducing stress 'status solutions'. At the other end, the construal may be that such relationships are concerned simply with role as distinct from status; I shall call these attempts at reducing stress 'role solutions' or 'definitional solutions'.

Status solutions and role (or definitional) solutions share the objective of reducing stress, though the former achieves this through codifying responsibilities and power and locating these more clearly in specific individuals (teacher, support teacher, parent, etc.), while the latter achieves it through locating the sets of responsibilities in *roles* rather than *people*. The latter has clear advantages in terms of the attributions which may be put upon the behaviour of fellow team members. (The contribution of attribution theory will be examined shortly.) The relationship of these notions may be drawn schematically, as in figure 5.2.

If one feature had to be isolated as characterising the majority of the difficulties revealed in the previous two chapters, it would be stress or tension. Attempts to relieve stress are seen in the building of status and autonomy, which in turn are promoted by and rest on incongruence over role and style. Such incongruence may be found in any of the areas highlighted at the outset: interpersonal, ideological or definitional.

This model may help in understanding the processes taking place in the various interrelationships occurring among adults in classrooms. Differences in role and status will clearly affect the nature of interpersonal perceptions, and the ways these are construed will in turn determine the stability, harmony and effectiveness of the teams comprising these varied personnel.

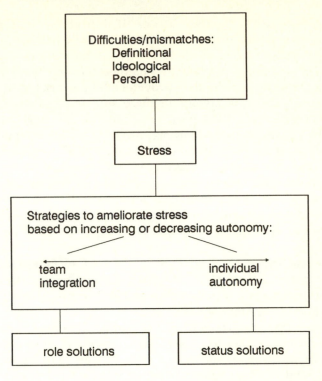

Figure 5.2 Strategies adopted by classroom teams

THE CONTRIBUTION OF ATTRIBUTION THEORY

Attribution theory provides a useful vehicle for examining these inter-relationships and constructions more closely. Heider (1944, 1958) assumed that people perceive their social environments as predictable, and that the observed behaviour of others could be attributed to inferred intentions. He writes:

> Of great importance for our picture of the social environment is the attribution of events to causal sources. . . . Attribution in terms of impersonal and personal causes, and with the latter, in terms of intent, are everyday occurrences that determine much of our under-standing of and reaction to our surroundings.

(Heider 1958: 16)

The working of the classroom team, then, and the success or failure of teams to work in the classroom, will be attributed by team members either to impersonal factors or to personal factors.

Already attribution theory appears to offer an insight into some of the processes involved in classroom teams. If difficulties occur in shared classrooms they may be attributed either to factors in the situation outside the team members' control (a windy day, 3R, a Friday afternoon); or they may be attributed directly to the other member(s) of the team. The value of attribution theory here is that it provides a framework for interpreting and analysing adults' behaviour in these situations. It can do this by looking at variations in the ways in which individuals make attributions about those problems. Individuals may attribute problems to other team members and to the dispositions of those members based on intentions those members are assumed to have. Or they may attribute problems to wider contextual features of the situation. The success or failure of the team – in a 'team' situation which allows for little on-the-job communication – is bound to depend crucially on these inferences. The contribution of attribution theory to the model proposed in figure 5.2 is shown in figure 5.3.

Clearly, the way in which attribution of success or failure of the team is made to personal factors ('it's me that's making the team work badly') or to others in the team, or to the team itself, will be crucial in determining the motivation to improve the situation.

The distinction that Heider's (1958) model drew was principally in assigning causality either to causal forces of persons, or to causal forces of situations. In *autonomy solutions* we may be seeing attribution to team members, while in *team solutions* may be seen a tendency to attribute success or failure to the nature of the team. Clearly the latter is more amenable to change, and thus to resolution than the former.

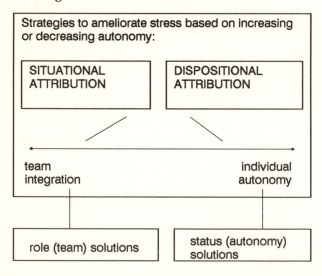

Figure 5.3 The contribution of attribution theory to understanding stress-reducing strategies

Jones and Davis (1965) refine the ideas of attribution theory to provide a model which can be borrowed to help account for the differences between teams, where those teams may comprise members of very varying backgrounds. They suggest that inferred intentions are built upon assumptions about the knowledge and ability of actors – in the case of this research, fellow team members. They say:

> the perceiver [in our case the 'host' teacher] typically starts with the overt action of another [the team teacher, parent, ancillary, etc.]; this is the grist for his cognitive mill. He then makes certain decisions concerning ability and knowledge which will let him cope with the problem of attributing particular intentions to the actor.
>
> (Jones and Davis 1965: 222)

Clearly the educational backgrounds and personal philosophies assumed to be associated with various personnel, from parents to ancillaries to support teachers, will strongly influence the attribution of intentions in observed action in the classroom. The professional–lay relationships will fare differently from the professional–professional ones, if attribution theory is correct. Jones and Davis' model builds on Heider's original model to suggest that the kind of responsibility attributed to the co-worker is assignable to different levels. Those levels are:

1 association (i.e. responsible for all effects with which the person is associated);
2 commission (responsible for effects instrumental in producing);
3 foreseeability (only for those which could have been foreseen); and
4 intentionality (only for those intended).

Team members will, it seems, build more or less correct impressions of their co-workers' biographies and these will determine the level of responsibility assumed for success or failure. In other words, attribution theory predicts that heterogeneous teams (comprising perhaps teacher, parent, ancillary) will fare better than professionally homogeneous teams (teacher–teacher) because of the lesser likelihood that in the former there will be responsibility assigned by the host teacher to her co-participants for tensions or disjunctions in the activity of the class.

Paradoxically, perhaps, there is not a simple extension of this argument along the continuum from most unlike teams (say, parent–teacher) to most alike (say, primary team teachers). Different kinds of teachers with different backgrounds and ideologies (say, support teacher and mainstream teacher) may have little sympathy with each other. Intentionality may be attributed to a support teacher with a different ideological framework for certain difficulties within the class in the way that it might not with a teacher who is perceived to come from a similar ideological stable. In other words, if things go wrong in such a team it may be easy for the mainstream teacher to think of the support teacher 'It's *you* with your stupid ideas about special needs that's messing things up here'.

The model proposed here, based on attribution theory, is employed to account in part at least for the findings of the literature that has so far been reviewed. It will be used to generate ideas and formulate hypotheses which will be tested in the research which follows in chapters 8 to 11.

6

INVESTIGATING CLASSROOM TEAMS

How should we investigate classroom teams? Should we make detailed systematic observations of teams in operation? Should we ask participants about their experiences of working in classroom teams? Should we send questionnaires to teachers to find out about the nature of the teams? Whether we do any or all of these depends very much on what we are trying to find out. Simple questions can very often be answered by using simple methods. But often in education the question to be posed is not simple; indeed, it may not be at all clear what the important questions are at the investigation's outset. It is only by beginning to look at the area that the real questions become apparent.

It is in both formulating relevant questions and helping to answer them that theory has a place. Theory, in education at least, has come in for something of a hammering of late, but I subscribe to the view of Kurt Lewin on this subject. He said that there is nothing as practical as a good theory. Theory represents a distillation of the ideas of those who have taken the time and trouble to study an area in depth. To ignore it is to cast aside masses of accumulated wisdom. Theory should enable us to frame our ideas; it should enable us to provide a mental scaffold for our experiences and our reading. It should be a stimulus to new ideas and new understandings.

Two important theories – construct theory and attribution theory – are drawn on in this research. I use them for the reasons I have just mentioned: to organise thought and experience; to stimulate new ideas; to help to understand what sometimes seems perplexing behaviour. Without them, the reviews, reports and reflections in this book would be much impoverished.

In this chapter I attempt to explain my use of these theories, as well as the methods I have chosen for doing research into classroom teams.

THE COMPLEXITY OF CLASSROOM TEAMS

Teams are complex social phenomena. Where these very complexities are the subject for study, the methods of analysing the processes taking

61

place within them must adopt an appropriate form – one which is able to address, assimilate and explicate this complexity.

The traditional methods of psychological and educational research have sought to simplify this complexity. They have tried to look at single, isolated variables by stripping away or controlling all variables which are of no obvious relevance to the situation. There are problems in dividing complex phenomena into discrete units for individual study in this way. There is the danger that we may so over-simplify the situation that the study of it and the subsequent analysis become meaningless. The acknowledgement of this fact has led many fields, including psychology, sociology and education, increasingly to seek new, more sophisticated methods of analysis – methods which are able to address the very complexity from which traditional methods shy away.

However, many in education have eschewed the insights offered by new methods of researching into complex questions, tenaciously relying on more familiar paradigms. While there has been a move towards illuminative enquiry (via, for instance, symbolic interactionism) as a means of unravelling the increasingly complex and diverse ways in which people organise themselves and negotiate their roles in relating with one another, research based on such perspectives is still regarded as 'soft' by many educational researchers. They hold to the notion that the only kind of meaningful research is research that is rooted in what Parlett and Hamilton (1987) call 'the agricultural-botany paradigm'. (Experimental psychology and its use of statistics took shape in the 1930s following Ronald Fisher's work with agricultural botanists.) By this paradigm they are referring to research which will yield 'objective' numerical data to permit statistical analyses.

But methods of enquiry which belong to this tradition are, many would say, unlikely to be adequate to make an explication or even a definition of the kinds of processes to be recognised and understood in the classroom teams under study here. If, as Popkewitz (1984) suggests, our paradigms provide lenses for illuminating the processes which surround us, traditional paradigms may distort our understanding by over-simplifying it.

DIFFERENT IDEAS ABOUT HOW TO STUDY GROUPS

Much of the traditional research into groups and teams was framed at a time when people fitted into institutions, rather than institutions adapting to their personnel – when McGregor's (1960) Theory X (the idea that people are at root work-shy and need to be forced or cajoled to work) had not given way to Theory Y (the idea that people will enjoy work and work well if the conditions are right, and if they feel they belong). As X gives way to Y, as the pervasive power of institutions, organisations and other structures gives way to the increasing power of smaller autonomous collections of people, including the teams of classrooms, so the nature of more traditional kinds of enquiry involving experiment are seen to be limiting or even distorting. The displacement of system-led phenomena by phenomena that are constructed out of negotiations among partici-pants in complex networks has to be reflected in appropriate methods of enquiry, methods which explore the very richness and complexity which experimental-analytic method would, on its own, attempt to simplify.

Scott (1983) notes the contrast between the differing perspectives in the following way. He notes that in the traditional model it was assumed that:

> variations in the way that organisations are structured were likely to have substantial consequences on the way that work was done.
> (Scott 1983: 13)

Scott goes on to assert that organisations cannot be viewed in this way; it has, he suggests, been discovered that many administrative arrangements have no impact on the activities of the organisation. The common-sense view that organisational arrangements profoundly affect the behaviour of the organisation's members is, he says, based on *rational myth*. Rather, he sees institutional environments determining organisational structure. Rules, belief systems and relational networks – which will surely exist in an especially fragile form in classroom teams – comprise these environ-ments; they determine purposes and then specify what activities are to be carried out and the kind of actors required to achieve them.

Toffler (1985) suggests that the organisational changes that are occurring are characterised by far looser relationships among people, and are marked by what he calls 'ad hocery'. In other words, the sharp managerial and procedural lines drawn in many organisations, including schools, will become increasingly blurred. The neatness of these lines at one time may have disposed researchers to believe that research using traditional methods would have been appropriate for the explication of processes drawn within them.

But the new blurring of these lines – the ad hocery that increasingly exists – sees the demise of the tidy-mindedness which gives rise to a requirement for theory and hypothesis in educational research. If in 'harder' fields scientific advance is now seen not so much resting in strict adherence to the progeny of positivist method, but rather in a 'series of non-cumulative developments' (Kuhn 1970) or, as Quinton (Magee 1982) puts it, in 'the piecemeal dissipation of confusion' we should in education be less self-conscious about departure from a self-imposed attachment to this methodology. The search for tidy theory and neat experiment is perhaps misplaced. Indeed, Glaser and Strauss, in sociological analysis, concur with this view in saying that theory should be seen as a process, 'that is, [we see] theory as an ever-developing entity, not as a perfected product' (1967: 32). This, essentially, is the view taken in shaping the central research of this book.

Another set of difficulties confounds the researcher into teams and that is concerned with the fragility, or sensitivity to observation of the subjects under study. The possible influence of the researcher and the investigation itself on the group under study has been well-recognised since the time of the Hawthorne study (Roethlisberger and Dickson 1939, reviewed in Tajfel and Fraser 1978: 218).

Such effects have recently been taken seriously even by natural scientists, as the phenomena they study become increasingly transitory, fragile or in other ways susceptible to observation and measurement. Recent years have seen a developing interest in the effects of observation in the 'hard' sciences that behaviourism and functionalism originally sought to emulate. Thus, the physicist Stewart (1990), for example, talks of 'quantum indeterminacy' in explaining the fact that events such as the decay of the radioactive atom are now held to be determined by chance, not law. In the context of the recent interest in the mathematics of chaos he draws also upon Heisenberg's Uncertainty Principle to note that in doing research we change the very subjects of our observation.

Whatever the validity or correctness of Stewart's conclusions, it is at least worth noting that even the 'hard' scientists who were the role models for the experimental-analytic tradition in the social sciences are now concerning themselves with doubts about the validity of the search for natural laws and about the effects of experimentation on the subject of study.

There are, then, two main reasons for mistrusting the traditional methods of enquiry. One is that these methods are inappropriate to study highly *complex* phenomena, and the other is that they are inadequate to deal with *fragile* phenomena. If complexity and fragility are thought of as continua, anything that is being studied could be placed somewhere along these continua. If instead of lying side-by-side with one another, the continua are rotated so that they are at right angles with one another, a clearer distinction between them can be made, as shown in figure 6.1.

Thus, many traditional natural science experiments would be placed somewhere in the bottom left quadrant, while those of quantum physics, and perhaps certain areas of experimental psychology would be in the top left. Certain engineering investigations might appear in the bottom right. However, it is in the top right, where both complexity and fragility are at play, that any investigation into the working of classroom teams would have to be placed. This combination of complexity and fragility calls for a variety of methods and instruments.

Shulman and Carey (1984), in a comprehensive review article about educational methodology, specifically draw on the case of team teaching as one that demonstrates how unamenable education is to the traditional methods of the natural sciences and psychology. They focus on team

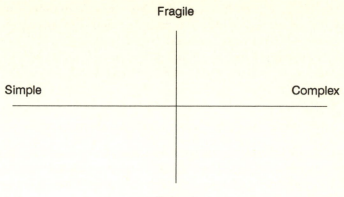

Figure 6.1 The relationship of complexity and fragility as
features of subjects of study

teaching as an example of the kind of practice that merits a different kind
of analysis from the one traditionally used in education. They say that
'attempts must be revised for understanding the failures of team teaching
and other strategies for rendering teaching a less isolated, more
collaborative exercise'.

ALTERNATIVE METHODOLOGIES AND SOCIAL
PSYCHOLOGY

A study of classroom teams and the interactions of their participants falls
most obviously into the area of social psychology. It is interesting to note
that Secord (1986), as one of the principal voices in the field of social
psychology, articulates an analogous debate here to the wider debate
about methodology in the social sciences generally. He draws a distinction
between two branches of social psychology – psychological social psychology (PSP) and sociological social psychology (SSP). He proceeds by
noting that PSP adopts a predominantly positivist stance, concentrating
on isolating variables and constructs such as role, status and group satisfaction; latterly, this interest has been superseded by interest in individual
behaviour and mental processes. By contrast, SSP adopts a more holist
stance, seeing behaviour as structured by the societal context. What is at
issue, says Secord, is the same long-standing debate over methodological
individualism and holism applied to history and the social sciences.

Secord goes on to note that PSP has been dominated by one approach,
while SSP is split into opposing camps: for example, those of symbolic
interactionism and ethnomethodology.

The 'staying power' of the methods of PSP may lie in their consistency, although PSP has evolved with changes in the mainstream of psychology, to become more cognitively oriented. Thus, Secord sees Heider's (1958) advances, for example into attribution theory, as a major marker in this process, and attribution theory has been (see chapter 5), and will be, drawn upon in this study.

THE IMPORTANCE OF LANGUAGE

However, Secord notes that despite the search for cognitive processes, language has been neglected as a topic for investigation by this branch of PSP. The significance of language to the meanings human beings create in their social lives, in teams or anywhere else, has relevance also to the more fundamental nature of social enquiry and social study as science, discussed above. Wittgenstein came to view human discourse as set within a series of language 'games', in which the rules of the game were constantly being reformulated by the participants; one has to understand the context and the rules of each game before being able to illuminate the meanings therein. Quinton sums it up thus:

> Wittgenstein's theory of action seems to imply that there can be no social and human sciences which use methods parallel to those of the natural sciences. Instead the study of man and society has to be interpretative in character . . . the form of social life being studied is, one might say, language-impregnated. Wittgenstein insisted that languages themselves are 'forms of life'.
>
> (Magee 1982: 92)

So, if we are to understand what goes on in classroom teams, appropriate methods for disentangling the meanings which inhere in the discourse therein are necessary. Appropriate methods for eliciting accounts about such discourse will be discussed in each of the pieces of research undertaken.

One of the strengths of newer methods of study such as ethnomethodology, according to Secord, is that they have grasped the importance of language in human action. (Wittgenstein would no doubt have approved.) Although behaviour in groups and teams is richly impregnated with language, traditional PSP studies, in common with the structuralist–functionalist branch of SSP, do not characteristically permit the individuals under study to speak freely about their experiences. Secord might as well have included construct theory among those models that have grasped the importance of language; Kelly (1955) suggested that people look at the world through 'templates' which they construct for themselves. He called these templates 'constructs', seeing them as people's ways of construing the world. We can gain access to these ways of construing via people's own accounts. This notion of *elicitation* of constructs is central to his philosophy and at variance with many of the techniques that have been built around construct theory, relying on a superimposition of these constructs. The methods to be used in this research are, by using participants' own verbal accounts, congruent with Kelly's thinking and also congruent with those models noted by Secord.

It is in this last respect that the disjunctions between the various approaches have most significance for the study of classroom teams. If an aim is to unravel and understand the constructs being employed by participants in relating to teams, then the instruments traditionally employed by PSP, including the repertory grid analysis of construct theory, are less adequate than they might be. The methods of SSP, including accounts, interviews and participant observation, provide powerful means for gaining insights into these processes, and should be drawn upon.

THE NOTION OF RESEARCH DESIGN

There is a corollary to the debate on competing methodologies. This is concerned with the understanding and use of the notion of *design* in research. Burgess (1984) makes it clear that many presentations of educational research are misleading, suggesting, as they do, a linear process with a beginning, a middle and an end. He says that the reality is far more complex than the presentation suggests; social research is not just a question of neat procedures but a social process whereby interaction between the researcher and the research directly influences the course that the research programme takes. The design of the research reported in this book, comprising in large part qualitative study, conforms to the description given by Burgess. The temporal sequence of field study and analysis envisaged at the outset is confounded both by the exigencies of the real world of schools, and by the fact that findings and analysis are being made continuously. To this extent the design is *emergent* and developmental, continually in the process of revision in the light of new knowledge and understanding.

Sadler (1984) summarises the advantages and disadvantages of emergent design neatly. He says that a design is said to be emergent if the plan for collecting the data depends on the data already gathered. The plan changes in response to incoming information, and he quotes Cronbach (1982) as saying that emergent design is evaluation at its best. However, there is the risk that 'rolling with the punches' may produce research that is compliant, opportunistic or unscientific. I take the view that the question of 'compliance' rests in the purpose of the research – there can be no question of compliance if those who are the subject of study have no interest in the outcome of the research, as they might in a funded evaluation study. The charge of opportunism can be met by showing that the study maintains the integrity laid down by the theoretical and structural parameters established at the outset. On the last point, I cannot see how a study can be called unscientific simply on the basis of an emergent design; whether or not work is scientific rests, as I shall show later, on factors unrelated to the rigidity of the design.

RESEARCH DESIGN IN THIS BOOK

Much of the research reviewed so far relates to the roles people fulfil in small teams. This notion of role is central to the classroom teams under study. In such teams, role definitions are, it seems, often only loosely defined or absent altogether. Research appears to indicate that in such a vacuum, or when there are other sources of role tension, team participants will seek first to define roles for themselves, and then to ameliorate that tension by a variety of strategies. The research further suggests that clear definition of roles will assist team participants and shape positively the process by which the team culture is established. Classroom research indicates that there exist clear guidelines by which such roles may be defined in the classroom.

The design of the research studies that follow is therefore centred on the notion of *role*: I shall examine role and its *existence* and *nature* at the outset in the new teams; its *definition* by participants; the *transformation* of these definitions by participants and the construals and attributions they use in making those transformations; the *process* by which such construals transform the original ideas and the effects this may have; the extent to which clear role definition at the outset can *support* the team process. This broadly corresponds to three stages in the research.

Stage one

The first and most unproblematic area for research relates to the extent to which teamwork in classrooms is actually happening. This research rests on the assumption that informal teams are working in classes to a far greater extent than ever before, yet in the UK there is no research directed toward assessing the extent of this trend. A review of the literature produces only patchy information, with the most substantial research on amounts of teamwork coming from the area of parental involvement, though even here information on the extent to which the trend is occurring is tangential to other information. The extent to which others – support teachers, welfare assistants, ancillary helpers – are involved in classrooms has not been examined at all in UK schools. The dearth of knowledge about the extent of adult participation makes one of the first tasks of this thesis to ascertain how many other adults are involved in classrooms, what their status is, how often they are involved and what kinds of activities they do when they are there. Survey is the most appropriate means of accessing this information.

Stage two

The second broad element of this research concerns the dynamics of the new teams and the status and role of the teacher in her relationships with others in these teams. The literature already reviewed enables me to frame those issues in the context of relevant models and theories, and, further, to test ideas against those theories. From chapter 2 came the notion of roles existing as both structural variables and emergent processes. Thus, roles as they are originally and logically defined in the classroom (structural variables) become transformed in the messiness of real life to determine the nature of emergent processes to generate what I shall call *emergent roles*.

The means by which roles are defined and the nature of their transformation will be examined through the use of account-based data, through participant observation and through analysis of semi-structured interviews. The notion of roles being defined, understood and transformed by participants is consistent with the views and methods of ethnomethodologists and those of the ethogenists. Thus, Secord says that:

> What underlies both perspectives [ethnomethodology and ethogeny] is an appeal to rules and convention, sometimes encapsulated into roles. Roles are normative and involve consensus across a wide spectrum of society. . . . But the ethnomethodologists in particular stress tacit practical rules that help individuals in interaction to put a construction on the local situation. They make much of the idiosyncratic nature of situations and the repeated construction of their meanings in new forms from day to day.
>
> (Secord 1986: 157)

A tentative model put forward in chapter 5 based tensions in teamwork on various mismatches between the participants. Those mismatches were in turn resting on construals made about the nature of the task and about fellow participants, and it was in turn postulated that such construals depended upon inferences which participants make about the behaviour of others.

A synthesis of personal construct thinking and attribution theory seems apposite in exploring this further, though I know of no instances where such a synthesis has been attempted, perhaps because construct thinking has been in the main limited to applications in clinical and educational psychology, while attribution theory has in the main been employed in social psychology. Proponents of construct theory would no doubt eschew its promiscuous linkage with other theories, partly because of its very comprehensiveness as theory: to suggest that insights from construct theory may be enhanced by linkage with another theory is to imply inherent weakness in construct theory – and that wouldn't do at all.

However, in the specific situation under study here the consonance of the theories' starting points, together with the power of construct theory as a means of interpreting behaviour, and the specific strength of attribution theory in enabling a discussion of the attributions being made when construals take shape provides for a rich analysis. Each of the theories also has its repertoire of preferred techniques. Thus construct theory has relied very largely upon the interpretation of 'repertory grids' (e.g. Shaw 1981), while advances in attribution theory have rested upon conventional experimental procedures in what Secord (1986) has called psychological social psychology. Despite the lack of coming-together of these two approaches, they are marked by a fundamental contiguity. Eiser puts Heider's (1958) position in attribution theory thus:

> Heider assumed that people are motivated to perceive their social environment as predictable and hence controllable.
>
> (Eiser 1978: 238)

while Bannister and Fransella sum up personal construct psychology as

> an attempt to understand the way in which each of us experiences the world, to understand our 'behaviour' in terms of what it is designed to signify and to explore how we negotiate our realities with others.
>
> (Bannister and Fransella 1986: 27)

The emphasis on negotiation is interesting in the light of the methodological discussion above. Construct theory has not been generated from mainstream sociological social psychology, and its choices of methods do not reflect the evolution in methodologies in that field, which seek to tap the verbal encounters that are made in these negotiations. If 'negotiation' is as central as Bannister and Fransella state it to be, then the use of the methods of symbolic interactionism and ethnomethodology in construct theory is wholly consistent with its tenets and is justified in this research. Indeed, ethnomethodologists explicitly seek the tacit practical rules which enable individuals to make *constructions* about the meaning of personal interactions.

The model outlined in chapter 5 viewed the mismatches between classroom participants as existing primarily on ideological or personal grounds. I suggested that these various mismatches may be attenuated or exaggerated by the participants in the team, and that participants may or may not seek autonomy. An autonomy–teamwork continuum was postulated whereby participants are seen to be increasing their autonomy, or alternatively seeking to promote teamwork.

I suggested that at both ends of the continuum there is a desire to reduce stress, although different sets of construals are responsible for the alternative strategies. At either end are sets of constructs which rest in attributions made about fellow participants and about the situation in which they collectively find themselves. This research, from the framework of construct theory and attribution theory, has to determine the nature of those constructs and those attributions.

As already stated, construct theory and attribution theory are each associated with their own 'technologies' or sets of methodological procedures and practices. It is only relatively recently that such procedures have begun to be developed and expanded, for example by Jones (1985) in her 'cognitive mapping' (to be discussed more fully in chapter 10), though even she does not locate the looser, more qualitative interpretations she seeks in the wider set of procedures which have been developed by ethnomethodologists and symbolic interactionists. It appears that a useful synthesis may be derived from these methods coupled with the notions of construct theory and attribution theory. I shall discuss the use of construct theory and attribution theory further in chapter 10.

Consistent with the position taken by qualitative researchers, the use of these procedures will not be associated with any antecedent hypotheses. As Jones puts it, the starting point is

> a concern to understand the world of the research participants as they construct it. . . . Theory which is 'grounded' in the concepts and theorising of the people it is about is likely to 'fit and work' as the basis for explanation and prediction.
>
> (Jones 1985: 264)

She draws on Glaser and Strauss (1967) for a notion of grounded theory, in which the central idea is that categories emerge out of an examination of data by researchers who study it without preconceptions about categories, variables or hypotheses. However, the problem is that categories simply do not emerge out of thin air, but are – even if they are drawn from participants' own accounts in this way – in themselves intimately bound up with researchers' beliefs, prior knowledge and preconceptions. The precise nature of the methods which Jones uses to circumvent – or, at least, take account of – these difficulties will be discussed later. Suffice it to say here that the central notion is that categories are located not in the researchers' preconceptions, but in the participants' understandings, and the purpose of the research is to shed light on these.

Thus, unstructured interviews, semi-structured interviews and participant observation will form the basis of the second part of the research, with the aim being to generate categories and discover relationships among them.

Stage three

The third, experimental, element of this work, will relate to operational strategies. Certain ideas about elements which comprise the teacher's role will have been drawn from the literature on classroom management. From these it will be possible to arrive at a model which may be tested experimentally. The thrust of the review so far has been towards stressing the circumspection with which conclusions drawn from experimental research in education must be held. Nevertheless, as has been noted, certain limited goals can be held in sight in experimental analysis. Thus, methods of organisation of classroom teams drawn from the literature will be tested against a measure (children's 'engagement') shown to be a robust (if insensitive) index of classroom success, and the results will be discussed in terms of the constructs highlighted in qualitative parts of the research. Specific details of the research design for this analysis will be discussed in chapter 13.

SUMMARY OF METHODS TO BE EMPLOYED

Stage 1 will use surveys of the extent of the new teamwork, investigating the nature of the people who are currently working in classrooms, what kind of work they are doing there, and how they are delivering help to children (chapter 7).

Stage 2 will employ:

1 Unstructured interviews with parents, teachers and ancillary helpers employing *network analysis* to determine the nature of the roles they construe themselves and others fulfilling and the attributions they make in so doing (chapter 8).
2 Semi-structured interviews with support teachers employing *cognitive mapping* of transcript data to determine the nature of the constructs participants are employing in themselves shaping the nature of the team-work in which they engage. I shall test the results obtained here (chapter 9) against the model developed at the conclusion of chapter 5.
3 Participant observation over a term in the support department of a secondary school, further examining the nature of these constructs and similarly testing the results against this model (chapter 10).

Stage 3 will use experimental analysis of, to date, the most developed system of operational strategies for organising the work of classroom teams. The analysis will assess and compare children's engagement under three different organisational regimes in the classroom (chapter 13).

A diagrammatic representation of these elements in figure 6.2 shows their interrelationship around the focus of the nature of roles within the team. First there is the establishment of what people are actually doing:

their default roles, to be established through survey, asking teachers what tasks adults in their classrooms actually performed, and who those adults were. Second there is the broad and complex question of the transformation of these roles via the attributions and personal constructs of the participants. Third, there is the question of whether the clearer definition of these roles may facilitate the team process.

From the documentation of the roles operating in classrooms, I proceed to explicate the processes by which team participants define roles for themselves, and the problems they perceive in teamwork which lead them to make these definitions. The need for such personal definitions rests in part at least on the absence of other definitions or the existence of role conflict. I seek to illuminate some of the personal constructs which participants employ in making various interpretations of the team process. Thence, I seek to throw light on the nature of the emergent process and emergent roles. Finally, I examine the effects of supporting that process through making clear role definitions.

Survey
Do the teams exist?
How are they comprised?
What are the team participants doing?
What are the *prima facie* sources of tension?

Unstructured interviews
Establishing the nature of the roles as participants see them.
In particular establishing nature of participants' role definitions in heterogeneous teams.

Semi-structured interviews
Establishing the nature of the constructs participants use in making transformations

Participant observation
Examining the evolution of the unsupported *emergent process* in practice.

Experimental study
Examining the effect of supporting the team process through clear definition of participants' roles.

Figure 6.2 A summary of the methods and their relationship

THE EXTENT AND NATURE OF THE NEW TEAMWORK

Throughout the review of literature on teamwork the importance of team participants' understanding of role keeps emerging. I have examined the tensions that may arise from different kinds of role conflict and role ambiguity and I have looked at the strategies that team participants may employ to relieve these tensions.

Before going on to look in more detail at these tensions it is necessary first to know a little more about the teams as they are actually arising and the roles which people are seemingly filling in them. This chapter therefore assesses the broad shape of those roles. Who are the team participants? What activities are they doing? Are they involved briefly or over long periods? What, in short, are the characteristics of the classroom teams?

This chapter reports on three surveys in which headteachers and teachers completed questionnaires about the nature of teaming in their schools and their classes.

THE FIRST SURVEY

A preliminary survey canvassed information from headteachers and served to provide information on which to base categories for the main, subsequent surveys. Specifically, it determined categories of additional people involved in the classroom, and it determined in a general way the nature of the commitment of those people.

Sample of schools

The headteachers of 100 primary schools in North Oxfordshire were questioned for this survey. The sample was chosen for its internal consistency and its ease of access rather than its representativeness of a wider population of schools. Familiarity of the target group of schools with the institution from which the questionnaire emanated increased the likelihood of a high return rate. As I make clear later (p. 79) the sample is likely to possess some special characteristics, given some innovatory moves on parental involvement in Oxfordshire.

The results which follow are based on an 86 per cent response to the first questionnaire. At first 59 per cent of schools responded to the questionnaire, but following one prompt to those schools which had not responded, this figure was increased to 86 per cent.

A note on definitions

Oxfordshire County Council uses the terms 'welfare assistant', 'ancillary helper' and 'auxiliary' to describe different kinds of non-professional employees. Ancillary helpers will be the most common form of non-teaching help found working alongside the classteacher since all schools, until the introduction of Local Management of Schools in late 1990, have had an allocation based on the number of children in the school. (The formula on which this allocation was based is one hour for each four children on roll in the case of junior-age children or each five children in the case of infant-age children based on the estimated roll for January.) Welfare assistants, on the other hand, are appointed specifically to help a particular child or group of children with special needs. (In most local authorities this would be for children who are the subject of statements of special educational need; Oxfordshire however, has, until LMS, had a low statementing policy which has meant that, uniquely among LEAs, welfare assistants are provided for children with special needs in ordinary schools who are not the subject of statements.) Auxiliary help will not normally be employed in the classroom; this category includes bus and taxi escorts, cleaning assistants and school meals supervisors. No specified qualifications are required for any of these appointments.

The questionnaire

Five categories of people were identified for the purposes of the questionnaire: peripatetic teachers, paid non-teacher support (including welfare assistants, ancillaries, auxiliaries, teaching assistants), parents, support services and nursery nurses. Others specified by the headteachers turned out to be home tutors, ESL teachers, secondary school students and volunteers such as school governors and retired people.

It was anticipated that the variety of classroom activities in which the various people engaged would be very wide; rather than constrain the respondents by delineating these in this first questionnaire, respondents were asked to explain briefly by means of an open-ended question the nature of the activity in which each participant engaged. Individual responses would subsequently be coded (in this and the main survey) according to a framework derived from the general response.

Findings

Surprisingly, in all of the responding schools people were reported to be working alongside classteachers in the classroom. In most of these a variety of people was involved. Respondents chose to describe the involvement of extra people in two main ways: either by stating the form of organisation adopted (groupwork, work with individuals, etc.) or by stating the kind of task/activity done (e.g. reading). Most teacher and ancillary involvement is described in the first way, while most description of parental involvement takes the second form. As neither form of description is complete in itself these variables were isolated and asked about specifically in the subsequent questionnaire.

Within the second category (kind of work done), parents are predominantly described by headteachers as doing three types of work: hearing reading; cooking, swimming, needlework, etc.; and language and number games. 'Cooking, swimming and needlework' is the most frequently reported kind of parental involvement, with twice as many instances reported as 'hearing reading'. This makes for an interesting contrast with classteachers' responses in the main survey, where hearing reading is the most frequently reported activity undertaken by parents.

No support service involvement in the classroom was reported in these mainstream primary schools and this is of interest given the commitment of some physiotherapists and speech therapists to classroom-based provision in special schools; it does not appear from this survey that integration has resulted in a transposition of this kind of help to mainstream schools. Nevertheless, the 'people categories' identified at the outset proved to be broadly accurate and needed little revision for the second survey.

Responses to the open-ended element of the questionnaire were also of interest in terms of the comments that headteachers made about the roles of additional people in the classroom. I have grouped the comments and I shall report typical comments and remark on these consecutively.

Institutional ethos

Comments indicating the institutional framework within which teachers had to operate revealed the sources of tension emanating from discontinuity between the views of the teacher and those of the institution as a whole, and represented by the headteacher. Thus,

'School policy of parental partnership'

perhaps indicates that there is an expectation that parents will be participating in classrooms, which might engender doubts in those who are uncertain about this kind of development. Ideological tensions may thus occur within the team and/or superimpose themselves on the team process.

Teacher as manager

The next set of comments stress the role of the teacher as manager with an emphasis on the teacher's status and importance as leader of a team:

> 'Parents in classrooms help with all aspects of the curriculum, under direction of the classteacher.'

> 'Parents carry out a full range of activities, as do ancillaries, under the control of the classteacher.'

> 'Teachers, ancillaries, parents and other helpers follow directions of teachers to help support class work.'

All these comments explicitly or tacitly emphasise 'under the direction of'. This is probably related to the concerns over teachers being seen to be undermined by strong-minded ancillary staff or parents. It is also made explicit that teachers will be 'in charge', with a recognition that entropy rather than synergy may be the result of introducing extra people. Headteachers perhaps feel constrained to make it clear that they acknowledge the possible tensions, but despite these their staff are adequately managing the group. One perhaps recognised that staff had not managed:

> 'I am wholeheartedly in favour of the proper involvement of parents in the life of the school [but] . . . now I do have some reservations about the way it is done' [doesn't elaborate].

Unproblematic nature of parents' role

There were many comments indicating that parents were involved in relatively unproblematic areas, which would provide no danger of a clash with the teacher's role in teaching 'academic' skills. This, as I shall later show via the second survey, is at variance with what teachers reported as actually happening. Thus, headteachers are indicating that parents are fulfilling the traditional parent role – cooking, needlework, etc. – while teachers say that parents are involved in a far wider band of activities, including the 3Rs. The difficult position of the headteacher politically is evident here, with their unwillingness (despite a clear pledge of anonymity) to divulge the nature of parent activity where there is sensitivity about parents usurping the teacher's role or that of other paid personnel. Thus, there were many comments of the variety:

'Parents: soccer, cooking, woodwork, book club, mounting and display of work.'

A similar set of clear-cut – but perhaps not entirely accurate – definitions about the roles of the participants is evident in:

'Peripatetic takes small groups with learning difficulties; parents help with craft skills, cooking, reading games, etc.'

Lack of role definition

By contrast, a lack of definition, or understanding, of the role of participants is shown in three similar comments, defining activity solely in terms of the individual nature of the work the participants undertake:

'Welfare assistant for one child.'

'SNAST [special needs advisory and support teacher] works alongside one child.'

'Support teacher for malad [maladjusted] child.'

'Auxiliaries work with small groups or individuals in support of teacher. Peripatetics ditto but from their own ideas.'

Even further lack of role definition for the participants is expressed as the desire to be 'flexible':

'We are quite flexible; we work out what is best for everyone.'

'We use everyone in every combination according to needs and situations.'

Already a set of role-related concerns emerges here.

THE SECOND SURVEY

The teachers questioned

In the first questionnaire headteachers were asked whether they would be prepared to take part in a follow-up. Thirty-six of the 86 who responded said 'yes', and these were used as the basis of the sample for this second questionnaire. The possibility exists that a skewed sample has therefore been drawn from the original population. However, comparisons of mean numbers of people involved in the schools of each of the two sets of respondents (i.e. those willing to be involved further in the research and those not) show that the difference between the means is in the opposite direction from that which would be predicted on the basis of an assumption that willing headteachers had more people involved in their schools ('willing': mean number of people = 13.6; 'unwilling': mean number of people = 14).

Headteachers were sent questionnaires which they were asked to distribute to each of the teachers in their schools. Results were obtained from 82 teachers in 22 schools (i.e. a 61 per cent response from the schools – there was no follow-up to attempt to increase this response).

The sample of 82 classes is broken down by age as follows: 1 nursery class, 37 infant classes, 23 lower junior classes, 14 upper junior classes and 7 vertically grouped junior classes. The sample of classrooms is broken down by school size as follows: 20 from schools with fewer than 100 children; 24 from schools with 100–199 children; 26 from schools with 200–299 children; and 12 from schools with 300 or more children.

As the sample was taken from Oxfordshire schools it is likely to possess some special characteristics which should be borne in mind when interpreting the results: Oxfordshire is a county that encourages parental involvement in education through a range of projects and initiatives, such as introducing the role of *animateur* to facilitate involvement (see Brighouse 1985); its peripatetic services have been innovatory in the way that they have provided help in the classroom to children with special needs, and it provides ancillary help in the way that some LEAs do not.

Measures

Eliciting information about classroom involvement poses a number of problems. Specifying categories for respondents perhaps constrains responses, with restricted information being an artefact of such a measure. Providing for open-ended responses presents difficulties in coding and comparing data from different sources. Given the nature of the information being sought – about type of person, type of activity, group size being worked with and length of time working – it was also a consideration that information about the associations among these variables be preserved without generating a form which would be intimidatingly complex and time-consuming for busy teachers to unravel. The familiarity of a timetable format was decided upon; the maximum possible information from specified categories could be obtained through having derived appropriate categories from the responses to open-ended questions in the first questionnaire.

Teachers completed timetables for one week of their work. They coded the type of people working with them in the classroom, the type of activity, the group size being worked with and the length of time worked. Respondents were asked to put the initials and title of the participants alongside the codes and using these it was possible to determine (a) the number of times a particular individual *within* a category worked during the week and (b) the sex of each individual. Most of the data are handled in terms of sessions of help, a session being an uninterrupted session or consecutive sessions (i.e. only interrupted by break or lunch) undertaken by one individual. Non-consecutive sessions are counted separately. Other information obtained from the form concerned the age range of children in the class and sex of the teacher. The only other variable used during the analysis was the size of school and this information was obtained independently of the forms.

Procedure

The first level of analysis consisted in providing descriptive statistics for the variables 'activity', 'group size' and 'person'. Subsequent analysis included the variables 'school size' and 'age of children in class' and sought differences between subgroups of these in terms of values of the classroom variables. Throughout, data handling and statistical analysis were undertaken using the SPSS-X statistical package.

Results

A wide variety of people was reported working alongside classteachers for the week of the timetable. Apart from the categories outlined in the questionnaire (parents, peripatetic teachers, ancillaries [i.e. general non-teaching staff], welfare assistants [i.e. non-teaching staff appointed to help meet special needs] and nursery nurses), the following groups of people were identified from the *other* category:

> *school and college students* (including young people on training schemes), 22 people;
> *voluntary helpers*, 11 people;
> *teachers* (e.g. specialist teachers of hearing impaired children; E2L teachers; seconded teacher working in school), 11 people;
> *special school staff* (working on integration schemes, or on 'outreach'), 6 people;
> *home tutors* (for children with special needs), 3 people;
> *school governors*, 3 people;
> *speech therapist*, 1 person.
> (Students on teacher training were omitted from the analysis.)

Although nil returns were requested, only one was received. Therefore 81 of the 82 respondents had other adults working alongside them for some portion of the week. Some 87 per cent of the responding teachers had one or more parents working alongside them during the week.

Tables 7.1 and 7.2 give an analysis of the way in which help was apportioned. Table 7.1 shows the numbers of sessions of help completed by each person group.

Table 7.1 Sessions in class broken down by person group

	Number of sessions	% of total sessions	Mean no. of sessions per person
Peri. teacher	68	9.6	1.39
Parent	251	35.4	1.33
Ancillary	179	25.2	2.81
Welfare asst	128	18.1	4.41
N. nurse	5	0.7	5.00
Other	78	11.0	1.53

Analysis also shows that people mainly work on one kind of activity, though the ancillaries tend to have their time spread over more activities than other person groups. The length of the sessions worked by the person groups is as shown in table 7.2.

Table 7.2 Length of session worked by person groups

	Percentages of sessions in blocks of:			
	Less than 1 hour	1–2 hrs	2–3 hours	More than 3 hours
	(actual number of sessions in brackets)			
Peri. teacher	16 (11)	66 (45)	18 (12)	
Parent	17 (43)	38 (94)	41 (102)	4 (10)
Ancillary	9 (17)	38 (68)	34 (61)	19 (34)
Welfare asst	16 (21)	31 (40)	34 (44)	18 (23)
Other	6 (5)	49 (41)	31 (26)	13 (11)
All	14 (97)	41 (288)	35 (245)	11 (78)

Most help therefore occurs in the 1 to 2 hour band though inspection shows (and chi-square confirms, $p < 0.0001$) that the proportion of instances for each of the person categories differs from time group to time group; the cross-tabulated categories show hardly any interdependence (Cramer's V, 0.18). The distribution of the time of ancillaries and welfare assistants is more evenly spread than that of parents, who as individuals – although there are more of them – worked in the classroom for fewer, shorter sessions.

The distribution of people's time according to activities undertaken is as given in table 7.3. Roughly one-third of all parental sessions were therefore involved with hearing children read. Just under two-thirds of the sessions of peripatetic teachers and welfare assistants were devoted to

Table 7.3 Type of activity undertaken by each person group as a percentage of all activities undertaken by each person group

	Reading	Cooking	Swimming	Needle	Art	Computer	Language	PE/Games	Teaching	Special needs	Expert	Cleaning	Mounting	Music	Unspecified
Peri.teacher	1					3	9		3	62	6	1	4	9	3
Parent	31	6	13	7	14	1	9	1	1	2	2	3	2	1	4
Ancillary	19	5	1	9	15	4	15	1	3	10		8	6	2	4
Welfare asst	12		1	1	8	4	11	1	3	52	2	3	2		
Other	13	2	4	3	11	4	16		4	25	1	2	6	4	4
All	20	4	5	6	12	3	12	1	3	20	2	4	4	2	4

Note: Some of the activity categories used in Tables 7.3, 7.4 and 7.5 have been abbreviated for ease of inspection. The full categories used by the teachers correspond to the abbreviated categories as follows: reading: 'hearing reading'; needle: 'needlework'; art: 'art/craft'; language: 'language and number games etc.'; teaching: 'teaching specific curriculum area'; special needs: 'work with slow learners/children with special needs'; expert: 'employing special expertise not covered above'; cleaning: 'cleaning, tidying, etc'; mounting: 'mounting children's work, cutting paper, etc'; unspecified: 'unspecified/other'.

working with children with special needs. Both of these person groups split their time for special needs evenly between work with individuals and work with small groups.

Table 7.4 shows how involvement was distributed by school size. No significant trend can be discerned in the way that involvement occurs according to size of school (Jonckheere trend test not significant at 0.05). It is worth noting, though, that help of additional people on computer work was far more common in the larger schools (more than 300 pupils) while large schools are correspondingly under-represented in help with art and craft.

Table 7.4 Mean number of activities (x10) per class broken down by school size

No. of children	Reading	Cooking	Swimming	Needle	Art	Computer	Language	PE/Games	Teaching	Special needs	Expert	Cleaning	Mounting	Music	Unspecified
<100 chn	22	3	6	7	12	2	13	2	7	22	2	2	6	5	7
100–199	21	3	3	4	17	3	10		2	17	1	4	3	2	5
200–299	25	7	7	9	15	2	14	1		25	2	9	5	1	2
300 +	22	3	8	7	4	11	20	2	5	29	4	3	4	3	5

Note: Decimal points are omitted merely to allow easy inspection.

Table 7.5 shows how involvement is distributed by age of children in class.

Table 7.5 Mean number of activities (x10) per class broken down by age of children in class

	Reading	Cooking	Swimming	Needle	Art	Computer	Language	PE/Games	Teaching	Special needs	Expert	Cleaning	Mounting	Music	Unspecified
Infant	22	6	9	10	20	6	16	1	4	17	1	7	6	1	3
Lower junior	33	3	4	6	9	2	10		1	21	3	4	3	3	1
Upper junior	11	3	4		1		10		5	34		2	2	4	5
Vert. grouped junior	17			7	14		13	4	3	30	3	4	4	3	14

The amount of involvement with reading peaks in the lower junior range, while help for children with special needs peaks in the upper junior range. Leaving out the vertically grouped junior group because of its mixed-age nature, there is a gradual decline in involvement overall as the age range of children in the class increases. Trend analysis however (using Jonckheere's test) only shows a significant trend existing in this decline (at $p < 0.05$) if help with special needs is omitted from the overall data.

Analysis of the group size used for each of the activities shows that most of the reading undertaken takes place on an individual basis (132 instances individual; 36 instances small group) while the activities of cooking, art, swimming, needlework, computer work, language and PE/games were all done far more frequently in a small group. Help for children with special needs was split fairly evenly between individual help (82 instances) and work with a small group (89 instances).

Each of the groups is shown to be working on broadly the same activity over the period of their work. Peripatetic teachers have the highest level of consistency (presumably because they have a specified reason for their presence) while ancillary helpers seem to show the greatest diversity. This is shown in table 7.6.

Those working in the classrooms were overwhelmingly female. Some 97 per cent of all the sessions were provided by females. Of the 192 parents reported, only 2 were fathers. (Corresponding figures are not given for the other person groups as they may be misleading: analysis was at classroom level and there is no way of determining how many of the individuals from other person categories worked in more than one classroom of the sample.)

Table 7.6 Number of activities undertaken as a percentage of total activities in a session for each person group

	Activities undertaken in a session				
	1	2	3	4	4
Peri. teacher	95.6	4.4			
Parent	83.7	15.1	0.8	0.4	
Ancillary	64.5	17.8	10.6	4.4	2.8
Welfare assistant	82.0	16.4	1.6		
Other	84.6	9.0	2.6	3.8	
All	79.6	14.2	3.5	1.7	.7

THIRD SURVEY

In order to check the possibility that an unrepresentative picture might have been picked up from the Oxfordshire schools of the first two surveys, this third survey was sent to a sample of schools across England and Wales.

The sample

A selection of 150 schools was randomly made from a list of all schools in England and Wales. Eighty-three (55 per cent) of these provided returns. Although this is a lower return than in the previous two surveys, I was satisfied that it was adequate to fulfil the purpose of the survey, i.e. to act as a check on the general validity of the findings of those surveys. The lower rate of return here can at least partly be explained by the fact that the schools approached had no personal knowledge of the institution from which the survey came. Neither had the headteachers been involved in a preliminary survey, as was the case with the Oxfordshire sample. They thus had had no opportunity to express a willingness or unwillingness to become further involved. Added to this is the fact that the questionnaires arrived at a busy time of year in a period of rapid change. The returns from the 83 schools yielded returns from 282 teachers and data are available on 1,507 sessions of help provided during the week of the survey in those teachers' classrooms.

The returns are divided regionally as follows: 10 per cent from the North-east, 15 per cent from the North-west, 16 per cent from the Midlands, 40 per cent from the South-east, 14 per cent from the South-west and 7 per cent from Wales.

Broadly, the sample is very similar to that of the Oxfordshire sample, with the main exception being that this sample contains a far higher proportion (15 per cent) of its reported sessions from nursery classes. This disparity can be explained by the fact that Oxfordshire had, at the time and in the area of the survey, only a very small amount of nursery provision.

A similar questionnaire format to that used in the second survey was used in this survey. The only change to the original format arose in adding two 'people categories' (student and voluntary worker) to the options available, while removing one (nursery nurse). One activity (assisting on visit) was added. As before, teachers completed timetables for one week of their work, coding the type of people working with them, the type of activity, the group size being worked with and the length of time worked.

Results

The number of sessions provided by each of the person groups is as given in table 7.7. Numbers in the Oxfordshire sample are given in the second column for comparison.

Table 7.7 Sessions in class broken down by person group

	Number of sessions	% of total sessions	Number of sessions	% of total sessions
		National		Oxfordshire
Peri. teacher	179	11.9	68	9.6
Parent	515	34.2	251	35.4
Ancillary	219	14.5	179	25.2
Welfare asst	101	6.7	128	18.1
N. nurse	–	–	5	0.7
Other	139	12.5	78	11.0
Voluntary worker	85	5.6	–	–
Student	218	14.5	–	–

The next table (7.8) shows the type of activity which the people were undertaking in the classes. The first line repeats the Oxfordshire figures while the second line for each person group gives the national figures. The extra people mainly worked with small groups or individuals. For instance, 59 per cent of parental sessions were spent in small groups and 20 per cent in work with individuals.

Table 7.8 Type of activity undertaken by each person group as a percentage of all activities undertaken by each person group

	Reading	Cooking	Swimming	Needle	Art	Computer	Language	PE/Games	Teaching	Special needs	Expert	Cleaning	Mounting	Music	Unspecified	Assisting visit
Peri. teacher																
Oxon	1					3	9		3	62	6	1	4	9	3	
National	8		2				18		13	41	3			15		
Parent																
Oxon	31	6	13	7	14	1	9	1	1	2	2	3	2	1	4	
National	18	10	10	13	11	4	10	4	1	1		2	5	2	2	7
Ancillary																
Oxon	19	5	1	9	15	4	15	1	3	10		8	6	2	4	
National	15	4	2	4	15	2	13	3		12		7	16		5	2
Welfare asst																
Oxon	12		1	1	8	4	11	1	3	52	2	3	2			
National	2	5	2	9	11		13	2		17		10	12	5	8	5

DISCUSSION

The possibility that certain trends are responsible for the influx of extra people to the classroom is supported by the responses to all three question-naires. The parental involvement movement clearly is of importance. Help with special needs is also a major reason for extra people to be in the classroom, with help for children with special needs accounting for one in five of all the sessions undertaken by additional people. The influence of wider social trends, in for instance young people from training schemes being involved in the classroom, is also in evidence.

The finding that involvement declines with age of children in class was expected. But reasons for involving people in the classroom extend across all age ranges and it is to be hoped that the older age ranges will ultimately catch up with the younger. Reasons for the greater involvement with younger children are explored further in the following chapter, but seem to be concerned again with role definition. There is a clearer set of tasks to undertake with younger children and fewer uncertainties about 'doing the wrong thing' when it comes to academic matters.

Differences between involvement in curricular areas in schools of different sizes (such as the increase in computer work in larger schools) can only be guessed at; they may simply be a reflection of more general curricular bias which in turn may reflect differences in ability to marshal and pool the kind of resources necessary for computer work. Similar general differences might be advanced for differences in activity with age, e.g. the increase noted in special needs work as age increases: special needs often become more conspicuous as children get older.

The third, national, survey reported here generally supports the findings of the Oxfordshire survey. Proportions of categories of people working in the classroom are similar over the two samples, with the important difference that proportions of welfare assistant sessions seem to be lower in the national sample, almost certainly as a result of the low statementing policy of Oxfordshire, which I have already discussed.

There are interesting differences between the local and national samples in the activities which the various people are reported to be undertaking. Peripatetic teachers are seemingly undertaking a broader range of activities in the national sample. This may reflect the ethos of different peripatetic support services across the country. Some may have less of an explicit emphasis on special needs; the work of the individuals who comprise these services may therefore have been coded not as 'help with special needs/slow learners', but rather as 'language work', 'hearing reading' or 'teaching'.

The main difference between the work of parents over the two samples is in the amount of time spent hearing reading. In the regional sample, hearing reading took nearly a third of all parent time, while in the national sample it took less than a fifth. The sensitivity of this central curricular area may be an explanation of this difference. Seemingly, only if the involvement of parents has been legitimised through an LEA-wide policy (as is the case in Oxfordshire) are teachers secure in allowing – or admitting to – parents to become so involved.

Although the pattern of ancillary helper work is very similar over the two samples, that for welfare assistants is not. For welfare assistants, the Oxfordshire pattern reflects a group of people employed for a specific purpose – that of helping children with special needs. However, the national sample reflects a less clear-cut brief, with welfare assistants holding the most diverse range of responsibilities of any group. Interestingly, welfare assistants in the national sample spend only a very small proportion of their time in the sensitive area of reading, perhaps reflecting notions about their status. Even if job definitions are lacking, status seems to play some part in defining role.

There are already findings here about which a note of caution ought to be sounded: parents are being involved in a wide range of curricular activities, and maintaining their confidence in undertaking these activities may require more structured support, guidance and feedback than is currently being provided; the 'vanishing effect' which attacks innovatory practice after the initial enthusiasm for it has waned is well understood

87

(see Hackman and Oldham 1980). There is perhaps the need for the development of a range of organisational formulae out of which teachers and those working alongside them are able to work out their own unique operational strategies for working effectively as teams in the classroom.

Guidelines on operational strategy for the survival and development of these innovations will have to be drafted on the basis of the patterns of development which actually emerge and which will be rooted in particular regional circumstances – in the traditions, the resourcing policies and the other idiosyncrasies of particular regions. However, a number of clear indications emerge: that there are large numbers of extra people working in the classroom; that there may be ideological disagreement about the place and proper purpose of these people; that they are doing a variety of activities; that teams are in constant flux – people come and go and are in the main employed for short blocks of time; and that uncertainty is articulated about the role of those personnel.

Further conclusions and insights from this study are discussed in the introduction to the following chapter, where the nature of the roles as understood by team participants is explored.

8

TEACHERS, PARENTS AND ANCILLARIES IN TEAMS
How they make their roles

From the surveys in the previous chapter a number of conclusions can be drawn about the composition of the new teams and their participants' activities, concerns and tensions.

First, there can be no doubt that classroom teams exist and that they exist in a variety of forms.

Second, a wide range of people is involved, with parents involved in nine out of ten classrooms. The admixture of people, from parents with no special skills to highly trained specialist teachers, indicates the existence of heterogeneous teams.

Third, people were typically involved for relatively short periods (relative, that is, to the teacher). The brevity of these periods (one or two hours) perhaps has implications for the ways in which these individuals are perceived by the classteacher. She may raise questions about the commitment or reliability of the voluntary participants, or the effectiveness of the specialist teachers. These short periods of involvement also point to unstable teams, with constantly changing members, and an inability to establish clear roles or working practices.

Fourth, participants are involved in many tasks about which they may be uncertain how to help. Hearing reading and working with children with special needs accounted for just over half of all the sessions of help, with, as I have indicated, implications for the confidence of people taking on roles about which they may be unsure – away from the traditional roles of the parent or the ancillary. As has been indicated, certain of the personnel who comprise the classroom teams, such as welfare assistants, are fulfilling specialised tasks for which they have no training.

Fifth, involvement declined as age of children in class increased, reflecting the perhaps implicitly held belief that it is in some way more appropriate for 'help' to be provided for younger children, with a clearer set of activities to be performed when helping them. The readiness of potential participants to become involved when there is a clear set of expectations – in other words, when their roles are well defined – is significant.

Sixth, headteachers' replies to open-ended questions suggest that they hold a range of beliefs about the roles of other adults. Mixed in with these beliefs is a certain amount of ambivalence and tension about the roles of these adults in the classroom.

The purpose of this chapter is to illuminate the nature of the roles as understood by some of these participants, elaborating on these six themes. In this chapter I report on interviews with a number of team participants – teachers, parents, ancillaries and welfare assistants. A number of questions are addressed: How do participants define their roles? In what contexts do they define sources of tension? What for them are the key areas of conflict and how do they define that conflict? How do they resolve conflict?

METHOD EMPLOYED FOR THE INTERVIEWS AND THEIR ANALYSIS

Classroom teams provide a fascinating exemplar for the study of role. It is beginning to become apparent that role is only very thinly defined in these teams, if indeed it is defined at all. In the absence of this definition, role appears to be constructed by participants out of their own beliefs about appropriate behaviour.

Of the methods reviewed in chapters 5 and 6, it is those providing a framework for illuminating social encounters that will assist in disclosing these beliefs. In continuing from the surveys previously undertaken, the aim is to elucidate the nature of roles as participants define them, but also to locate these in the social frameworks perceived by the participants.

The position taken by ethogeny is appropriate here. Participants recount their experiences of episodes; in this case episodes of working in classroom teams. Ethogenic research focuses on the thoughts, feelings and intentions of those taking part. The elicitation and analysis of these can take various forms, but in this case elicitation will be via:

1 unstructured interviews and analysis using the isolation of tentative interpretive schemata; a schema is defined by Deaux and Wrightsman as 'an organised configuration of knowledge derived from past experience which we use to interpret our current experience' (1988: 105).
2 systematic network analysis (Bliss, Monk and Ogborn 1983), drawing on these schemata.

The sample who were interviewed

Though there are differing views on the sample, or the subjects on whom to draw for interviews, in qualitative research, one or two criteria seem appropriate to note. The notion of what Glaser and Strauss call 'statistical sample' is antithetical to qualitative research. There is no a priori assumption that the sample is representative of the wider population. Rather, there is the assumption that the views of informants are of interest in and of themselves. Each situation is personally defined and has meanings personal to the informant.

Having said this, it is worth at least noting that the sample in this study is probably not *un*representative. The respondents in this case have been drawn from those in the survey research (chapter 7) who had expressed a willingness to become further involved in the research. As I made clear then, these do not appear to form a biased sample in terms of their views about involvement drawn from the original population. There are a total of eight respondents: four teachers, one welfare assistant, two ancillary helpers and one parent.

How participants were interviewed

McCracken (1988) suggests a five-stage process in interviewing. First, there is the process of looking at each utterance in its own terms, without reference to models or to other elements of the data. Second, these are interpreted in the light of the rest of the data and the wider literature. Third, the interconnections between these second-level observations are made. Fourth, the observations at previous levels are subjected to collective scrutiny. Fifth, the themes from several interviews are subjected to a final process of analysis.

Broadly, this will be the process followed in this analysis. However, in order to systematise the analysis, network analysis will be used for parts three, four and five of this process.

In terms of the write-up of the results, then, there will be two parts. First, before network analysis, the interview material will be introduced by means of selected quotations; this is of value, McCracken says, because it takes 'advantage of the fact that qualitative research can take the reader into the mind of the life of the respondent' (p. 54), setting out the main themes in the interview material. The context of each of the quotations will be mentioned and commented upon. Second, the formal analysis will be undertaken, using the instrument of network analysis.

Each interview, lasting between 45 minutes and one hour, was tape-recorded and transcribed onto disc, and edited for the purposes of this research by word processor. Editing conventions will be explained via footnotes in the text.

91

Respondents were told that the interviews were for research on the work of additional people in the classroom and that the responses they made would be anonymous. Since the focus was on roles and participants' definitions, the questioning began, after appropriate preliminaries, with questions about what the respondents did and how they felt about it.

Since the subject was participants' role definitions, discussion was directed towards the contexts of those definitions, with the focus on the additional people in the classroom. The interview would follow interest in the teacher's role if it appeared that the respondent was suggesting that the presence of the additional person modified the teacher's role. Since the emphasis was on what was assumed to be a collective process of definition, the interviews were not formally differentiated by 'occupation' of participant; the definition was the subject of interest, not the activities *per se* about which they spoke.

While the interviews were unstructured, the conversation was none the less guided towards certain areas where it was clear from the literature that there were issues for further study. These were as stated earlier:

1 the perception of heterogeneous teams by the team participants;
2 the instability of team and the ability or inability to establish clear roles;
3 the quality of role definition as articulated and perceived by the participants;
4 the significance of clear sets of expectations;
5 ambiguities and tensions concerning the role of others in the classroom.

Network analysis

In network analysis (Bliss *et al.* 1983; Cohen and Manion 1985) a system of categories is developed and via this, qualitative data are classified while preserving the integrity, the wholeness of the material being classified. Network-like structures are generated via a notational technique. After examining transcripts of the interviews, classificatory divisions are established and these may be further divided and subdivided.

RESULTS

Part 1 – an introduction to the interview material and interpretive schemata

Interestingly, the interview material initially divides itself fairly clearly into two parts: one relating to what I have called role definition, and another relating to what I have called role conflict. These two categories encapsulate the concern over points 2, 3, 4 and 5 above. Point 1, the perception of heterogeneous teams, was not specifically articulated by the participants, though its importance is implicit in certain of their comments relating to the differences between team members. Where these occur, they will be commented upon.

The following are therefore divided primarily according to two schemata: role definition, and role conflict. Another schema, which has been termed 'effects of being observed', emerges distinct from the two primary schemata and is discussed after these.

Role definition

The question of role definition is raised in a number of ways. There is general confirmation of the supposed looseness of those roles and the 'on-the-job' role definitions. This is from a teacher:

Q: Do they have any difficulty with that, sort of telling them how you want it?

R: Well, I think *they sort of say what do you mean*[1] and do I tell them the word because if I say 'Tell them the word, just fill in the words' they don't. . . .[2] Well, shouldn't they try and sound it out and that sort of thing. Well I would try with some children but I don't want them to be forcing them so just fill in the word and I will, er, do it, you know with them . . . [IND][3] . . . . *so I think they know what to do*.

The quality of this explanation suggests that parents may remain confused after the supposed clarification.

A parent emphasises the importance of getting to know the teacher's expectations:

Q: Is there anything else you would like to be doing?

R: What, as well?

Q: That you are not doing.

R: No, *I don't get asked,* no I don't think so actually. I think *you get to know the teacher* you help and they are very fair. I suppose they get to know whether they like you as well, *you work together really, you know, I find it's, as you go along,* you get more familiar, well not familiar, I don't mean like that but they sort of know what you're perhaps better at or what the children like you for as well, I think you've got to like each other.

---

1 Italicised text represents the key point about which commentary will be made.
2 Three dots '...' without spaces represent a pause or discontinuity in the respondent's account. Dots with spaces '. . . ' represent editing of irrelevant material.
3 'IND' is an abbreviation for 'indistinct', where the exact words used are unclear from the tape recording.

A welfare assistant makes it clear also that she has picked it up on-the-job:

R: *I mean I find it easier now, the first few weeks I was there I didn't know where
things were,* I didn't know what she [cerebrally palsied girl the WA
was employed to help] was capable of doing. And *as time has gone on
I found it easier,* I know where things are in the classroom, I know
that she concentrates better in the morning.

The welfare assistant emphasises the 'picking it up' aspect:

R: Well we went to the museum one day last week because obviously
we're doing things about that. So he'll [teacher] sit down with the
children and say to them well this is what I want you to do in the art
work and I'll *just sort of pick it up from there.*

A welfare assistant points to the lack of any formal guidance on how to
help and the importance of 'learning together':

Q: Did you have any training?

R: No, no, I came to the interview and on that afternoon I went to see
Parkside School [for physically handicapped children] and on the
Friday I came into school to have a look around the classroom and
saw where the books were going to be kept and everything and
started on the Monday. (*laughter*)

Q: Did you find that daunting?

R: No – pause – (. . or was it just common sense)[4] it was common sense,
I mean the biggest thing was knowing what she was capable of doing,
which *we sort of learned together.*

One teacher comments on the very broad categories of tasks on which she
is prepared to see the parent working:

R: I wouldn't ask them to help with the other work, just the reading or
the creative activities and *I wouldn't let them do the reading until I let
them know exactly what I wanted done.*

It is reinforced by this welfare assistant, who makes it clear that she almost
has to 'sense' what the teacher wants:

Q: . . . and what do you do in the classes?

R: It varies from watching the art corner, mixing the paint and
generally doing that and reading stories if I'm needed there or um,
mounting work. *Really getting to know what the teacher wants and working
in co-operation with her.*

---

4 Round brackets with two dots (..) represent a 'probe' from the interviewer.

Q: It's very flexible.

R: Yes very flexible.

Q: And depends on the day, whatever's going on?

R: What topic is going on, yes, and er some teachers like to do their own mounting so I won't do that I'll do something else. *It all depends on what the teacher wants you to do*, as I say it's just building up that extra pair of hands in the classroom wherever it's needed really.

In the following, the welfare assistant actually uses the word 'sensing' to describe the process by which intentions are communicated from teacher to assistant:

R: I suppose it works both ways, um, because I'm a crafty person (*laughter*) crafty in more ways than one! I do like that sort of thing, so I find that comes into it, so when it comes to craft work I can perhaps offer ideas there. Yes, I think we just talk about the topic that's coming on, suggest ideas together and it goes on I suppose. *Really knowing the teacher, knowing the teacher well, how much she expects from a helper, and sensing when she doesn't want you there*. I mean, um, responding to it really. Yes, I think, well any helper in school, or any mother could get bossy or too big headed about it, and it's knowing where to stop.

What seems to be 'sensed' here is a threat to the teacher's autonomy or status. In the next passage, the teacher seems to suggest that role definition is important for those who are helping. She seems to suggest that partici- pants clarify these roles for themselves by going for the simple options:

R: I think they're happier doing something that they're confident in. If you ask them to do something a bit complicated, like some practical maths, or something like that, then they'll probably be a bit, you know, it depends on the parent really, but *I think they're happier cooking and sewing*; most are quite willing to do anything really.

There are parents that you discover have got this talent or something they do, but *they don't always want to take it up*. I mean *you obviously have to get to know the mums*, in order to feel that that situation is going to work. And they have to feel comfortable, coming in.

Here, another teacher is saying that the parent's role is a matter for dialogue, for resolution between parent and teacher.

R: It's nice to give the parents, not a free hand but to [let them] come up with suggestions. Because then it makes them feel that they are actually doing a really good job. *Otherwise it's a bit, 'do this and do that'*.

Parents' ambivalence about both tasks and what to do if children 'mess about' is shown in what the same teacher says here. She talks about the parents not daring to raise their voices, as though they see themselves as marginal to the situation, not fully aware of its routines and accepted practices:

R: Well, it's awful really, because *a lot of parents don't have a great idea of what's going on*. It depends on the parent (. . yes) and it depends on the child who's being a bit frisky . . . Whereas, you know we [teachers] can say, 'And you can stop doing that!' and maybe be a bit loud about it, they are very much calmer and quieter about it, almost as if they *dare not* raise their voice, you know.

The comparative ease of defining one's own role (in the absence of other guidance) with younger children, as the survey (chapter 7) indicated, is confirmed by this comment from a teacher:

R: Basically they get on with it. The thing is, we are talking about quite young children, I think it's different when the children are older. Because having taught upper juniors and having parents in, they look upon it as something very different to the younger ones.

The following from a teacher represents an unusual degree of definition of the ancillary's role, with the corollary of specificity about the teacher's role. Even so, this definition is in terms of what the ancillary will *not* be doing:

R: I don't ask her [the ancillary] to read. I use that time when she's in to hear all my readers, as much as I can. Because she's got groups of children and because she's doing other activities it enables me to hear readers.

The line drawn over reading is consistently held, and seems to relate to the maintenance of professional status. However, the nature of the role definition thus articulated to the parent is interestingly limited to an implicit understanding; simply to 'veering away' from the subject:

R: I think it's a difficult problem really, when they [parents] come into your reading, because it depends on how they deal with it, if they just sit and listen then it's not too bad *but if they start trying to teach how to read then you're up against problems*. I would, I think if they did ask to hear readers, I'd try and *veer away* from it, to be honest. Just in case, you know it does cause . . .

The absence of role definitions, or even the addressing of a potential issue about how to use and manage ancillaries by the school as a whole, is disclosed in this comment from a teacher:

R: [talking of the ancillary helper] I mean I find it peculiar because I've never had, sort of, any helpers in the classroom at all. And I couldn't get used to somebody else being there, because I was suspicious I suppose. And I kept saying *'What do I give her to do'*. I thought she was really bored, you know.

A teacher talking of another ancillary helper draws on the particular ancillary's personal abilities and experience to solve the 'problem' of defining a role for her:

R: No its quite easy. Because she's been here such a long time as well, she knows, perhaps better than me (*laughter*) you know, if I don't give her anything to do she will always find something to do.

One teacher selected roles for the parents in terms of their perceived skills: parents would be invited in if they had a special skill to offer. Interestingly, the articulation that a certain set of tasks is legitimate for a teacher helper to do, reveals the implicitly held status-related belief that there is a corresponding set of tasks which it would not be legitimate for a non-teacher parent to do.

R: Sometimes I ask if a mum is particularly good at a particular craft. I say would you like to come and help us. One or two of my mums are infant teachers, so they help – I've got several tapes, we have a language tape which the *two mums that come in who are teachers will take a group of children and will do the language tape*.

In the absence of any clear definition about what she expected parents and ancillaries to do, this teacher was asked what they don't do. Roles were not made very much clearer from her response:

Q: Is there anything you wouldn't ask Mrs P [ancillary] to do in a class?

R: Well she doesn't talk to the parents, you know if a parent comes in with a query she always refers them to me.

Q: Is there anything you wouldn't ask parents to do?

R: The same sort of thing really. I think I don't perhaps expect parents to sit with children and I can't say work, but for want of a better word you know, sit with a group and do some uh new work, you know, I'd do that myself. I wouldn't ask them to take the class as a whole.

Definition is helped by organising frameworks which are imposed on the situation from outside. Bronfenbrenner (1979), calls such frameworks 'exo-systems'. The existence of a contract for paid employment is a good example of such a framework:

R: Well it makes it easier, having other people, especially if its an ancillary – you do have ancillaries as well – because you know then that *they are paid and I will say can you please go and wash the pots*, will you please make up paint *whereas with some parents they tend to want to come in and to do nice things*, (laughter) *they don't want to wash the pots.*

The voluntary nature of the parents' contribution, not formalised in any way by contractual arrangements, seems, for this teacher at least, to loosen the definition possible; in these circumstances the teacher seems to feel inhibited about defining roles, and concomitantly it is perceived that parents see themselves, by the voluntary nature of their contribution, protected from menial tasks. The tentativeness with which roles can be defined is shown by this comment:

R: *I find six very reliable mothers* to come in every morning unless a child is ill, or the car won't start (*laughter*) (. . yes) . . . IND . . . or there's snow but they're very good. I *started with a few more but they dropped out*, they found it was *too much of a commitment.*

Communication, then, will depend on the network of shared understandings which have evolved in this loose framework. These understandings seem to take the place of role definition. Because they are substituted for this clearer definition a premium will be placed upon regularity and dependability where those understandings can remain fairly consistent. This is shown in the use of 'reliable', to describe those parents who appear regularly. The 'dropping out' or 'commitment' of others emphasises the contexts (Bronfenbrenner's exo-systems) within which the roles they take on in the classroom are framed.

This ancillary makes it clear that she defines a role for herself in the absence of any other definition:

R: If the whole class is doing the same thing, like sitting there and it's storytime, I would probably go off and tidy paintbrushes, sharpen pencils. Because obviously I would just be sitting there listening to the story as well so *I'd rather be kept busy* IND ask me to do something which I'd much rather do *than just sit there.*

The following from a teacher shows that the children at least are confused about the roles and status of the parents who help:

R: The parent might say go and wash your hands and the child will come up to me and say is it all right if I wash my hands, to check.

The confusion is also used by them:

R: You have to be quite careful because Mrs. P will say do so and so, and um, find it yourself and they will come round to me and say 'Do you know where such and such is Mrs. A'. But you've always got, well you get used to them.

Role conflict

However loosely the roles are defined in the examples above, it is clear that 'role' exists, at least implicitly, as a construct in the excerpt that follows. Here, talking about a new teacher coming into the class, it appears that the role that the ancillary perceives herself filling (because of the expectations of the children) might in some way cause the teacher to feel herself displaced from that position.

R: Well I suppose if a new teacher comes in, they [the children] respond to me but that's before a new teacher gets to know them.

Q: So almost the roles are reversed there.

R: Yes the roles are reversed, and if it's a very new teacher I feel for her in a way because I feel that perhaps *she doesn't want an extra body in the classroom when she's just starting and she's not sure how to deal with perhaps situations, so I hide in the cupboard then,* do some mounting in the cupboard, so that she can get on with it.

There appears to be a perception by the ancillary in the latter of a likely infringement on the teacher's status or autonomy. The conflict thus engendered induces a need to 'hide'.

A teacher in the following passage talks about a parent, indicating that roles may be implicitly defined at least in the teacher's mind, by the existence of a selection procedure for parents, or as she calls it, 'sussing them out', but the implicitness of the definition perhaps allows the way for 'competition' where the teacher feels that the parent sees herself in the teacher's role.

R: I try and sus them out first, so I know whether I actually want them in (. . yes), and I did have one last year who was overpowering and it ended up that she would stop in at lunchtime and she just wouldn't go, she wanted to come in everyday (*laughter*) even at breaktime she wanted to stay in the classroom and I kept saying well, come on let's have a drink before we come back but she wanted to stay with it and boss them around *so there was a bit of competition between us*.

Another teacher gives a very similar account:

R: It's a horrible atmosphere, actually, *a mother who thought she was a teacher* and wanted to take control all the time and had her eye on her child all the time.

The same conflict inflicts itself, this time on a parent in the following passage; but here the perception of inappropriateness of role, of not having the 'right', comes from another parent:

R: But one mother did challenge me in my other daughter's class and

99

she said 'Do you think you have the right to listen to children read and say what books they should be on' and all this. *Well I don't have any right*, 'I just come in to help', I said, but I don't recommend or anything you know. This is a mother who doesn't actually help herself but I think you get *some people who think you are being a busybody and just poking your nose in.*

A parent here reinforces the view that there may exist some tension occasionally when parents want to assume the teacher's role:

R: You're just a helper [but] I suppose some people do it because they are frustrated teachers, you know, um.

Effects of being observed

The last set of comments isolated here relate to a feeling about being on trial or being observed, which relate only tangentially to role definition, but which occurred frequently enough during the interviews to be worthy of note. They represent, perhaps, the most direct expression of a desire for *autonomy*.

R: I think part [of parents coming in] is just to see what the teacher's like as well, just to see how their child's getting on really . . . *you feel a bit on trial* (*laughter*) – especially when they first come – they get used to you and to know how you work – I think part is just to see what the teacher's like as well. But at first it's like – 'What's she doing?'

Similar feelings came from this teacher who had to work with an established ancillary:

Q: Did you actually find it a constraint at all, having somebody strange in the classroom when you first came here?

R: It could have been difficult, I think.

Q: Someone who's established like that, did you particularly . . .

R: It was just strange having somebody in the room with me for a whole morning or a whole afternoon. And I thought of it, *it was almost like having an adviser in at first.* You're not used to somebody else being in. But after about half a term I was getting used to the idea, and realised that she was a plus.

There seems in the last comment to be a relaxation of the need for autonomy and a suggestion of the possibility that autonomy is equated in some way with security. With familiarity, or 'getting used to the idea' as the respondent puts it, she ceases to feel on trial. It is possible, then, that a lack of role definition creates insecurity and thus the conditions necessary for a need for autonomy (and perceptions of 'being watched') to emerge.

Preliminary discussion prior to network analysis

The first conclusion which needs to be drawn from these interpretive schemata is that the roles that exist at the outset, if they exist at all, exist as very loosely held views stemming broadly from two main areas, namely

1 pedagogic concerns and expectations, and
2 affective concerns and expectations.

The literature suggested that role is a central determinant of small group effectiveness, and there is no reason to doubt that this is the case. However, the constructs employed for explicating the part which role plays in the workings of the team – for instance in role definition, role ambiguity, role tension and role conflict – do not figure in the accounts of these classroom participants. While role definition is clearly of importance, the process of its definition, in classroom groups which comprise people from varied backgrounds and varied status, is more subtle than the process of definition in most of the teams which have been the subject of research in other settings. A range of pedagogic and affective concerns shape those definitions.

Thus, while role definition and role conflict have been the categories that have so far suggested themselves for organising the interview data, further analysis under these categories would take us no further forward in terms of determining the means by which roles are defined, which in broad terms is the aim of this chapter. For the next subsection to take this analysis forward, it is necessary, then, to invert the categories of role definition and role conflict. Preliminary analysis suggests that role is tentatively defined via pedagogic and affective concerns, and these will form the framework of the network analysis.

Part 2 – network analysis

Each of the interviews undertaken will be subjected to a network analysis. Each of the utterances is examined to see whether it represents a pedagogic or an affective concern. The fact that seems to be emerging is that role – in the absence of definition – is built around participants' already-existing notions of what constitutes 'proper' behaviour, and how they *feel* about behaving in certain ways in the classroom. These notions and these feelings are the pedagogic and affective concerns that I highlight below.

Pedagogic concerns are split into two main sub-categories: professional and routine (see figure 8.1). The former is further subdivided into status concerns, leadership concerns and skills concerns. The other main category, affective, is divided into personal and interpersonal concerns. Thus each of the utterances related to the roles of these individuals in the classroom may be placed in one or other of these categories.

Certain aspects of role are defined by status considerations, for instance about the central pedagogic role of the teacher, and the importance of instructions coming from her.

Leadership emerges as an important category of response. Several participants mentioned the difficulties which could arise from a 'struggle for power' in the class.

Certain skills are seen as legitimately falling in certain groups' ambit, though even here 'rules' are broken when a certain individual is seen as having extraordinary skills.

The clearest definitions are provided in the area of 'routine' descriptions of tasks to be done, though even here they are sometimes limited to descriptions of 'picking it up' or 'sensing' what the teacher wants.

The role is also defined by personal and interpersonal factors. Personal factors generally relate to what the participants like or find comfortable doing, while interpersonal factors relate to relationship between participants (generally the teacher and the co-worker) and its importance in the effectiveness of the partnership or team.

Thus, the following network of contributory schemata has been established on the basis of analysis of all the interviews. Individual network analysis for each of the interviews is given after this summary, together with sample quotations from the interviews.

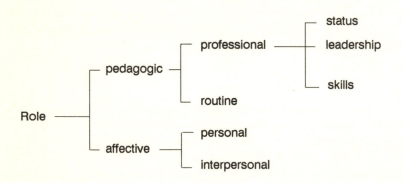

Figure 8.1 Summatory network of schemata

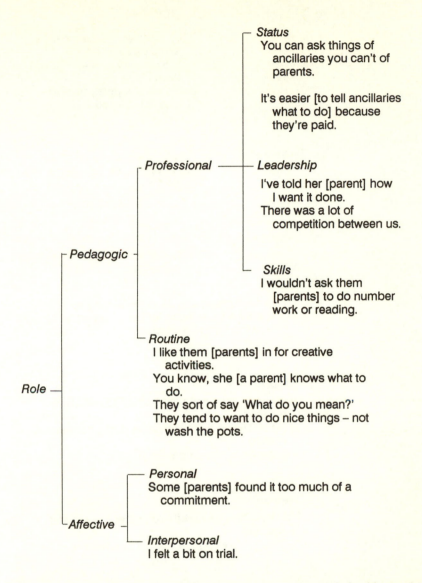

Status
You can ask things of
ancillaries you can't of
parents.

It's easier [to tell ancillaries
what to do] because
they're paid.

Professional ——— *Leadership*
I've told her [parent] how
I want it done.
There was a lot of
competition between us.

Skills
I wouldn't ask them
[parents] to do number
work or reading.

Routine
I like them [parents] in for creative
activities.
You know, she [a parent] knows what to
do.
They sort of say 'What do you mean?'
They tend to want to do nice things – not
wash the pots.

Personal
Some [parents] found it too much of a
commitment.

Interpersonal
I felt a bit on trial.

Commentary: Professional–pedagogic concerns seem to help this teacher to define team members' roles by delimiting the activities which categories of people can undertake. 'Routine' activities are primarily negotiated. Affective factors clearly contribute to definition, with external influences playing their part, and interpersonal rivalries shaping any negotiation which may take place.

Figure 8.2 Interview network 1: teacher

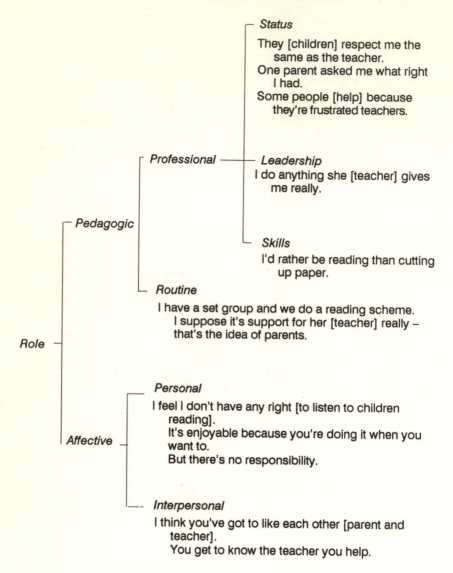

Figure 8.3 Interview network 2: parent

Commentary: A certain degree of uncertainty is expressed about role here, both in terms of her status, and in terms of routine. A view about the 'idea of parents' in class is given to justify the view of parental involvement as the loose notion of 'support' for teacher. The quality of the interpersonal relationship in cementing this loose set of expectations is reaffirmed.

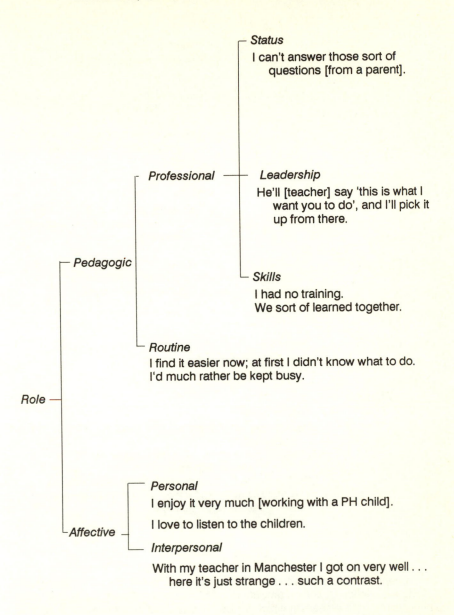

Status

I can't answer those sort of
      questions [from a parent].

Professional — *Leadership*

He'll [teacher] say 'this is what I
      want you to do', and I'll pick it
      up from there.

Skills

I had no training.
We sort of learned together.

Pedagogic

Routine

I find it easier now; at first I didn't know what to do.
I'd much rather be kept busy.

Role

Personal

I enjoy it very much [working with a PH child].

I love to listen to the children.

Affective — *Interpersonal*

With my teacher in Manchester I got on very well . . .
      here it's just strange . . . such a contrast.

Commentary: An individual who clearly finds her place in the team difficult to define.
Even the professional schemata do little to contain the role for her. Affective factors
both provide her main source of satisfaction for doing the work, while providing a
certain amount of tension.

Figure 8.4 Interview network 3: welfare assistant

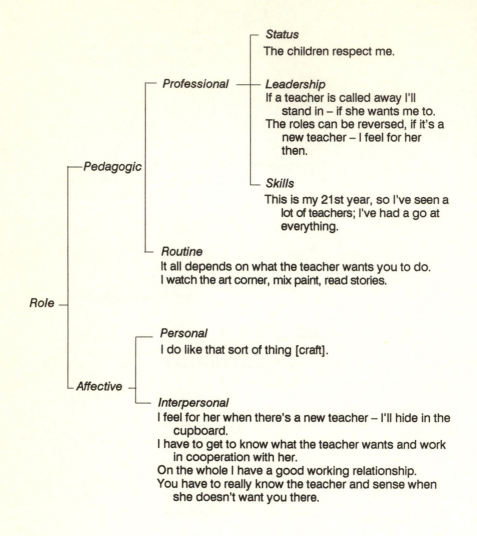

Figure 8.5 Interview network 4: ancillary helper

Commentary: An individual with the confidence to define her role for herself, given her long experience. A certain amount of conflict arises precisely because of this experience and the esteem in which she is held: professional constraints work to elevate her status, a process which she evidently has to try and minimise. Affective factors are important in helping to define the role, though she has to rely on 'sensing' that the teacher may not be at ease in her presence.

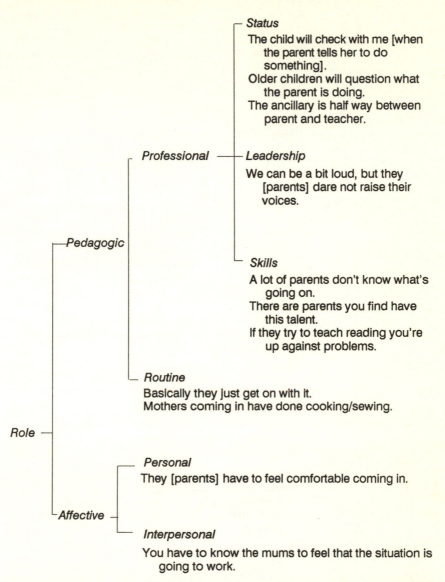

Status

The child will check with me [when the parent tells her to do something].

Older children will question what the parent is doing.

The ancillary is half way between parent and teacher.

Professional — *Leadership*

We can be a bit loud, but they [parents] dare not raise their voices.

Skills

A lot of parents don't know what's going on.

There are parents you find have this talent.

If they try to teach reading you're up against problems.

Pedagogic

Routine

Basically they just get on with it.

Mothers coming in have done cooking/sewing.

Role

Personal

They [parents] have to feel comfortable coming in.

Affective

Interpersonal

You have to know the mums to feel that the situation is going to work.

Commentary: Role here is defined very largely around the respondent's view of the professional, bounded by a set of activities which it is not appropriate for untrained people to do. Participants are assigned a limited set of activities and 'get on with it'. Not surprisingly, relationships are monitored for suitability; those unwilling to stay inside these professionally-oriented role boundaries are screened out.

Figure 8.6 Interview network 5: teacher

107

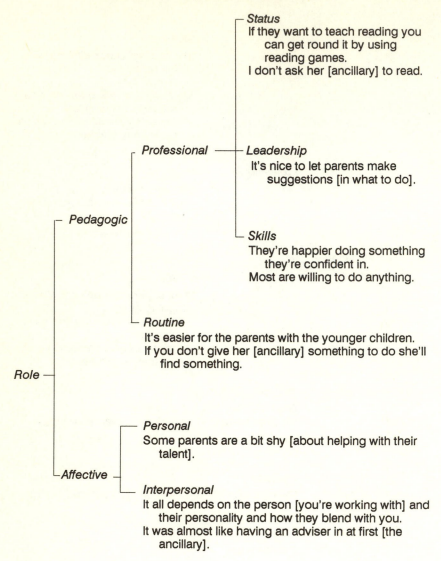

Status

If they want to teach reading you can get round it by using reading games.
I don't ask her [ancillary] to read.

Professional —— Leadership

It's nice to let parents make suggestions [in what to do].

Skills

They're happier doing something they're confident in.
Most are willing to do anything.

Pedagogic

Routine

It's easier for the parents with the younger children.
If you don't give her [ancillary] something to do she'll find something.

Role

Personal

Some parents are a bit shy [about helping with their talent].

Affective

Interpersonal

It all depends on the person [you're working with] and their personality and how they blend with you.
It was almost like having an adviser in at first [the ancillary].

Commentary: Again here role is defined for this teacher by factors outside this particular situation – mainly by her beliefs and ideology. These shape her views of status-appropriate activity and shape her ideas about a set of activities with which parents are assumed to be comfortable. Again, then, suitability rests on a certain set of taken-for-granted assumptions about the views, background and status of the participant.

Figure 8.7 Interview network 6: teacher

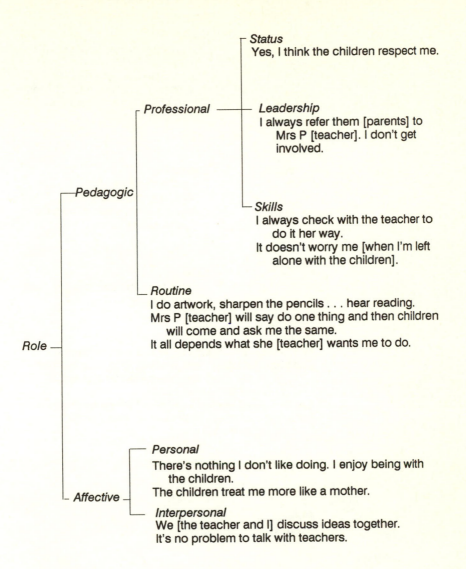

Commentary: The professional concerns of the teacher have been taken on board but some concern is expressed over the room for ambiguity which exists in routine expectations. The importance of the relationship is reaffirmed in the absence of firm guidance; personal motivation is important.

Figure 8.8 Interview network 7: ancillary helper

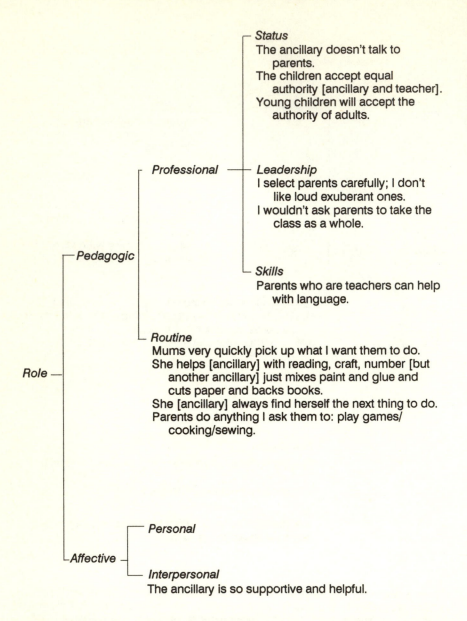

Status
The ancillary doesn't talk to
    parents.
The children accept equal
    authority [ancillary and teacher].
Young children will accept the
    authority of adults.

Professional

Leadership
I select parents carefully; I don't
    like loud exuberant ones.
I wouldn't ask parents to take the
    class as a whole.

Pedagogic

Skills
Parents who are teachers can help
    with language.

Routine
Mums very quickly pick up what I want them to do.
She helps [ancillary] with reading, craft, number [but
    another ancillary] just mixes paint and glue and
    cuts paper and backs books.
She [ancillary] always find herself the next thing to do.
Parents do anything I ask them to: play games/
    cooking/sewing.

Role

Personal

Affective

Interpersonal
The ancillary is so supportive and helpful.

Commentary: This teacher also prescribes a role in terms of professional exclusions, while asserting the equal status of the ancillary in the eyes of the children. While much was said about routine, this in the main related to the 'pick up', 'get on', 'do anything', 'finds herself' dimension.

Figure 8.9 Interview network 8: teacher

CONCLUDING DISCUSSION

Role definition in these teams does not appear to take place in the sense meant by commentators such as Kahn *et al.* (1964) and Lippitt *et al.* (1958) when they wrote about role. The Krech model (Krech *et al.* 1962) drew on a fairly formal notion of role and assumed that roles as originally defined undergo a process of adaptation while the group is working.

Such original roles do not exist in the sense meant by these commentators. When asked questions about what they do, respondents were often unable to give clear or explicit replies about routine expectations, relying rather on comments such as 'I sense what to do' or 'I do whatever's wanted'.

Participants commented on lack of training or initial uncertainty about how to help. This leads potential participants into work where activity is perceived to be more clearly defined, such as working with younger children, a fact noted by more than one respondent.

The potential for unstable teams was noted at the outset, following the surveys in the previous chapter. The importance of 'commitment' among parents was noted by one teacher, given this potential for instability. Commitment by a 'reliable' caucus may be seen as a necessary element in classroom teams, given that so much of the everyday discourse and activity rests on tacitly developed understandings within a regular 'fraternity'. Given the lack of explicit rules about how to behave or what to do, it appears that parents seek those options that will involve them in the least opportunity for 'doing the wrong thing', while teachers place a premium on acquiring a set of helpers with whom they have been able to develop such understanding.

However, network analysis supports the view that role is nevertheless described, albeit in a more amorphous, tacit way. The analysis revealed that the heterogeneity of the team is important and that there are, in Bronfenbrenner's (1979) terms, macro-systems and exo-systems within which people work and behave which shape for them the roles they fulfil and those they are prepared to see others fulfilling. In other words, belief systems and ideologies (macro-system) and other settings such as the home (exo-system) affect the way that individuals consider their role and the roles of others at 'work' in the classroom.

The network analysis revealed that for the teachers interviewed, a pedagogic–professional schema dominated their thoughts on the work of additional people, with certain activities proscribed as far as parents and other non-teachers were concerned.

Compensating for lack of routine advice or a formal set of professional expectations is a reliance on 'getting on' with the person you are sharing with. In the conflict and ambiguity which research tells us is the result when definition is poor, these self-selecting teams appear to rely heavily on affective schemata – essentially found in good personal relationships – for providing motivation and maintaining the process of the team. Thus, personal and interpersonal reasons are given for staying with the team and with the other team members. Without guidance (on management for the teachers, and simply on what to do for the non-teachers), participants resort to being able to laugh, joke, muddle by and generally 'get on with each other' in order to submerge tensions.

Bate uses the term 'root construct' to describe these collectively held beliefs about a team situation, ascribing the term 'unemotionality' to this root construct in his own industry-based study. In these classroom teams the word 'fraternity' might best describe the set of beliefs which characterise the ability of the team to work well – in other words to submerge role conflict.

This set of interviews broadly supports the notion that the heterogeneity of classroom teams is significant in shaping the nature of the team dynamics. It suggests that in the absence of clear definitions of participants' roles, broad schemata frame the means by which participants describe their behaviour. A premium is placed upon the participants' positive interrelationships and unspoken understandings in this situation.

This study sought to reveal the means by which classroom roles are defined from the participants' point of view. It has shown that the idea that these roles are clearly laid out at the outset is invalid. It has revealed instead a continual toing and froing among participants whereby roles are assumed rather than defined. Factors in the wider systems within which people operate and frame their views provide the parameters wherein this process takes place: certain behaviours are prescribed while others are proscribed. It is assumed that the stresses thus engendered are contained and attenuated by the fraternity contrived among the team members – a 'getting along with one another' – in which it can be assumed that no one in the team will 'step outside the limits'.

Further analysis in the chapters which follow will focus on these interrelationships and this communication to illuminate the process by which original role definitions, loose and tacit as they are, are changed by the participants.

9

SUPPORT TEACHERS
The construction of roles

The previous chapter showed that roles are framed for classroom team participants not by clearly articulated rules, guidelines or job descriptions. Rather, in the absence of these, they are framed by the participants' own views about teachers, teaching and classrooms. Roles are framed, for instance, by the participants' notions of status: do they believe that a teacher is a professional with a set of skills inaccessible and untransferable to others – or do they believe the converse of this? Their views will clearly affect the way that they behave as team members in the classroom.

Those were teams of teachers, parents and ancillaries. I suggested that for them ideas about role in the classroom team revolve around certain expectations which exist when teamwork begins. These expectations are constructed around notions which the individuals hold concerning professionalism, status and leadership. There is no reason to believe that role will be framed differently among other kinds of classroom teams, though the constructs which are used to frame role may be very differently shaped.

In this chapter the focus is on teams comprising classteachers and support teachers, though my contention is that role is indeed framed in much the same way in these teams as it is in other kinds of team. I wish here also to look into the idea that the fragile, tentative roles set up at the beginning of classroom teamwork undergo reconstruction as the enterprise progresses. This process of reconstruction – suggested by Krech *et al.* (1962) in other kinds of team – is important since within it lies the possibility of the team process getting better or getting worse.

ROLE RECONSTRUCTION BECAUSE OF MISMATCH

I proposed earlier (chapter 5) a model to account for the varied kinds of role construction which may take place in classroom teams. I suggested that mismatches between the expectations of team members are resolved by means of participants adopting certain strategies which would have the effect of either attenuating or exaggerating the original mismatches.

It has been substantiated by the previous chapter that mismatches indeed occur. But in that chapter it was found that possible grounds for tension in the lack of role definition are minimised or circumvented altogether by selection of team members who will get along with one another and by reliance on what was called fraternity among the members of the team. A high premium was placed on this fraternity, which was seen to exist as a substitute for role definition.

It was originally suggested in chapter 5 that mismatches may occur on ideological or personal grounds, or because ground rules for cooperation have not been clearly set, thus generating ambiguities and mismatches in expectation. The previous chapter confirms this and suggests further that in the absence of role definition, tacitly developed understandings take the place of role definition. Such understandings are built around the pedagogic and affective concerns of the participants. However, fraternity is now seen to camouflage ambiguities.

The review of the literature suggested that participants, in particular the team leader, would adopt strategies which ameliorated for them the effects of stress arising from these supposed mismatches. The process of arriving at a *root construct* of fraternity in the previous chapter was not anticipated, but is now seen to form part of this process. It was anticipated that teams became either more team-like or less team-like by adopting either status solutions or definitional solutions to the problems they faced. A summary is shown in figure 9.1.

Status solutions and *definitional solutions* share the purpose of reducing stress, though the former achieves this through codifying responsibilities and power and locating these in specific individuals, while the latter achieves it through locating the sets of responsibilities in roles rather than people.

I suggested in the previous chapter that fraternity was achieved either

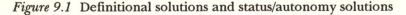

Less team-like ←――――――――――――――→ More team-like

| | |
Status/autonomy solutions Definitional solutions

| | |
Collection of individuals Team working together
working autonomously with clear aims and
 definitions

Figure 9.1 Definitional solutions and status/autonomy solutions

through the use of a selection process or through a deliberate decision to 'get on'. There is no reason to suppose that achieving fraternity is in any way incompatible with the process of establishing status solutions or definitional solutions.

INVESTIGATING THE WAYS IN WHICH ROLES ARE CONSTRUCTED

Analysis of the ways in which the collection of people who are formed together in a team in the classroom come to change the ways in which they view themselves and others as team members will be taken forward with the help of attribution theory and using methods adapted from construct theory. As I made clear in chapter 6, these models are compatible, each drawing on a view of people as scientists, discovering cause-and-effect relationships and seeking to predict and control the situations in which they find themselves.

The means by which roles are transformed, I suggested earlier, rests on the constructions made by the individual and the consequent attributions made about the working of the team. The linking of construct theory and attribution theory requires some further elaboration for the fullest explanation of the methodology used in the work reported in this chapter.

CONSTRUCT THEORY

According to Kelly (1955) we all evaluate the phenomena into which we come into contact according to a finite number of constructs. He suggests that each of these constructs is bipolar, capable of being defined in terms of polar opposite terms such as 'quiet–talkative'. The phenomena to be evaluated by these constructs are termed 'elements'; thus, people, schools or teams may constitute such elements.

An important aspect of Kelly's theory as far as this research is concerned is what he called the 'organisation corollary'. This states that people evolve, for their convenience in anticipating events, a construction system embracing ordinal relationships between constructs. The constructs people employ are interrelated hierarchically. The example Bannister and Fransella (1986) give of this, 'good jazz versus bad jazz', may be subsumed under the 'music' end of the construct 'music versus noise', where the former is the subordinate construct and the latter the superordinate.

Another important corollary for this research is the *sociality corollary*, which states that 'to the extent that one person construes the construction processes of another, they may play a role in a social process involving the other person' (Bannister and Fransella 1986: 18). In the interviews that follow, much of the time the respondents are indeed construing about the constructions of their colleagues, in trying to understand their reactions in the team.

It was noted in chapter 6 that construct theory shares much with ethnomethodology in its seeking of personal interpretations and constructions, and in its eschewal of externally imposed categories as valid means of analysis in interpreting the worlds that others perceive. It is worth noting here the point made in chapter 4 that many of the techniques that have been associated with the development of construct theory (e.g. Shaw 1981) ignore this central feature (i.e. the importance of the *elicitation* of participants' own constructs) by providing subjects with preconceived categories. The semi-structured interview technique to be used in this chapter will be consistent with the notion of elicitation.

ATTRIBUTION THEORY

Attribution theory has been already been discussed. Its particular importance for this study will be taken further here, especially in so far as its interconnection with construct theory is concerned.

Attribution theory has taken an important place in social psychology over the years. Its central aim is to examine people's perceptions about the causes of social events. Do people attribute the occurrence of an event, or the success or failure of a project, to themselves or to others? Do they assume it is outside their control or do they feel they can do something about it?

To cut a long story short (see Deaux and Wrightsman 1988, for a fuller discussion), attributions about the behaviour of others in a team (indeed, of one's own behaviour) may be either 'dispositional' (that is, personal) or 'situational'. The choice of either of these areas has been called the choice of a 'locus of control'. Deaux and Wrightsman (1988) note that there is a tendency in our culture to attribute causes to personal responsibility; this over-attribution to dispositional (personal) causes has been called the 'fundamental attribution error'. The tendency for this to occur in the teaching culture is noted by Doyle (1977), who says that assessments of teacher success generally rest on 'personalistic' interpretations of teaching.

Weiner (1974) suggests that there is another dimension to our judgement about dispositional or situational causes, which he calls the temporary/stable dimension. Extending this model to the classroom team situation, Weiner's model would organise the kinds of attributions which might be made about the working of the team as shown in figure 9.2.

In other words, if things go wrong (or right) in the team, do the team members attribute this failure or success to the intelligence, personality, education or status of their colleagues? Do they attribute it to the mood

	Temporary	Stable
Dispositional	Mood Fatigue	Intelligence Personality Education Status
Situational	Luck	Nature of task Home situation School policy

Figure 9.2 Weiner's attribution model applied to the classroom team

or fatigue of the team members? Or do they attribute success or failure to the nature of the task being done, or to the wider whole school ethos within which the team's work is being framed? Or is it all simply a matter of luck?

In Weiner's model, those who I have suggested seek *team solutions* to the problem of the team working will look to the situational/stable quadrant of figure 9.2, while those who seek *autonomy/status solutions* will look to the stable/dispositional quadrant. In other words, educational background, ideology and personal and professional philosophy will all be 'used' by the latter to determine whether they attribute what Jones and Davies (1965) call 'intentionality' to particular events, or whether they link the person with the event only if they think that the outcome could have been foreseen ('foreseeability'). The willingness of the participants to make these distinctions rests on their inclination to overestimate dispositional causes. It might be posited that the establishment of fraternity is more closely linked with dispositional factors than with possible situational solutions; in fraternity there was repeated evidence of a search for harmonious personal relationships, possibly as a screen for unsatisfactory role definitions.

It may be helpful to represent the links between these ideas diagrammatically, as in figure 9.3. This figure attempts to make it clear that it is participants' personal constructs that determine their perception and interpretation of the variables in the situation. My contention is that certain kinds of constructs will predispose participants to certain kinds of attributions and that it is therefore these constructs which determine the nature of the teams that ultimately emerge.

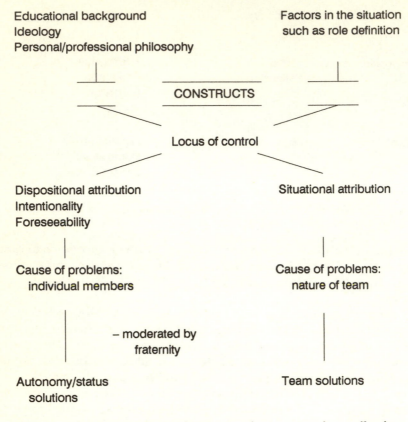

Figure 9.3 The mediation by personal constructs in attributions about the team process

RECAPITULATION

So, the notion of fixed roles which was suggested at the outset appears to have been refuted by the last chapter. Instead, a different process marks the formulation of people's working characteristics in these teams. This process is characterised by roles crystallising out of a set of loosely held views; these in turn give rise to the tacit, if firm, roles characterising the *autonomy* or *team* solutions outlined above. The process by which this happens is the subject of this chapter. In particular, the nature of the constructs the participants employ in making attributions in this process will be examined.

This chapter reports on interviews with a number of support teachers with a view to illuminating these processes.

The support teachers who were interviewed

Questions about samples in qualitative study have already been discussed in chapter 6. Suffice it here simply to say that in this study there is no attempt to sample a representative selection of team participants, but rather to gain an in-depth understanding of the perceptions and understandings of those being interviewed.

Those interviewed were all teachers working alongside other teachers in a supportive role, working with children with special needs. They are, therefore, primarily being interviewed about their work in homogeneous teams; the contrasts between the processes in homogeneous and heterogeneous teams will be noted and commented upon where they are clear. However, the main focus in interviewing this group of people is neither on these differences, nor on the special problems of support teachers. Rather, it is on the constructs which a relatively homogeneous set of individuals employ in making attributions about the behaviour of other team members and about the team process.

In-depth interviews were conducted with eight support teachers. Two were heads of support departments in secondary schools; two were support teachers in support departments in secondary schools; two were support teachers in middle schools; and two were members of primary support teams. All were known to me to use support (as opposed to withdrawal) as a means of working and all were approached informally about participation in this research.

Research instruments

The value of interviews in general as a means of eliciting participants' own ideas (their perceptions, interpretations and personal constructs) has already been discussed in chapter 6 and needs no further elaboration. However, the use of *semi-structured* interviews has not yet been discussed.

The semi-structured interview comprises, according to Borg and Gall (1983), structured questions which are complemented by open-ended questions from the interviewer. It is similar to what Cohen and Manion (1985) call the 'focused interview'. By this, they refer to a situation in which an interviewer has already, having reviewed the literature and other elements of his or her own research, deemed certain aspects of a situation as of significance. Using this analysis as a basis, an 'interview guide' is constructed which identifies the relevant data to be obtained. However, the actual interview is not rigidly determined by the guide, but rather is shaped by the interviewee within this framework, focusing all the time on the subjective experiences of the interviewee.

To make an analysis of these interviews, the same basic procedure outlined in chapter 8 will be adopted. In summary, this comprises: first, examining the raw interview transcripts; second, interpreting them in the light of previous studies; third, establishing interconnections between second-level observations; fourth, subjecting observations to collective scrutiny; and fifth, subjecting several interviews to analysis.

While network analysis was used in that chapter to systematise the analysis at stages three, four and five, in this chapter an adaptation of *cognitive mapping* developed by Jones (1985) will be adopted for this systematisation. Jones describes cognitive mapping thus:

> Cognitive mapping is a method of modelling persons' beliefs in diagrammatic form.... A cognitive map comprises two main elements: persons' concepts or ideas in the form of descriptions of entities, abstract or concrete, in the situation being considered; and beliefs or theories about the relationships between them, shown in the map by an arrow or simple line. An arrow represents a relationship where one thing leads to, or is explained by, another.
>
> (Jones 1985: 266)

She suggests that the cognitive mapping process enables a *fracturing* of the data of an interview without losing its Gestalt.

How the interviews were made and analysed

As in the last chapter, each interview, each lasting around 45 minutes, was tape-recorded and transcribed onto disc, and edited for the purposes of this research by word processor. Respondents were told that the interviews were for research on support in the classroom and that anonymity would be guaranteed.

The interview guide comprised, after opening preliminaries, ten questions relating to: whether interviewees felt accepted by mainstream colleagues; whether mainstream colleagues tended to seek their advice; whether there were regular meetings with colleagues; what sort of role they normally took in the mainstream class; whether they sometimes felt that they didn't have the specialist knowledge to cope; how far they felt that the success of support depended on the teachers they were working with; what the main problems of providing support were; whether they felt pupils gained from their presence; whether they were available to help all pupils; whether they felt there were occasions when their presence was of little use; and what changes they would introduce to make their work more effective.

Following transcription, the interviews were edited. This first edit removed my own questions and comments (where these did not relate integrally to the context of the reply) and comments from the respondents which were not related to the team process. Key words or phrases in each respondent's reply were then highlighted. There followed a process of coding and re-coding each of these replies, grouping them together until they generated a limited set of schemata capable of concisely accommodating the key ideas put forward during the interviews. These would form the building blocks for the next process of cognitive mapping.

The purpose of these interviews and this chapter is to determine the nature of the constructs participants use in making transformations from the 'given' variables to the actual situation. In so doing, I examine the schemata the participants appear to be employing as well as those they appear to infer about the colleagues with whom they are working.

As in the previous study (chapter 8), there will be two parts to the results. First, before cognitive mapping, the interview material will be introduced by means of selected quotations, grouped according to interpretive schemata, setting out the main themes in the interview material. The context of each of the quotations will be mentioned and commented upon, and the quotations will illustrate the schemata under which they are grouped; the quotations will also help in the reformulation of schemata, which have been drawn from the literature and from a primary review of the transcripts. Second, there will be an analysis undertaken using cognitive mapping. In the first part, therefore, organisation will be via the interpretive schemata, while in the second part the linkages which characterise individuals' own accounts will be drawn out.

RESULTS OF THE INTERVIEWS

Part 1: an introduction to the interview material and interpretive schemata

As noted already, a number of schemata can be proposed which will accommodate most of the key ideas about teams' success or failure put forward in the interviews. These are summarised thus:

1 Status and self-esteem
2 Territoriality
3 Threat/suspicion
4 Interpersonal factors
5 Ideology–professional
6 Communication
7 Organisation
8 School policy
9 Role clarity

Each of these will be illustrated by quotations[1] from respondents.

---

1 Notation here is identical to that in chapter 8.

Status and self-esteem

The following teacher feels her own role in the eyes of others is low; she is 'used' and has a low status. There appears to be a kind of work for which she is suited and another kind for which the classteacher is suited.

R: I have asked next year not to be a support teacher. I've had enough. I feel that my self esteem as a support teacher er, my *self-esteem as a teacher, has gone down through doing support.* And it is only because I have had confidence beforehand in my ability, in my own subject and because I, er in my own right as a teacher that I have managed to do it this long this year, because er, you become ... support teaching can bring with it a terrible feeling of er just er just *being used.* You've got a, well it's very hard to describe, a *very low, yes, a low status* . . . there's a feeling of, er, *I don't hold my head up.*

The same teacher, a support teacher in a secondary school, continues. The poor image, poor status is at least in part due to a lack of special skills – a lack of professional markers which distinguish you from the rest:

R: *A teacher is not the same as a support teacher.* You can't just pick somebody up and throw them into a room and say 'Now on you go and support'. And that's what they do and that's why I think it's got such again a *low image*, because you're not seen as being, having had special qualifications, you know, to do it.

Linked with this is a range of comments which came from nearly all respondents, articulated as a perception of status difference. The following, from a teacher in a middle school, relates the idea of being a good colleague with being on *equal terms.*

R: So I've gone to all their [first year] em, planning meetings and everything, because I've got the most input there, and also because em, I mean they're very *good colleagues*, if you like, and they're, it's very *easy to, to discuss* things, sort of on *equal terms* with them, and have some influence on em, how the curriculum's going to be planned and organised and so on. So I feel that's good, good use of my time. Now, in the case of some other year groups, em, it's either *a question of luck*, or what tends to happen anyway is that the most inputs [are] with the youngest children.

This secondary teacher reinforces the idea that she feels that classteachers do not see her as an equal:

R: They accept me, um, because they know I'm going to be able to help, *I'm an extra pair of hands*, I'm going to be able to help, *I do not necessarily think they look upon me as an equal in terms of a teacher*, a fellow teacher when I'm in the room, they look upon me as a fellow teacher in my own subject but not necessarily as when I'm a support teacher.

She makes it clear that this impression can be transmitted to the children. Some teachers make it clear that status is equal (which is part of clear role definition), while others imply to the children that it is not:

R: *The pupils don't see you as being accepted by the teacher there on a level with the teacher.* In other words when they say 'Now there are two of us today, er, any questions, we're both ready. Any queries ...', you know, constantly referring to the fact that *we're on a par here*, where er, we're both capable of doing, fulfilling whatever it is you need today, and if this is built up week after week after week then you find the support begins to work. And the children will willingly call you over. *If it isn't* then they will put their hands up and then when you go across you can even get children who say '*I don't want you, I want so and so*, because she knows this, or I need sir because they know'. And then you know it hasn't worked. There's always that little feeling, and they look at me and think 'Yeah, well she's a textiles teacher, she's not an English teacher, and *I'm just not sure whether or not, you know, what she's going to tell me is right*'. And I've actually noticed that some of them will listen and they'll go ahead and write whatever it was they were writing anyway.

The status of the teacher appears to be linked with being marginal:

R: The English department are all *together. But you're outside it*. And it's, and I think it's the same in other subjects.

The marginal nature of the work is attested to by this comment:

R: I think that er, the heads of departments like to have their meetings regarding special needs at the beginning of the year. *Let's get it over and done with* in September, 'Let's get special needs done, nice and quickly, get it out of the way.'

This notion of this marginality is strengthened by a middle school teacher who talks of the feeling of being part of a team in those classes where there appears to be an attempt to avoid the support teacher becoming marginal:

R: Well the good ones are good because, like in the last school for example, because the first year team, I go to all their year meetings and *I feel part of, of the team*, and we work out work together, and I'm in on all the planning and em, they ask me things like 'Do you think so and so will cope with this' and they don't mind how often I chip in and say 'Oh, well I think that's a bit above them', and so on. They never mind. Whereas some of the other teachers are a bit more formal and have been doing the same sort of lesson, year after year.

That's their lesson and it's just sort of seemed to me, you know they can't alter anything and *they wouldn't mind if I actually went away.*

The following comment relates this feeling of marginality versus teamness ostensibly to different professional ideologies adopted in different halves of the middle school:

R: There just seems to be quite a division [between the upper and lower school]. You know, but it's probably partly as well because I, *I'm seen just as the extra person up there, whereas in the bottom half I'm just one of the team*, like all the kids just see me as another, as *one of them*, you know I think I can cover a lesson and so on, and it's just another first year teacher, *whereas in upper school*, I think it's seen as oh, *the reading lady*, or the something lady. Though it shouldn't be like that now, because I've been there over four years.

The question of status is again raised here, where the support teacher seems very much to be associated with the low status of the child she is helping in the classteacher's mind. This clearly hinges on the classteacher's view of special needs:

R: He [child in home economics class] was punished and had to do the dishes, you know wash up the dishes, and I was expected to go along and help him wash up the dishes. And a couple of times I was spoken to in a manner that I didn't feel was, you know, wasn't on – not for a *fellow colleague; I wasn't seen on equal terms* and I have had to work very hard to put myself on an equal footing with that person; I think that's an exception rather than a norm but you do run into it and it's very, very hard.

The question of status is here interestingly linked with partnership, with the support teacher noting that she hasn't led a lesson; the lack of partnership also implies a lack of status in this situation

R: I haven't introduced a lesson, no, we haven't had that *partnership*. Partly because in the five classes . . . the teacher has the momentum, knows where she is, knows what they want to accomplish.

This head of special needs relays the feelings of his colleagues on the status accorded to them by some mainstream colleagues even more bluntly. He relates the feeling of subservience to teachers not giving away elements of their role:

R: Some of the supporters are a bit cynical . . . and they say 'Well you know we are allowed to be in charge of the class when they want to go and make a phone call but another time *they want you to take the, the sort of servant role'* um, but in general I think people are gradually coming around to the idea that if you have got two adults working in the class then *both of them have got to be seen as having a role in all respects* in the classroom.

Territory

The next major schema which appeared to be held by these teachers related to the territory or property which they perceived themselves infringing when they worked alongside a classteacher. It is the more interesting for the fact that at no time was the word 'territory' used in the questioning or in probes. This schema seemed to be important for all of the respondents. The following teacher links the need for territory strongly with her own identity and status:

R: It's, this is my room – I'm, I'm going into my room. I feel here I am now going in with another teacher, to help yet again. And *I feel as if I'm a bit of a dogsbody. And I've lost that identity* of having *my own, my own base*, and *for teachers in school it's important; they'll fight for their own room*. They want their own room . . . *that's their identity*. That is their room, their subject. You start to take those things away and you start to lose an awful lot of your em, of what you feel is your esteem in pupils' eyes. And that's important when you go back to take up your own subject again, because you've got to work even harder to show them *that you know what you're talking about* now in your own room. And I'm not here supporting any more so you do just what I say. Whereas it's different when you support. *You're the second person.*

This middle school teacher, while not mentioning territory specifically, talks of being 'shut out', not being 'wanted', in contrast to some teachers who are welcoming:

R: I haven't actually come across anybody who hasn't accepted me in the end. In some senses of them word, I mean, you know there's different levels of acceptance but there's, there have been people who, when I first started working with them, I felt they, *they've been really trying to shut me out, and not really wanting me there at all*. Um, and I think in all cases that's improved. But obviously you feel *more comfortable with some people than others*, and you feel *more welcome into some classrooms* than others.

A head of special needs in a secondary school here reports an even more stark rejection:

R: But there are others where *I'm still asked to sit in the corner of the classroom* or sit in a particular chair and those are the ones that we are still fighting, we're still trying to win that battle.

There even seems to be a feeling that the teacher is discomfited by the physical movement of the support teacher, though here there is the suggestion that this is linked with an ideology which sees support as remedial help in the classroom:

R: In some lessons we are treated as, 'oh you've just come in to help him', and you're very much put with one child or two children, we get up and try and *move around and it's obviously not appreciated*.

This secondary support teacher links the idea with that of personal space which may be *violated*:

R: It's their *territory, it's their classroom, it's their subject area. . . . It's their personal area. Yes, it's their space* . . . I think teaching is a very personal situation and the interaction with the class can be very personal and as, and a person coming in, whoever it is, head, parent, whatever, they move into that area so *I see it as a very personal sort of space and so if you go in as a support teacher in some respect you are violating that*.

Interestingly, this teacher attests to the fact that such feelings evaporate when she is supporting the supply teacher; she seems to experience a freedom which she does not feel when working with the classteacher.

R: If I go in to support the *supply teacher* then I will talk to that teacher at the beginning and I will say the class has not been behaving, we are not getting the work accomplished and I will *feel responsibility for the whole class* in that I will take over the discipline . . . we're *sharing this territory together*, we're both inputs and I wouldn't do, I don't think I would have done it with a regular teacher, no.

The following teacher interestingly links territory with the notion of *ownership*, seeming to feel that a true partnership – true teamwork – is not possible while such ownership exists in the mind of the classteacher:

R: I'd like to have more of a *partnership* situation in the classes that I am supporting, team teaching, when it does work with another teacher, the two of you are working in a class then it's great. But sometimes you really have to sit back and look at it and er . . . People you don't know as well you really have to sit back a wee bit and I'd like more give and take. But again *it comes down to ownership of class* and material.

Suspicion/threat versus confidence

This next major schema is represented as bipolar because of its clear and universal representation in this way, almost explicitly on this continuum, by the respondents. It appears to be linked with the previous schema. The following teacher perhaps sees this suspicion as related to a threat over professional status, ideology or skills:

R: I think that, er, that teachers in general are rather *suspicious* of outside so-called experts. Um, so I think you have to win them over, I think you have to be very careful, you can't go in and try and change the world if you have to fit into their model and maybe if you think there should be changes or you have suggestions, do it over a period of time or you would get people's backs up.

It is linked here with the notion of fear of being watched, with perhaps the intimation that watching is equated with monitoring of professional skills:

R: I think it is difficult for some people to have somebody else there. Because *they feel that you're going to be watching them.*

The following makes the contrast with those who are *secure* and those who are *threatened*; she talks about people she can work easily with:

R: Well, I think they're people who feel *secure* about what they're doing themselves, mostly. I mean, I think it's harder for somebody who doesn't feel secure in what they're doing anyway. And people who are sort of fairly *open*, you know who don't mind disagreements, or who can cope with that sort of thing. Not very easily, *people who are not very easily threatened*, I suppose.

In the following, there is the implication that being welcoming or otherwise is related either to mistrust/threat, or alternatively to ideological differences over appropriate action for children with special needs.

R: [We will say] 'Would you allow us to come in and support them?' The response at that level varies tremendously. Some people say *'Yes, lovely I hadn't thought to ask'* and other people say *'Well you can come in if you want'* but it will be more use you taking him out and doing something on his own with him.

The following teacher brings out the fact that people vary in their ostensible perception of threat:

R: I think it [the success of support] depends a lot on it [the person you're working with]. Not entirely, I mean I think you can, you can make some progress even if, even if they're not the easiest person to work with . . . But it's obviously much easier if it's somebody who, who, say basically who *isn't going to feel threatened* by an extra adult there.

Here, the teacher seems to suggest that the perception of threat comes from the classteacher's vulnerability, perhaps linking this vulnerability both to personal and professional factors:

R: I think a lot of it is the *confidence* of the teacher themselves, a lot of teachers don't want to have somebody else in the classroom and they are not confident enough about their own style or their own discipline or whatever . . . I think without exception those are the ones where there are discipline problems within the class and the teacher isn't saying, yes I'd be glad of somebody else in there can we talk about how we can work it out, like some teachers do, yes, it's a very difficult class and can we talk how to work it out between us. But other teachers simply *seize up* and don't want you to be in there.

Here, the middle school teacher actually perceives that the classteacher can feel *under attack*:

R: I think *people who've been isolationist* in their own classrooms and you haven't been used to having other people in there, *feel under attack really*, they feel on the defensive. And they don't like, I mean I have teachers and they don't like anybody else in the classroom.

Interpersonal factors

Personal and interpersonal factors have already been implied in the extracts that have been used. The need for these skills was identified strongly in the previous chapter, and the congruence between those findings, and the findings here will be discussed after the results have been presented. The importance of interpersonal factors is stated quite simply here:

R: I mean I think there are obviously personal things with people, you know *you get on better with some people than you do with others* and I think that's quite an important factor.

A different teacher makes a similar comment, relating more to personal than interpersonal features:

R: It [resistance to support] may be, em, something to do with the fact that *this particular teacher is a very very quiet and very withdrawn person* anyway, who is not happy teaching. And, therefore those kind of *personal attributes* that he has or not. I think that has a lot to do with it.

The importance of *getting along* is perhaps masked, this teacher seems to suggest, by the fact that it is so 'obviously' important:

R: *So much obviously depends on personalities and who you get on with*. I wouldn't dream, although I should do I know, with some of the teachers, with even bothering to suggest that I took the lesson.

Here, having an 'open personality' is linked with the ability and need to communicate:

R: [It's easier with someone] who's *willing to discuss things* and, and, is a sort of *open personality*, where you're actually able to talk things over with them.

Personality and the ability to communicate are here linked with the perception of threat noted earlier:

R: This particular teacher is not . . . very flexible *as a person* really and she won't vary her approach and she's *not very responsive* to someone saying, if you tried this, do you think it would work better, she feels that's a *criticism of her*.

The contrast in the following extract between those with whom relationships are easy and those with whom they are difficult perhaps marks a continuum:

R: Yes, there are um, definite differences [between teachers]. It depends very much on the relationship between the two teachers. In, for example, English there are two teachers who regard me as being extremely helpful, value what I do, and do actually say, you know it's great having you, I don't know what I'd do without you. With one other, I am, *I could just be a piece of furniture in the room*, basically, I have to make, walk around, no introduction is ever made, no er, at no point does he ever say, 'You have two of us today to help you', which is what the other teachers would say, er it's just him in the room and me at the side and it's up to me to make the move to go around the room and help, quietly. There's no feeling of being a part of the lesson in any way.

Professional–ideological

Another schema emerging in accounts is the professional–ideological. It seems to be felt that one's effectiveness as a team member is determined in large part by a congruence in ideology between support and classteacher.

The need for some similarity in thought, style or ideology is evidenced here:

R: I think [support teaching is of little use] almost exclusively in very formal situations. *Where someone is teaching a class as a class, I think that the services of a support teacher will very rarely be needed.* I'm not even sure that the presence of an extra person is of any benefit in a situation where there are behavioural problems. I tried to work with a notorious third year group last year in French lessons because the main problem there was a behavioural one and I don't think I made any difference, and if I did make any difference being there it was probably a detrimental difference, in that there was a play-off between two teachers or I was causing distractions to people who were easily distracted.

This middle school teacher seems to indicate that there is a limit to the professional 'sharing' that can go on, though the amount of sharing wanted or permitted by the teachers is on a continuum depending on their place in the school and perhaps the associated expectations of formality in the curriculum:

R: Um, they don't seek advice about the structure of the lesson, particularly, but the majority of them would take comments that I said afterwards, or in it. They don't mind me sort of butting in. If they're saying something and I can see that some of them aren't quite with me, or it's been a bit vague, or, that type of thing, sometimes *they sort of call across*, you know, 'Wouldn't you say so Mrs __', or something, to give me my chance to say 'Well actually I was just standing here thinking, I'm not quite sure what we've got to do here' . . . *but a lot of the time with the upper school, it's still 'What're you going to do about so and so', and so on, not sort of 'How will we do this?'* There's a marked difference between the two halves of the school.

A primary support teacher affirms the importance of this similarity in professional outlook for communication and clarity of shared goals. Such clarity seems to be an example of a *role solution*:

R: People are in a different range of things aren't they *depending on attitude to special needs* and there is one colleague that I work with who is absolutely superb, she's an infant teacher and has a psychology degree, I don't know if that helps, but she manages the whole class, she obviously enjoys teaching, she's very imaginative and she's just really easy to slot in with. She's very *clear on what she's doing*, she's very good on telling you in advance what she's doing, um it's quite easy to have a kind of shorthand communications, because a lot of the problem is time, so you need to find a quick way of *communicating* together, so, *we do think the same way about teaching* which helps, because you are immediately on the *same wavelength*.

Here the middle school respondent suggests that this ideological similarity is more important than personality:

R: I mean obviously some personalities make it easier in that they might be more sympathetic. *The hardest thing is a person that actually feels a child should just be withdrawn* and given a dose of this, that and the other.

Another, a secondary head of support, verifies that professional style is more significant than personality:

R: I think in our experience the thing which has made the whole difference between whether it's easy to work with someone or difficult is *the way in which they organise their classroom and the way, the types of teaching methods they use* and the stand up chalk-and-talk people were the last to actually see the point of anyone coming in the classroom and I found the most difficult to work with. Um, not necessarily on a personal level, they were very often very accommodating and happy to have you there after they'd tried it and pleased to try and make it work. But then most difficult in terms of methodology to work with because you find that you're spending about 75 per cent of your time sat down with the kids listening, and very little time actually doing anything actively.

Equality in role seems for this teacher to depend centrally on the underlying philosophy of the classteacher:

R: There is for instance, there's one teacher who very much likes the children to work in *mixed ability groups*, all the time, or very much as far as possible. And there you, that does make it easier, because, em, you know you maybe have a group to work with who are, who are whole range, and then you're really working alongside the teacher on a sort of, some kind of *an equal basis*.

Communication

It has already been shown that communication is linked with personality factors and similarities in ideology. However, communication emerges repeatedly as a discrete schema in respondents' accounts, although of course it may be tacitly encapsulating these other schemata in so doing. The simple practicalities of adequate communication, such as finding the time for it, emerge as important. This teacher seems to indicate that roles cannot be developed without adequate communication; however, the exigencies of school life mean that adequate communication is relegated to the odd moment:

R: It [communication] is almost exclusively informal and very often taking place at break time or lunchtime or even at the end of a lesson when the kids are moving on to another place you can grab a few minutes.

An extract from another teacher's account reinforces the perfunctory nature of communication:

R: Em, when I go up to them and say, er, 'We're all right for tomorrow morning', something like that or 'We're OK this afternoon'. Em, they'll say 'Yes, em em, I'm going to be doing such and such today, er, so that'll be great having you in.' That's it, I mean *that's as much as I ever get.*

Another attests to its importance, and links it with the ability to *get on*:

R: [The success of support depends] ever so much [on communication]. I mean I'm not saying it's useless, I mean I do sometimes go into lessons, yes, which we haven't discussed at all before . . . but, *yes, the more we've planned and talked it over together, then the more I actually get on with that person.*

This teacher links communication integrally with the role she plays; without communication and time for planning, she resorts to withdrawal:

R: I sort of catch them [classteachers] at odd moments . . . I haven't managed to really talk about things in any systematic way with them. I found that quite often I end up saying that, well, I'm going to take these children out of this class, and work with a group. Which is not what I consider ideal. But, but *if you haven't done the planning together beforehand,* I think it's sometimes inevitable because otherwise *you don't really have a proper role in the class.*

The following extract emphasises the fact that the supporter has to *read* the situation in the class as a substitute for good communication:

R: I think the person coming in has to have a fair amount of sensitivity and flexibility; *you have to be able to read what is going on* and be able to slot that child into the programme because you don't have the opportunities for formal meetings and setting it up; I mean that's very nice, but you don't. You really have to be very adept at reading what's coming from the teacher and *melting in.*

Organisation

Methods of organisation emerged as a separate feature which would inhibit effective co-working. This respondent links it with personality:

R: I hope he hasn't seen me as being critical. But it could be that he's picked up some of my feelings about the way he has set out his class, which I have said to him on at least two occasions I think he should change so that I could get to the pupils I need, and it would do them good to be mixed up and spread around, because there is a tremendous amount of chaos and er noise in the class. Which I find difficult to work with anyway so maybe it's just a combination of personalities and a conflict, *I feel he's not using his, er, management of the class; the class is not working*.

This head of special needs attests to the fact that children are aware of the differences which exist:

R: Sometimes you will get a wry look from the child when something's going on in the classroom and they know *it's not the way that you would do something* um, they also are aware of differences between teachers' methods and so on.

The following teacher seems to perceive a lack of possible development in her role as linked with her own unwillingness to press the issue on organisation:

R: *They know that I'll fit in with whatever they have planned, I don't make a fuss.* I don't harass them to find out what we're going to do, and 'Could I have a four week plan, I'd like to work out something myself. Have you got a strategy here?', or whatever. I don't do that. So they probably see me as being quite happy to come in and er, do whatever is necessary. So they don't ask my advice on, on what . . . [how I'd organise]. They will ask after a lesson about specific pupils. How I felt they'd got on, or if they were worried about somebody. So we will discuss a pupil. But it doesn't affect what I do with them the next lesson.

School policy

Very few comments related to the importance of policy in determining the success of teaming. However, they are significant in terms of the attitudes which develop, as these comments show:

R: And also he [headteacher] agreed that they took people who were light on the timetable and built them up with support. No background in support work. *No help. No guidance. You are a teacher, off you get into somebody else's room. That's it.*

The following indicates that a policy obviates the need for some discussion, implying that such a policy lays out broad parameters for the role which should be adopted:

R: In schools that actually have a whole school policy for special needs, and they have a special needs co-ordinator, there are regular meetings. Um, but in a school that doesn't, where special needs are a low priority, um, no it's very difficult, you have to actually get consultation times, *you have to snatch times*, catch people at lunch times.

Role definition

This is presented as an addendum to this section, since it relates only peripherally to the question of schemata or constructs which participants employ in fashioning roles in the classroom. However, many respondents raised the point that an explicit allocation of roles had in fact substantially eased many of the tensions about which they had been talking. One teacher, seemingly frustrated by the tensions of support, split the class into two, with the approval of the support teacher:

R: He [mainstream teacher] says 'Right now, this week you lot can go outside with Mrs —— and, er, you're going to do some extra work quietly out there with her, which relates to what we're doing in here. Now then you'll do yours next week, all right OK. I know we're coming round to you.' He has made it an extra, a special thing. So it's not seen as you take the poor ones out. He's mixed his groups so that everybody gets support. It makes his class slightly smaller and more manageable, so he benefits, and they benefit because they've got an extra little group outside, and I thought that is really good.

She points to the fact that otherwise (i.e. outside this situation) role is not specified:

R: I'm not sure ... *how they see my role exactly, because it's never been stipulated.*

Another had addressed the need to have specific areas, perhaps specific *territories* in the class:

R: We tried to [specify roles] in the form of zoning in that, you know wherever you are in the classroom you would feel responsible for that area of the classroom.

Here there is evidence of explicit role differentiation:

R: We decided that that [another system of support] obviously didn't work. And so we ended making more use of splitting the class so that when . . . a particular problem in French was that when we were doing listening and speaking exercises, the whole class just couldn't concentrate on it. So *we were splitting it;* the French teacher was doing the speaking exercises with small groups while I was monitoring the rest of the group doing the rest of their exercises and *that works a lot better.* So it wasn't, a simple presence in the classroom wasn't the answer but I suppose in the end *what we did was to work out a whole new method of working which involved having two people to work with the class and having worked that out then it began to work better.*

Preliminary discussion prior to cognitive mapping

The nine schemata drawn out at the beginning of this section serve as a useful way of marshalling the diverse thoughts, meanings and constructions of these teachers. While they serve as a means of organising the interview responses effectively, they do not help to relate together into a meaningful whole the cognitive Gestalt which individuals were constructing for themselves. How are individuals, in Kelly's terms, construing the social world which they confront and of which they are a part? How are these constructs they employ interrelated? How do constructs mediate attributions about 'given' features of the team to give rise to the actual roles which emerge?

Part 2: the cognitive maps

As I noted earlier, an adaptation of Jones's (1985) cognitive mapping is being used for this study. Jones writes of the mapping of constructs in which subordinate and superordinate constructs are linked. She further talks of 'second-order' categorisations, grounded in those of the interviewee but nevertheless reflecting her own perspective and research interests. The adaptation I use will make no pretence at drawing such distinctions. The 'constructs' elicited will be related to the interpretive schemata isolated earlier, and interrelationships will be marked if they are evident. The personal nature of the respondents' own construct systems will then be discussed in the light of this analysis, drawing out the bipolar nature of these personal constructs where this is evident and any superordinate and subordinate features.

For the purposes of the mapping, key statements are summarised and boxed for clarity. Each box is numbered as an identification code for reference in the subsequent commentary. Numbers and the shape of the map are arbitrary in Jones's system; here, the numbers retain the temporal flow and logic (which may be of interest) by representing the sequence of the utterances. Where statements are interrelated they are joined by lines. A continuous arrowed line indicates a connotative relationship whereby the utterance at the end of the arrow appears to subsume or explain in some way the related utterance. Dotted lines represent tentative links between ideas. Shaded boxes represent the clearest elicitation of personal constructs and the labels in upper-case accompanying them represent what Jones calls *second-order categorisations*, which are schemata grounded in those of the interviewee, but framed in the context of the research already undertaken. The personal constructs are inferred from these schemata in the subsequent commentary. I have omitted the use of Jones's positive and negative signs accompanying the connotative links since examination of the data indicates that contradictions or inconsistencies (indicated by a negative sign) rarely if ever occurred in the accounts of these interviewees.

Map 1 – commentary and discussion

A head of a learning support department in a secondary school. Four themes dominate here. Roles are clearly shaped for this teacher by the perception of threat, and by interpersonal factors. The threat construct might be termed 'threat versus acceptance' – a fairly simple dimension in which the respondent appears not to perceive hostility or suspicion, but rather a fear which he is confident will translate into acceptance as the team situation progresses (1). Here, then, is explicit recognition of the ways in which roles emerge and change: this teacher is confident that with greater understanding between participants, *threat* will turn into *acceptance*.

This perception of threat (as is the case with this construct in other interviews) is a construing of the *colleague's* construct system (as in Kelly's sociality corollary discussed earlier).

Roles are also shaped, or transformed, to a much lesser extent for this respondent by the interpersonal manner of the participants; for him, this might be termed easy to get along with versus difficult to get along with. He sees himself at the easy end of this continuum, and perhaps because of this sees this construct as being of minimal importance. He can overcome difficulties by being able to 'get on with people', though here, as was made clear in the previous chapter, such *fraternity* may mask inadequate communication. Perhaps because of this 'easiness', communication appears for him to be less important than it is with some of the other interviewees. Communication for him is about 'planning' (9) and 'meetings' (8), which are related to the importance he places on the *professional* schema. He explicitly says that the style of teachers is far more important than their interpersonal manner (3).

In this last comment lies the kernel of this teacher's construing system and the central means by which he views the determination of roles in the shared classroom. This comment about style is echoed, as the map shows, in other comments about professional style and status (2, 10, 13, 18). For him, the professional schema is not one on which ideological differences figure largely; rather, there is the danger for him of not being seen as a professional (13) and this is caused by the style of the other teacher (2). It might be inferred that the construct is 'professional versus unskilled', with a subordinate construct of 'professional versus redundant', as evidenced in 'main problem is being seen doing something'. This would clearly be subordinate to the construct of status – for him, 'high status versus low status'.

The relevance of this last set of constructs for the transformation of

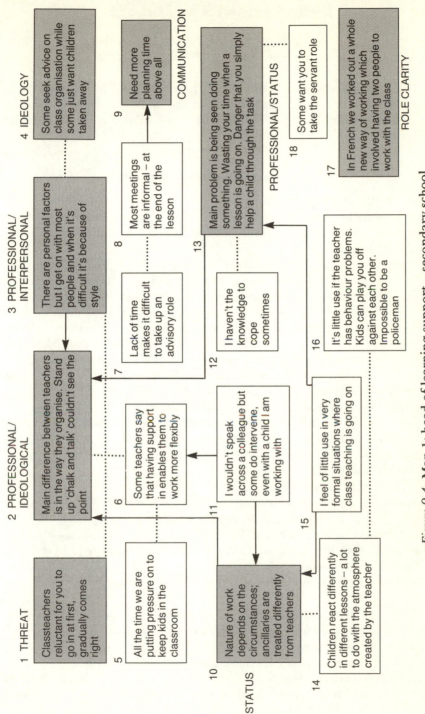

Figure 9.4 **Map 1: head of learning support – secondary school**

roles is manifest. The style of the classteacher is seen as a possible block to adequate role enactment; Adair (1986, see chapter 2) calls this 'role underload'.

Interestingly, the search for role clarity evidenced in comment (17) substantiates the notion that there can be with certain colleagues a situational attribution – a recourse to team solutions in the face of difficulties.

Map 2 – *commentary and discussion*

This teacher is a support teacher in a secondary support department. Clearly unhappy with her role, or lack of role, most of what she says is predicated on the notion of status, and her low status in the eyes of many of her colleagues.

For her, the superordinate construing system through which she views what happens in classroom teams is concerned with status and esteem. 'High self-esteem versus low self-esteem' is subsumed under 'equal status versus low status'. She sees herself as not being on a par with certain colleagues (10), concluding (17) apparently that support teachers do not fit even as a sub-set into the set of teachers in the way presumably that maths teachers or English teachers do. She is not a 'proper' teacher. She links this with not having any special qualifications. Her low self-esteem is linked with a lack of qualifications, providing evidence of her construct filtering the information available to account for the difficulties she experiences. She makes a dispositional attribution having seen the range of possible causes of her difficulties through this *status* construct; through this construct, this template, she 'sees' educational background as the explanation for this low status.

This status is linked for her with the schema of territory, which for her seems to emerge from a construct of 'marginal/alienated versus feeling part/included'. Marginality is determined by this low status. She says (3) that the welcome she receives is dependent on her relationship with other teachers, though interpersonal factors do not figure elsewhere in this way in her account. However, this 'good versus poor' relationship would seem in turn to hinge on the status which is accorded to her by the colleague (2).

Similarly, status is the superordinate construct also for communication. It seems to be taken as a given that communication will be perfunctory, done almost as a matter of routine duty, because of the low value which is placed upon the support teacher's contribution and status (5).

With this teacher, then, full development of her role is determined by the status which is accorded to her by others. This status construct comprises and accounts for many of the problems which are perceived in other areas such as communication. In contrast to the previous teacher,

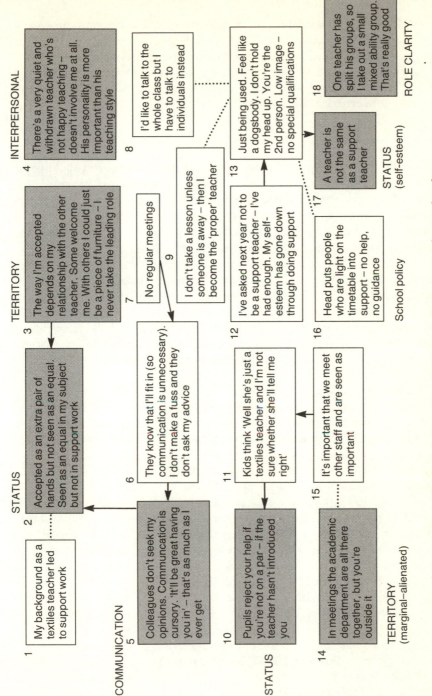

Figure 9.5 Map 2: support teacher – secondary school

the style of the classteacher is unimportant. The emergent process is determined by the 'equal status versus low status' construct.

Again with this teacher there is, with one other teacher with whom she works, the successful search for role clarity in splitting groups (18). A switch to a situational attribution resolves many problems for the two teachers concerned.

Map 3 – commentary and discussion

This is a teacher in a primary support team. Her emergent role appears very much shaped by her view of her colleagues' professional and ideological positions. Her peripatetic status compounds any difficulties which she may have; since she moves from school to school the scope for her perception of infringing on the territory of others is magnified, and communication must also be made more difficult.

Nevertheless, the central means by which she judges the success of her attempts to fulfil a professionally satisfying role is through this professional/ideological schema. For her, the construct that appears to exist is of teachers as restorative versus teachers as preventative (after the continuum proposed by Wilson 1988) in respect of their views about special needs. Those who take a preventative view enable her to work in one way, while those with restorative beliefs constrain her to fulfil a different role.

Though she does not make the links between different schemata explicit, they may nevertheless be inferred. Communication, for instance, is clearly centrally bound up in this mismatch of expectations, yet she refers to communication simply as a practical matter, where logistics seem to form the main obstacle to better understanding (6). At no point does she make the explicit link between communication and reduction in threat or resolution of ideological problems.

However, the link between the perception of ideological mismatch and that of infringing on another's territory is explicitly made in comment (2). Here there seems to be the feeling that in moving into the school, you may be moving into hostile territory – into a place where the ideology is alien to one's own; where people expect you to behave in a certain way. It is linked to comment (3), where she feels that she is being viewed as an 'outside expert'. The notion of *outsider* fits with the territorial analogy. She has to 'win over' these ideologically different teachers, but (one has to infer) she doesn't have the time to do so (6). She makes clear that the perception of this suspicion depends on the ethos of the school (4).

This notion of threat is echoed in comment (5), where she says she felt under attack herself. The construct might be inferred as 'attacked versus accepted', and this is clearly subordinate to the ideological construct.

For this teacher, then, dispositional attributions are created from

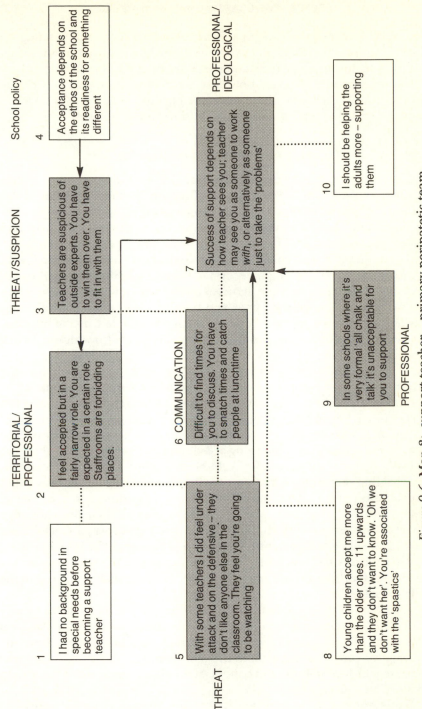

School policy

4
Acceptance depends on the ethos of the school and its readiness for something different

THREAT/SUSPICION

3
Teachers are suspicious of outside experts. You have to win them over. You have to fit in with them

TERRITORIAL/
PROFESSIONAL

2
I feel accepted but in a fairly narrow role. You are expected in a certain role. Staffrooms are forbidding places.

1
I had no background in special needs before becoming a support teacher

6 COMMUNICATION

Difficult to find times for you to discuss. You have to snatch times and catch people at lunchtime

5
With some teachers I did feel under attack and on the defensive — they don't like anyone else in the classroom. They feel you're going to be watching

THREAT

8
Young children accept me more than the older ones. 11 upwards and they don't want to know. 'Oh we don't want her'. You're associated with the 'spastics'

PROFESSIONAL/
IDEOLOGICAL

7
Success of support depends on how teacher sees you; teacher may see you as someone to work *with*, or alternatively as someone just to take the 'problems'

10
I should be helping the adults more – supporting them

9
In some schools where it's very formal 'all chalk and talk' it's unacceptable for you to support

PROFESSIONAL

Figure 9.6 Map 3: support teacher – primary peripatetic team

constructs that shape a view of colleagues' acceptance as depending on their ideological positions. This could be altered through communication, but the exigencies of her peripatetic role make this less than easy. There is the suggestion of a situational attribution in comment (4) with the recognition that school policy plays some part in her acceptance, but this is not extended to practical strategies at the classroom level.

Map 4 – commentary and discussion

This is a support teacher in a middle school. Her construct system seems to hinge centrally on the perception of the professional position of her colleagues. Practical considerations and constraints figure largely in her accounts, and she makes interesting distinctions between the upper and lower parts of the school in which she works.

The superordinate construct here appears to be concerned with professional practice; it might be termed 'formal teaching versus informal teaching'. It is reinforced and clarified by the way in which it can be used to distinguish between the upper and lower parts of the school. For this teacher, her role – as she would like to see it – is 'enabled' by the informal teachers, while constricted simply to the reading lady (5) with the formal teachers.

This superordinate construct is also seen as controlling the effectiveness of communication (rather than vice versa, as in some other accounts). In other words, the effectiveness of communication, and her acceptance is dependent on the way in which teachers organise their work.

Another linked and subordinate construct is in organisation. The practical details of lesson planning are viewed by this teacher as inhibiting or enabling her ability to work effectively as a support teacher – inhibiting or enabling her role. This organisational construct – perhaps 'tight organisation versus loose organisation' – is subordinate to the 'formal versus informal' construct. With the 'good' teachers (3) she feels accepted ('part of the team'), with the intimation being that formal teachers are 'bad'. This suggests that an overarching construct might be found in 'good teachers versus bad teachers'. The organisation of the class means that she might feel 'like a spare part' (2, 3, 11), or very much relegated to the role of 'helper' (8).

An ideological dimension enters in comment (4), but it is not clearly articulated and seems to be construed as subordinate to the organisational construct. Thus, 'formal versus informal' teaching subsumes any ideological concerns rather than the converse. It is these organisational matters which inhibit the enactment of an appropriate role rather than ideological concerns.

Throughout this account and from this analysis come dispositional attributions. The emphasis on organisation might have led to situational

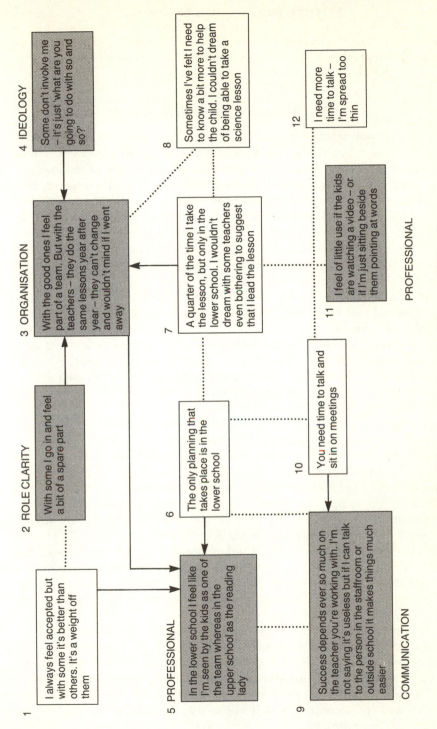

4 IDEOLOGY

Some don't involve me – it's just 'what are you going to do with so and so?'

8

Sometimes I've felt I need to know a bit more to help the child. I couldn't dream of being able to take a science lesson

3 ORGANISATION

With the good ones I feel part of a team. But with the teachers – they do the same lessons year after year – they can't change and wouldn't mind if I went away

12

I need more time to talk – I'm spread too thin

2 ROLE CLARITY

With some I go in and feel a bit of a spare part

7

A quarter of the time I take the lesson, but only in the lower school. I wouldn't dream with some teachers even bothering to suggest that I lead the lesson

11

I feel of little use if the kids are watching a video – or if I'm just sitting beside them pointing at words

PROFESSIONAL

1

I always feel accepted but with some it's better than others. It's a weight off them

6

The only planning that takes place is in the lower school

10

You need time to talk and sit in on meetings

5 PROFESSIONAL

In the lower school I feel like I'm seen by the kids as one of the team whereas in the upper school as the reading lady

9

Success depends ever so much on the teacher you're working with. I'm not saying it's useless but if I can talk to the person in the staffroom or outside school it makes things much easier

COMMUNICATION

Figure 9.7 Map 4: support teacher – middle school

attributions but the overarching construct within which organisation is framed appears to be of 'good teachers versus bad teachers'. The emphasis is on the people rather than on the system.

Map 5 – commentary and discussion

This is a support teacher in a middle school. Her construct system appears to turn on an overarching schema concerned with communication. While there are comments relating to the schema of territory, as noted in other accounts, a more prominent schema is in *threat* (2, 3, 7). However, this teacher opens up this schema more fully than the others, disclosing that it is integrally bound up with the willingness to accept a discourse (3, 7) about ways of working. She talks of colleagues who are 'open' (2) rather than being threatened. Her construct might therefore be labelled 'threatened versus open', indicating that it is subordinate to a construct she holds about communication.

Her concern over status means for her the interpretation of her professional role by both colleagues and children (6, 8). It is not, as in another account, related to whether or not she is seen as an 'equal' by them. This professional status is translated in (6) as being concerned with her specific role. It might therefore be labelled 'restorative teacher status versus teacher status'. The ideology of the teacher she is working with is of importance to her, though this receives only a brief mention (9). Organisation is also mentioned briefly (10).

Perhaps the briefness of these last two mentions hinges on the most interesting of her constructs, that of communication. It has already been noted that threat for her is bound up in the ability and willingness to communicate. The extracts in comments (5), (11), (12) and (13) indicate how clearly for her, her role is determined by this ability to communicate, which might simply be termed 'good communication versus poor communication'. In (5) is seen a clear demonstration of how her role is shaped by her ability to communicate with individuals, while in (11), (12) and (13) is seen the most manifest link between this need to communicate and the importance of appropriate role definition. This is more than a simple desire to 'get on' with others, to maintain a camaraderie, or to establish a fraternity. This is a desire to forge a discussion about appropriate ways of working.

In these comments relating to communication is signal demonstration of situational attribution. A need for role clarity is expressed in (11) particularly, and in (12) and (13) a need for the communication and 'reflection' which will enable its attainment. Only in (2) and (3) is there any sign of dispositional attribution. Here the idea of threat is subsumed under the communication which will enable the kind of role definitions which will facilitate easier team working.

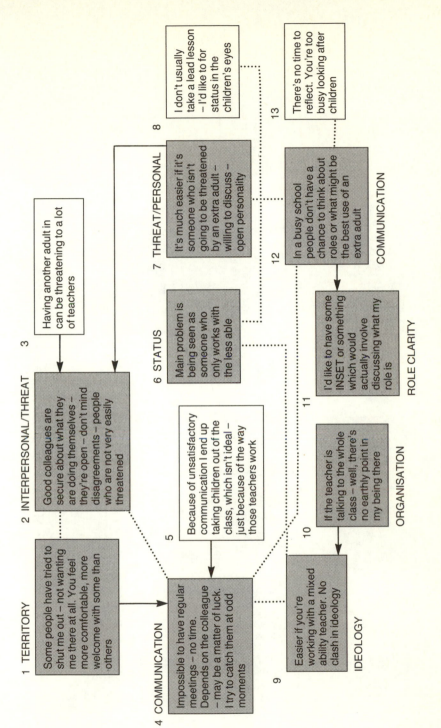

1 TERRITORY

Some people have tried to shut me out – not wanting me there at all. You feel more comfortable, more welcome with some than others

2 INTERPERSONAL/THREAT

Good colleagues are secure about what they are doing themselves – they're open – don't mind disagreements – people who are not very easily threatened

3

Having another adult in can be threatening to a lot of teachers

8

I don't usually take a lead lesson – I'd like to for status in the children's eyes

7 THREAT/PERSONAL

It's much easier if it's someone who isn't going to be threatened by an extra adult – willing to discuss – open personality

6 STATUS

Main problem is being seen as someone who only works with the less able

13

There's no time to reflect. You're too busy looking after children

12

In a busy school people don't have a chance to think about roles or what might be the best use of an extra adult

COMMUNICATION

11

I'd like to have some INSET or something which would actually involve discussing what my role is

ROLE CLARITY

5

Because of unsatisfactory communication I end up taking children out of the class, which isn't ideal – just because of the way those teachers work

4 COMMUNICATION

Impossible to have regular meetings – no time. Depends on the colleague – may be a matter of luck. I try to catch them at odd moments

10

If the teacher is talking to the whole class – well, there's no earthly point in my being there

ORGANISATION

9

Easier if you're working with a mixed ability teacher. No clash in ideology

IDEOLOGY

Figure 9.8 Map 5: support teacher – middle school

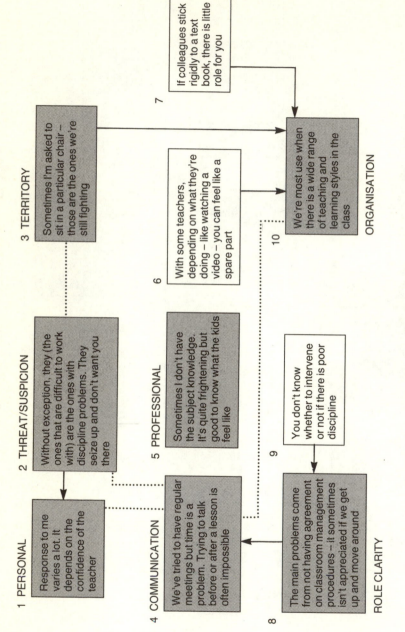

Figure 9.9 Map 6: head of learning support – secondary school

3 TERRITORY

Sometimes I'm asked to sit in a particular chair – those are the ones we're still fighting

7

If colleagues stick rigidly to a text book, there is little role for you

2 THREAT/SUSPICION

Without exception, they (the ones that are difficult to work with) are the ones with discipline problems. They seize up and don't want you there

ORGANISATION

We're most use when there is a wide range of teaching and learning styles in the class

6

With some teachers, depending on what they're doing – like watching a video – you can feel like a spare part

10

5 PROFESSIONAL

Sometimes I don't have the subject knowledge. It's quite frightening but good to know what the kids feel like

9

You don't know whether to intervene or not if there is poor discipline

1 PERSONAL

Response to me varies a lot. It depends on the confidence of the teacher

4 COMMUNICATION

We've tried to have regular meetings but time is a problem. Trying to talk before or after a lesson is often impossible

8

The main problems come from not having agreement on classroom management procedures – it sometimes isn't appreciated if we get up and move around

ROLE CLARITY

Map 6 – commentary and discussion

This is a head of support in a secondary school. The construct system is similar to the last one in several respects, notably in the situational attribution ultimately made.

Threat is not as clearly perceived as being due to inadequate communication as it was in the last interview. Rather, the perception of threat is ascribed to personal features of the teacher: confidence (1) or discipline problems (2) causing in this teacher's mind the perception of threat. The construct appears in this respondent's mind to be linked with personality: it might be called 'high self-regard versus low self-regard' on the part of the teachers with whom she works. She linked threat, at least in the sequence of her account, with territory: the specific territorial marking shown by (3) subsumes a range of expectations concerned with the proper role of the 'remedial teacher' and fear about having someone else present.

Organisation, construed apparently as 'formal teaching versus mixed ability teaching', restricts the role she is able to fulfil (6, 7, 10). She feels like a 'spare part' in some classes.

Although it is not as crucial as it was for the previous respondent, communication ('good communication versus poor communication') is important in the construct system of this interviewee. Subsumed under it is the notion of role clarity; in (4) and (8) are clear statements that good communication will be about establishing procedures. In turn, role will be positively shaped by a greater emphasis on this communication. In this interview, then, there are both dispositional and situational attributions.

Map 7 – commentary and discussion

This is a primary support teacher. Organisational concerns seem to shape her construct system. The utterances in comments (1), (2), (3) and (5) show a number of schemata interrelated; organisation is an overarching schema.

Threat, with the mention of defensiveness, criticism and confidence, is seen to depend on the perception of a teacher's organisation. This organisation is seen quite specifically in the ability to be flexible. Thus, 'rigidity versus flexibility' is suggested as the bipolar construct here. Rigidity inhibits the support teacher from enabling any development of her role. A different construct is also suggested under organisation in (10) and (11). Here, practical day-to-day matters impede effective working – and, it might be inferred, effective communication – with the host teacher.

Ideological differences also account for differences between teachers as seen in (4) and (8). She says that she has to be on the 'same wavelength'. Communication is seen as a secondary process here; it follows the similarity in thought rather than generating it. The emphasis is clearly dispositional rather than situational.

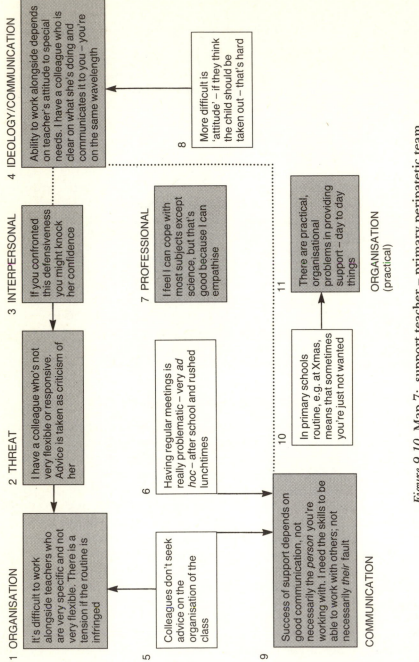

4 IDEOLOGY/COMMUNICATION

Ability to work alongside depends on teacher's attitude to special needs. I have a colleague who is clear on what she's doing and communicates it to you – you're on the same wavelength

8

More difficult is 'attitude' – if they think the child should be taken out – that's hard

3 INTERPERSONAL

If you confronted this defensiveness you might knock her confidence

7 PROFESSIONAL

I feel I can cope with most subjects except science, but that's good because I can empathise

11

There are practical, organisational problems in providing support – day to day things

ORGANISATION (practical)

2 THREAT

I have a colleague who's not very flexible or responsive. Advice is taken as criticism of her

6

Having regular meetings is really problematic – very *ad hoc* – after school and rushed lunchtimes

10

In primary schools routine, e.g. at Xmas, means that sometimes you're just not wanted

1 ORGANISATION

It's difficult to work alongside teachers who are very specific and not very flexible. There is a tension if the routine is infringed

5

Colleagues don't seek advice on the organisation of the class

9

Success of support depends on good communication, not necessarily the *person* you're working with. I need the skills to be able to work with others; not necessarily *their* fault

COMMUNICATION

Figure 9.10 Map 7: support teacher – primary peripatetic team

However, in (6) and (9) there is something of a contradiction to this. The success of support is seen to depend on the communication, not the person. The success of support depends on a set of skills for working effectively.

Here again is a mixture of dispositional and situational attributions with a clear move towards the end of the interview to the expressed idea that the effective fulfilment of her role depended on the acquisition of skills, rather than a set of amenable personalities.

Map 8 – commentary and discussion

A support teacher in a secondary support department. Most of her construct system revolves around the notion of personal space, which she mentions repeatedly.

Communication is evidently not much of a problem for her. However, status is mentioned in terms of how she is being seen by colleagues (4 and 5): 'equal status versus low status'. This however, is not related to any operational strategies in terms of specifying roles. It is a dispositional attribution. She links the lack of status with the lack of ownership of territory.

Organisation is mentioned as a practical problem (6 and 7). However, communication is not talked about as a means of structurally resolving these problems, but rather as a means of getting on, of 'having a little chat' (1) – promoting fraternity. The roles that emerge out of this process will be different from those that emerge out of a detailed analysis of the class activity when two or more people are present.

The need for territory or personal space, and the sensitivity about 'violating' (9) the space of another teacher emerges as the key idea. Her status is lowered because of the lack of personal space; host teachers may be sensitive (1) because she infringes on it and communication is relegated to informal chats (1, 2) perhaps because of sensitivity over the issue. Only limited development can take place here.

One might try viewing the world through this set of constructs. Towards which kind of attribution, dispositional or situational, will the gaze be concentrated? In Weiner's model (see p. 117), it is clear that such constructs will encourage the line of sight towards the stable dispositional quadrant of the diagram. The fault in support teams is seen as lying in the teacher's almost constitutional, inviolable desire for territory. Such a world view will tend the viewer towards the strategies that she has in fact adopted to ameliorate the tensions which emerge: informal chats (1) and the willingness to be adaptable (6).

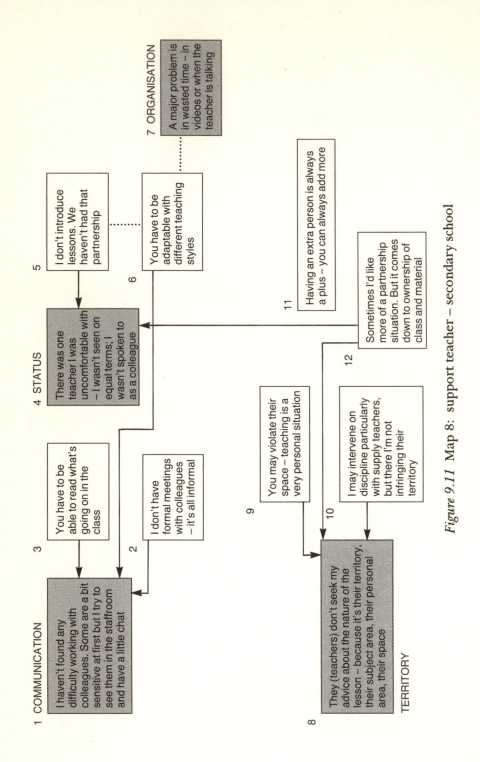

1 COMMUNICATION

I haven't found any difficulty working with colleagues. Some are a bit sensitive at first but I try to see them in the staffroom and have a little chat

3

You have to be able to read what's going on in the class

2

I don't have formal meetings with colleagues – it's all informal

5

I don't introduce lessons. We haven't had that partnership

4 STATUS

There was one teacher I was uncomfortable with – I wasn't seen on equal terms; I wasn't spoken to as a colleague

6

You have to be adaptable with different teaching styles

7 ORGANISATION

A major problem is in wasted time – in videos or when the teacher is talking

11

Having an extra person is always a plus – you can always add more

12

Sometimes I'd like more of a partnership situation. But it comes down to ownership of class and material

9

You may violate their space – teaching is a very personal situation

10

I may intervene on discipline particularly with supply teachers, but there I'm not infringing their territory

8

They (teachers) don't seek my advice about the nature of the lesson – because it's their territory, their subject area, their personal area, their space

TERRITORY

Figure 9.11 Map 8: support teacher – secondary school

CONCLUDING DISCUSSION

The central question with which I was concerned at the outset was whether team members were attributing difficulties in teaming to:

1 'failure' in their colleagues or themselves (dispositional attribution), or
2 'failure' in the more impersonal team system (situational attribution).

I wanted to look at the thoughts and feelings of support teachers to try and make some informed guesses about how they might be construing and judging the team process of which they were part.

Throughout the interviews there is evidence that respondents are making distinctions between the different team members with whom they work, and that the constructs which are employed, both by these respondents and by their colleagues, shape the ways in which their roles are formed and developed. It is clear here that roles are only loosely formulated at the outset, if indeed they are formulated at all, and that the degree of development that takes place in the understanding of these roles is dependent on the constructs employed by the participants.

Further, the constructs employed can be seen to contribute to the nature of the attribution made about the tensions in the working of the team. The constructs employed and attributions made show some interesting similarities. For instance, maps 2 and 8 (figures 9.5 and 9.11) share a concern about status and territory, with attributions in both cases being dispositional. Maps 5 and 6 (figures 9.8 and 9.9) share a view of communication as a means of establishing role definition (a situational attribution) rather than as a means of getting on better with the other person – the fraternity of the previous chapter. Indeed, fraternity emerges here also as an important ingredient in the working of the team. A further categorisation of the constructs identified in this chapter is made in chapter 10.

The distinction between dispositional and situational attributions put forward in the model at the outset proves to be a useful one. Evidence for it takes a number of forms in these analyses. In maps 1 and 2 (figures 9.4 and 9.5) the teachers talk of the need to split the class in one way or another to resolve the difficulties, while in maps 5 and 6 (figures 9.8 and 9.9) there is the desire through communication to come to decisions about the team process.

The other central distinction made at the outset was between status solutions and definitional solutions. Evidence is clear for both. Status figures largely in a number of interviews and its construal, either by the interviewee or her construal of this construct in the co-worker, will harden the attitude toward the working of the team. Here again, fraternity may be used to soften these difficulties. The resort to status serves, as was expected, to keep the participants in separate 'camps' with easing of tensions, but without their resolution.

On the other hand, definitional solutions exist as discrete schemata, unconnected in any important way with the complex set of constructs used to account for dispositional attributions. This is perhaps a symptom of the 'fundamental attribution error' that is part of our culture; we have a sophisticated set of mechanisms for allocating and apportioning 'blame' to individuals (including ourselves) rather than to the systems within which we behave.

Thus, the schemata for role clarity or role definition exist as discontinuities with the main stream of explanation which I have inferred from the cognitive maps. They exist almost as addenda to the thoughts of these individuals. This is particularly clear in maps 1 and 2 (figures 9.4 and 9.5), where no connection is articulated between these ideas and others. Where role clarity is connected to other schemata, as in maps 5 and 6 (figures 9.8 and 9.9), it is connected to the need for communication, to the need to discuss what the role might be with one's partner in the classroom.

In one sense at least the disjunction between this schema and others may be viewed positively. In the sense that the role solutions are not 'contaminated' with the dispositional attributions, they may provide a relatively unproblematic way forward and these are examined in chapters 12 and 13. Before doing that, though, I look in a little more detail at the particular problems of the support teacher in the following two chapters.

10

DIARY OF A SUPPORT TEACHER

If the previous chapters have shown anything, it is that the process of role definition in classroom teams is by no means simple. The culture of schools and classrooms seems almost to eschew clear role definition in these new teams, preferring to think of the collection of people in classrooms not in terms of teamwork, but rather in terms of concepts such as 'parental involvement' or 'learning support'. Participants are forced to arrive at understandings on the basis of their own personal ideas about the tasks to be done, and the kinds of things which they think they and the others in the team ought to be doing.

As noted in chapter 8 these tacit understandings are built essentially around pedagogic and affective concerns. Support teachers, as distinct from parents or ancillaries, centre their concerns more on pedagogic matters. In the previous chapter the support teachers seemed to be using a number of ideas to try and make sense of what was happening in their own teams. I tried in that chapter to categorise the kinds of explanations being made. Explanations about the success, or otherwise, of the team are given in terms of, for instance, the quality of communication between team members, or in terms of the security of fellow team members. These explanatory categories (such as communication and security) I term schemata.

In this chapter I report on my own experience as a support teacher in a comprehensive school. Although I make frequent reference to a diary I kept during this teaching, I attempt to make the account more than simply an annotated anecdote. I do this by relating my own thoughts and feelings to those of my interviewees in previous chapters. I seek evidence for the emergence of the various schemata and the constructs which accompanied them in those chapters. I shall also seek evidence for the resort to different kinds of solutions (status/autonomy solutions or role/definitional solutions) which I suggested were the likely result of holding particular construct systems.

PARTICIPANT OBSERVATION AS A RESEARCH METHOD

The method to be used here is participant observation. Burgess (1984) points out that in participant observation it is the researcher who is the main instrument of investigation. The value of participant observation is that it enables the researcher to collect rich detailed data based on observations in natural settings. He says that

> researchers can utilise their observations together with their theoretical insights to make seemingly irrational or paradoxical behaviour comprehensible to those within and beyond the situation that is studied.
>
> (Burgess 1984: 54)

Participant observation can take a number of forms. In the case of this study I behave as *participant as observer*. This is defined by Burgess as a situation where observers make their presence known but attempt to become a 'normal' or 'acceptable' person within the group's activities.

Denzin (1970a) notes that the participant observer uses a range of methods: collecting and analysing documents, interviewing informants, direct participation with introspection and direct observation. It is these last methods – introspection and observation – which will be employed most extensively in this study. The attempt was as far as possible to become one of the team; relevant comments made as part of normal interactions or lessons were recorded as faithfully as possible in the diary.

Research instrument – the diary

The record of participant observation is generally taken to be in the notes of the participant observer. These comprise a record of thoughts, feelings, interviews and observations.

A diary was kept of these thoughts and feelings. The term 'diary' is used in preference to 'notes', since its central purpose was to record personal insights and reflections. The diary – as an instrument – is the subject of surprisingly little discussion in the literature about qualitative research. However, its pedigree as an instrument is impeccable, and indeed, could be said to constitute the origins of participant observation in the work of Malinowski (e.g. Malinowski 1922, cited in Malinowski 1982).

The situation in which participant observation took place

The school is a comprehensive school in which the remedial department has become a support department. All details of the school and staff have been withheld or changed in order to protect complete anonymity.

Although some remedial withdrawal still occurs, much of the work is undertaken through support. The head of the support department, Mr Fairfax, is a person of some experience who works using both support and withdrawal. Mr Fairfax works with another full-time teacher, a part-time teacher and two ancillary helpers, Pauline and Queenie, and these together comprise the support department.

I worked in the classes of three teachers. Xanthe is a science teacher in her first post-probationary year. Yvonne is a teacher of French. David is a geography teacher. Both of the last two are experienced teachers. The reader is referred to the appendix in which extracts from the diary are given at the end of the book for a fuller understanding of the styles of these teachers. At times, the ancillary helpers, Pauline and Queenie, were working alongside me in these classes.

The school uses a system of 'non-random mixed ability grouping' – essentially, setting. This adds uncertainties and tensions to the support teacher's role, which are discussed in the results and in the next chapter. These tensions and the general atmosphere of the school can perhaps best be ascertained through reading the transcripts of the diary.

The school was visited for one afternoon a week for ten consecutive weeks. I told Mr Fairfax, the head of support, that I wished to be treated in every respect as another member of his team. I told him that I was updating my classroom experience (which was true) and that I would be using my observations in my research into classroom teams. This was explained to relevant staff, who were told by Mr Fairfax of my interest in support teaching and my desire to find out 'what it's really like'. The children were introduced to me in various ways, discussed in the diary, and the teachers' own perceptions of me are also discussed where these seem to represent more than an ingenuous acceptance of the given facts.

Further details of the situation under study and the procedure adopted are integral with the study itself and where necessary are discussed.

Analysing the diary

Becker (1970) suggests that there are three stages in the analysis of participant observation data:

1 the selection and definition of problems and concepts;
2 a check on the distribution and frequency of these phenomena; and
3 the incorporation of individual findings into a model of the organisation under study.

Broadly, this three-stage model is followed, though much in the way of definition and selection of problems has already been undertaken in the previous two studies. Thus, the first stage of establishing categories having been completed, the study concentrates on the second and third of

Becker's stages: checking on the frequency and distribution of the phenomena (this was done by highlighting key words or phrases in relevant diary entries and then grouping these under the schemata derived from the study reported on in the previous chapter), and incorporating the findings into a model. This model will be presented in the following chapter.

RESULTS

Categories

The categories which emerged from both of the previous studies proved, on analysis, to 'fit' the data from this participant observation. However, a different pattern of category usage emerged from that arising out of most of those results.

The frequency of each of the categories employed in accounting for the difficulties of teaming places them in the following sequence from most frequent to least frequent:

1 organisational differences;
2 lack of role clarity;
3 status concerns;
4 communication difficulties;
5 interpersonal factors;
6 perception of threat.

This selection is conjoined in a variety of ways depending on the colleague with whom I was working. The above represents an overall picture.

Comments from the diary categorised under schemata

Organisation/ideology

By contrast with the previous two studies, the main schema used in my own account was that of organisation. Organisation is used to describe the way in which the lesson is structured. At times this enabled me to fit in and work easily and naturally, while at others it stopped me from doing anything useful. Take this extract from my diary about Xanthe's science lesson:

> None [of the children] understands what they are doing or why they are doing it:

> GT: Why have you put the plant in that red liquid?
> Child: It's carbon dioxide.

Where do I begin to explain?. . . I suspect that even if I had a Nobel prize in chemistry I couldn't begin to get through the pupils' confusions. *Help is limited to procedural advice*: Put the card round this one; draw this here; now do this. But the confusion in the lesson generally is such that my presence merely acts as an aid to attention for the pupils for as long as I am present.

Much of my concern related to what to do when the lesson was taken 'from the front':

my presence is superfluous, as it seems to be with all 'central' activity, i.e. activity focused upon a central focus ... To break into such activity [lesson from the front] would be intrusive and counter-productive.

At times the concern turned to whether these organisational frictions could be ameliorated through my intervention in the organisation of the lesson. This, however, immediately led to concern over the effect on the status of the classteacher:

Throughout all this is the question, should I intervene by raising my voice and taking a higher profile, rather than merely supporting. To do so would undermine rather than support and would be de-skilling for this young teacher. Such team teaching would have to have been well-planned in advance, with agreed aims and methods.

I amplify the point here, in reflecting on the way that the children have been brought in at the beginning of the lesson:

This kind of error is so clear yet it is the kind of point which it is *extremely difficult to put over to a colleague*, especially when one is ostensibly at least trying to help those *children* who have particular difficulties. I suppose that the only real way is through example and team teaching.

Here, though, with the reference to 'example' is a resort to dispositional attribution, with the suggestion almost that indefinable qualities inhere in people. The implication is that these can be modelled but not defined or explicitly articulated.

The concerns over 'central' activity were also found in Yvonne's class, even though hers was a very different environment, more controlled and better organised:

Here again *I find it difficult to know what to do in this 'centrally' organised activity*. The teacher, Yvonne, is working with the whole class, asking them questions in French. How do I help the boy I'm sitting next to without seriously disturbing the flow and the sequence of the teacher's work.

Such concerns are, in the following extract, extended to the nature of the work expected of the children. Often this was such that there was simply no role for me to fulfil:

> 'Support' in this situation, where the children have a limited time to complete a task (filling the appropriate word in the blank space in sentences) essentially means telling the children the answer, or, hardly better, giving them such gross clues that they cannot fail. *The task seems meaningless and my support equally so.*

The same is true here, from Xanthe's lesson:

> My responses can also only be procedural, given the inappropriateness of the task for this group ... My support has been peripheral, and procedural, only serving very transitorily to focus the children's attention as I talk to them ... I feel frustrated at the inability to intervene in this confusion. Again, to do so would only undermine the teacher.

and here in Yvonne's:

> The lesson goes on mainly in a chalk and talk vein, in French. My help is again limited to merely repeating to the child what the teacher has said; it would be pointless to give the answer, and prompting or more elaborated help seems unproductive.

In the following, I suggest again that the method of organising the class and the children's work means that my role is very limited:

> To inject a new factor – such as a support teacher does not necessarily improve the situation – one can only dabble at the edges. The children's understanding of what they are doing in the lesson I'm supporting in at the moment isn't improved, neither is their understanding of why they are doing it. *I merely help them through the itinerary.*

The point is reinforced here:

> Of its kind the lesson is good – *it's just that there is nothing for me to do* in the actual lesson, partly because these children are setted already and this teacher has effectively addressed the question of how she will make the curriculum accessible to all children.

In the following extract the problematic nature of sharing the organisation is made explicit. However, the sharing is put in the context of being *fragile* again betraying the belief that the nature of this sharing process is almost sub-verbal, beyond explication:

> The centre of control moves back to Xanthe as I finish my talk and

the fragile nature of control and sharing of control becomes more clear as the carefully established rules of conduct I have established are immediately neglected and violated by Xanthe. It is surprising how quickly the children perceive this and how quickly the control collapses as she takes over.

Moving onto David's geography class, I here suggest that effective organisation of the lesson helps set the parameters of my contribution. There is no tension about how I can broach the fact that the work is inappropriate, because, in the main, it is appropriate:

It is in fact much easier in this lesson since the work is correctly pitched for most of them and they know what they are supposed to be doing and why they are supposed to be doing it.

Ancillary Queenie makes a similar point about the organisational styles of the teacher:

Differences between staff are seen [by Queenie] to be all important. She finds it extremely difficult supporting some staff: one teacher simply asks children to copy from books, and here her support, she feels, is totally wasted.

A conflict in ideology is suggested in the following, where the nature of special needs is at issue; lack of understanding or adequate communication would seem to be behind this. In an ideal world, support teachers would be able to discuss their understanding of the notion 'special needs' fully with their colleagues. The exigencies of school life make such discussion impossible.

I help those who David flagged to me as in most need of help, though to me it is not that obvious that it is this group who is most in need of support. They seem to be getting on OK, or at least no worse than anyone else. Those who need most support (of whatever kind) are the three girls, who are not concentrating at all, are talking and shouting at one another, and doodling in their books. *This raises questions about the nature of what is understood by 'special'*: here, where the work is fairly appropriate, the most special needs are those of the girls, even though they are among the brightest.

The following, a record of a conversation taken after a lunchtime meeting I had led with the staff, indicates that it is the routine, rather than the professional, aspect of support work which is most appreciated by this teacher (David). It might be inferred from this that by focusing on routine matters, he is saying that all the ambiguities and tensions generated from having an additional professional present are eliminated. He seems to be saying that not only is it *possible* to make the work of the additional person explicit, but it is also *preferable* to make it explicit through defining a set of well understood tasks. The sentiment is echoed in a comment also made by the deputy head.

> He [David] also makes the point that it is *extremely valuable having someone else competent in the classroom, not for any 'high falutin' academic reasons' but simply to assist with simple routine matters* because the teacher can't be in two places at once. What he is saying seems to reinforce the point made by the Dep Head at the end of the meeting: the support that one offers is appreciated more as an extra pair of hands than as a skilled teacher.

Role clarity

The simple issue of what one ought to be doing arose again and again in the diary. We can begin, here, to make the link between the *routine* schema of chapter 8 and the situational attributions of the last chapter. This is from my first lesson with Xanthe:

> I ask the teacher at the start how she would like me to provide support: to individuals, generally, or in some other way. *She's not sure – as they seem to need it.* Discussion with Pauline, the ancillary, has already revealed that *she is very unsure about what she should be doing.* She doesn't have a specific group of children to help.

This lack of clarity and definition is here seen to be enmeshed with the organisation of the lesson. Without clear goals for the children, it is not evident what one's role is:

> There is some extremely unclear instruction to get test tubes and undertake the experiment. *I feel redundant while the explanation is going on; more than redundant – embarrassed both for myself, and for my colleague.* Anxious to be providing 'support' now that the explanation has finished I look around to see if anyone seems to be unsure about what to do. There is a general air of disorganisation – pupils are wandering around, shouting in a fairly good-natured way to one another, spraying water at one another. *There is no obvious way to provide support to any of these groups;* they all patently need support since the instruction was so inadequate.

The same is evident in Yvonne's class, though hers is better organised, with clearer goals; with her, paradoxically, it is the clarity of these goals and the efficient nature of the organisation which leaves the supporter without a role:

> There are about fifteen children in the class and I sit (randomly – again, the teacher doesn't have any specific preferences about whom

160

I should support) next to a boy called Kevin [the following week was much the same . . .] I go to help the group of four children who are nearest to me; this seems to be as good a criterion as any for identifying children who need help . . . Discussion with the classroom assistant (Queenie) as we are going out reveals the same problems as I have been sensing: *not knowing who to help, how to help them, when to intervene, whether one might be intruding*.

I raised this matter in my meeting with staff, and there was clearly some empathy from the supporters:

I start by talking about *how to target those in need of help* – particularly if the organisation of the year groups is by setting and there is therefore a fairly homogeneous group of children in each set – and *there are assenting nods* from those who provide support in the school.

Concern over lack of effectiveness in Xanthe's lesson led me to believe that only joint planning could resolve many of the difficulties. Here, then, is a sign of a shift from the dispositional attribution being made earlier, to a situational attribution:

It can only be meaningful if I can share with the teacher some ideas about what tasks are useful and meaningful for these children, *if we have joint planning about the teaching objectives* and content.

However, in reflecting on Yvonne's lesson, I change my mind, in the belief that specialist subject knowledge should not be predicated on a concern for the discomfiture of the support teacher. I here seem to be suggesting that a support professional is in fact intruding into what seems an appropriately organised lesson. To introduce concerns about effecting team teaching would be to divert attention from the subject teacher's main focus. It would, in effect, subvert a carefully worked out programme, which has been planned to fit in with the school's organisation:

My reflection on this does not suggest to me that team teaching is the obvious and necessary answer to support in this situation. The children are doing the same work as the other children in this year group and it appears to me as a non-specialist that it is being well taught . . . is it possible to go into a whole set of classrooms, each with a different subject being studied, and be knowledgeable enough in each to enable one to team teach effectively in each situation? I doubt it . . . It is not for me to suggest that the children are achieving very little from these exercises . . . There appears to be a delicate balance between different factors: teaching style, content, expectations, children [i.e. nature of group of children] which teachers establish taking into account all these factors; each is dependent on the other and the result is the best possible result with the given constraints. To inject a new factor – such as a support teacher does not necessarily improve the situation – one can only dabble at the edges.

In the following I reflect on the kind of task I have been doing in classes. In so doing, in making such a 'task analysis', I make a point almost identical to that made by David and the deputy head earlier:

> One is providing procedural help to children and as often as not administrative and procedural help to the teacher. As such, a competent ancillary is as effective as a trained support teacher; indeed may be more effective. It may mean that there are *fewer tensions in the class, less ambiguity* about who should be doing what.

The way roles are framed by school policy is highlighted from this diary extract about a session in David's class:

> This perhaps also brings into play the whole question of a whole school policy for special needs and whether it should be stated at the outset that the support teacher is there to support the teacher as well as the children. This would put on the agenda at the outset the issue of establishing ground rules for collaborative work. My (our) rules in this situation are rapidly developing into teacher up-front, me as the assistant, only taking the up-front role when the teacher is out of the classroom.

Status

Status figured largely in my accounts, especially in Xanthe's class and in David's. My main concern here, I think, was with my own 'survival' if and when we went to team teaching. I was concerned that by association with certain styles of teaching I would be viewed as less than competent by the children. A number of factors compounded this: there was the concern that one could not establish authority with the class, since by so doing, one would be undermining the authority and self-esteem of the classteacher. The feeling of being a 'spare part' (which emerged also in interviews with support teachers) arose, and also the feeling of not being in 'control', an uncomfortable feeling for people who view themselves as professionals:

> [In French] I take the role of a 'native' [Frenchperson] like the other children; I realise in doing this how much of a *spare part I feel and how out of control I am of my own impression (in the kids' minds), and my own autonomy.*

The same occurred in Xanthe's class:

> *I have simply been an adjunct to the teacher – and one that seemed to the*

children to be insignificant and powerless – because of the in-between situation in which I placed myself, not wanting to undermine or usurp Xanthe's authority.

I make frequent comments indicating that I wish to make clear to the children my ability to maintain control:

> My main purpose, though, is in making clear to the class who I am and what I intend them to do, and also the fashion in which I intend them to behave.

At one point the children make explicit their own view of those who support in the class, and this reinforces my own fears. I do not share their view (of supporters as people who can't control the class), but it is quite clear from my observations how they come to perceive this to be the case: supporters are in a powerless, subordinate position, almost as if they were in a position of apprenticeship to the classteacher:

> there are a lot of questions about who I am – 'Are you the new headmaster?' 'Are you a student?' When I tell them that I am a teacher who is helping and that I am with the support department and Mr Fairfax, there is a telling question: 'Does that mean that you can't control the class?'

The view of the support teacher is confirmed in David's class, after I am introduced as helping Mr Fairfax in the support department:

> David introduces me as a member of the support department, and the mention of support invokes a snort from at least one child.

I continue with these reflections the following week:

> I wonder here whether the support teacher can achieve any status with the group, given that *s/he is always an adjunct to the status of the existing classteacher*. This is in addition to the problems noted last week (support teacher – that means you can't control the class, doesn't it). The answer is that you probably can achieve status, but at a cost – in terms of your own energy, and the time you have to devote each session to establishing the rules and also in terms of the cost of the possible injury done to the ego of the person you are teaching with.

My concern with my own status inhibits me from supporting effectively:

> I again position myself at the front and *try in a way not to associate myself with Xanthe's rather ineffectual attempts at establishing control*. Is this appropriate support from me – to look into the distance? Surely I should be coming in with banter with Xanthe to show that we can support and work with one another. Again I feel ambiguity about how to support. Will this undermine her?

163

The feeling of freedom which I express in the following extract when I am in charge of the class is unrelated by me to any feeling of territory, one of the schemata isolated from the last study. This may be because in reality, none of this was any part of my territory. Rather, it was, I think, related to a feeling of control – or at least the obverse of that: the feeling of not being subordinate.

> I'm left in charge of the class for a while and have a strange feeling of freedom. Immediately I'm able to address the whole class as well as addressing individuals.

It has a spin-off which further serves to reinforce my concern about the secondary nature of the support role:

> These kids seem to have a respect for me which I haven't noticed them expressing or showing to David, maybe because when he was out last week I managed to talk to them in a fairly matter of fact way without raising my voice, by treating them as adults and talking to them as though they commanded the respect that adults would command.

Communication

The constraints on communication lead one to understand how *fraternity* takes over in its place. Given the lack of opportunity for proper discussion or negotiation, an overlay of politeness and pleasantry is a simpler option, serving to mask tension and relieving the need to tackle sensitive issues about teaching style, curriculum or class management:

> Subsequent discussion with the teacher is a rather *hurried exchange* before the next class comes in. She is *embarrassed* by the clear failure of the lesson to achieve any aims which could be called educational, and I spend most of my energy trying to convince her that I am not being judgemental, but that I am interested in how support can best work. I can sympathise with teachers who *dread this kind of hurried exchange: the defensiveness, the lack of understanding, the perceived intrusion.* To explain what one really wants to do would take hours and only minutes are available.

The practical constraints are manifest:

> I arrive having prepared material to work with the science class. It is the lunch hour still and I have 20 mins to talk to Xanthe about the lesson ahead. I show her the materials and she approves. We agree roughly on a running order for the lesson, who will talk first and how we will take over from one another. The plans for this action are not very clearly drawn, yet this must always be the case with

support since time for this kind of preparation will always be in the squeezed lunch hour or after school.

The following week, although we have supposedly effectively communicated, there is still some difficulty in putting ideas into practice:

However, *there is still uncertainty* about who is to be doing what. We've only had a *short time to prepare* this session together and in any case the lessons don't reflect the preparation, if last week's was anything to go by.

A variant of fraternity is seen in the following extract, where David has made every attempt to involve me in the work that he has planned for the children. My failure here is in acquiescing in this rather than moving the discussion forward on to appropriate roles. It is easier to talk about curriculum than about style or management.

Afterwards I talk to David about what we will do next session and feel that there is some genuine attempt to include me in the discussion; but even though I am more competent in geography [than in science or French] I wonder about the value of my contribution to this debate. *The talk is about the content of the lesson, not the way in which I provide support.* While the content is important, I feel that *our working relationship together should be higher up the agenda.* At least we have more time to talk here since the school day has now finished – David is very keen and doesn't seem rushed to be on his way home.

The following, again from David's session, demonstrates this last point. David is at least willing to try and talk, but management turns out to be a very sensitive topic for discussion; certainly more difficult to discuss than curriculum:

The kids come in and the class as usual has to be rearranged into groups forming rows. The kids do this characteristically noisily, making as much scraping noise and banging as possible. Not the best way to start a lesson. However *I'm in a supporting role – not an inspectorial one so how can I mention this kind of simple management point?* With another teacher it may be possible, but not with David, who is fairly highly strung and rather defensive. It would take quite a time to build trust and teamwork before this kind of point could be made.

Interpersonal

The mere presence of another person – particularly another, possibly more experienced, professional – may in itself be inhibiting as I have noted elsewhere. My concern in the next passage over feeling redundant in Xanthe's class extends to a feeling of not simply being a useless appendage, but worse, to a feeling of actually contributing to a deterioration in the situation:

> Again I feel redundant – not only redundant, but worse that I am compounding the situation by my presence, and perhaps that Pauline, the ancillary, is in a similar position. *She [Xanthe] must feel some degree of inhibition* about doing what comes naturally to her to quell the sorts of problems that she is experiencing. Again, there is no way that I feel I can intervene in the immediate situation without making things worse. I am also slightly concerned that if we ultimately move to team teaching *I am losing credibility* by being associated with this degree of control.

The ancillary helper, in a subsequent discussion in Mr Fairfax's room, says she has felt the same:

> She (Pauline, the ancillary) notes exactly the same situation as I have: that in which *to assume a degree of authority with the class will take away from the confidence of the teacher* – she describes it as a vicious rather than a virtuous circle.

The confidence, experience and openness of the teacher are important in shaping the way that the extra person feels:

> *My relationship with this teacher [Yvonne] is rather easier as she is more confident.* She spontaneously comes over to me to explain in more detail what she is doing, the aims of this session, and how this class and activity fit in with this year group and the wider curriculum.

The meeting to which I spoke agreed:

> On . . . the way in which people interact next to one another the consensus seems to be that this is very much a matter of *personalities and teaching styles*. In some classes those who are supporting find it easy to team teach and work alongside colleagues; in others it is merely a matter of giving procedural advice to the children.

Interpersonal relations and the communication which accompany them are forever framed by the supportive relationship. This extract from the diary documents part of a field study session with David:

> On crossing the road, all of the kids have cut a corner across some grass and he [David] calls them back to walk across the road so they won't miss any of the shops – this in fact seems unimportant to me since I don't think there are many shops at the top of the High St (it turns out that in fact there aren't any). This highlights for me another problem of team teaching and support – that of the personality clash. In our case it's not so much of a clash as a mismatch, though if I pushed it it would

be a clash. In this situation, *I'd be far more laid back about what the kids were doing*, especially in view of the time constraints, which I seem to feel more acutely than David. *Can I say to him 'Oh it doesn't matter'* (which is what I want to say) if the kids are cutting this corner. I don't think he'd react to it well. *I'm supposed to be supporting him, not directing him.* It's up to him to set the direction and for me to support him in having taken it. This aspect of management could, I suppose, be shared if colleagues knew each other well enough and if they trusted each other enough. In this situation, though, I feel unable to intervene. Perhaps I should have done.

The following, also taken from the field study, demonstrates how a desire for fraternity almost seems to inhibit effective role definition:

I suggest that we walk down on different sides of the road to help kids as we are going along, but David thinks we ought to go down together and meet them at the end. It's almost as though he himself wants the support; *this would seem to be an ideal chance to use an extra person effectively*, where there is perhaps more opportunity for the kids to get lost or confused.

Threat/suspicion

The last of the schemata used to account for the problems of the team is the perception of threat and/or suspicion. It is mentioned relatively little, not because it wasn't perceived (it was) but because in my notetaking I recorded it using words other than 'threat' or 'suspicion'. The notion of threat or suspicion is not apparent in the notes. More often it is coded as interpersonal tension, or inhibition, perhaps reflecting my own personal constructs in conducting this exercise. It comes near to being explicitly articulated relatively little. This extract from David's class provides an example:

There is only one group of girls who are being overly a nuisance, talking over the teacher. He deals with this by loudly and shrilly drawing attention to them – the impression is that it is almost manic. *He is far from being relaxed and my presence probably is not helping.*

Here, then, are a number of categories which represent a distillation of the thoughts, feelings and anxieties which I experienced as a support teacher. These parallel very largely the schemata drawn from the interviews of the previous chapters. The ways in which these schemata frame the support teacher's role are explored further in the following chapter.

11

TEAM PERSONALITIES

In order to understand the ways in which individuals within the classroom team adopt particular working practices, there needs to be a coupling of the ideas from chapter 9 with those from the last chapter. In essence the ideas obtained in chapter 9 were similar to those found in the last chapter and the findings from those chapters validate each other.

It is now clear to me that during my time as a support teacher I attributed difficulties in the team to different things. Most of the time I would make dispositional attributions (i.e. 'blaming' the people I was working with or blaming myself), while some of the time situational attributions ('blaming' the situation or the system) were being made.

In order to tidy up my reflections about my support teaching, I tried to organise those reflections – thoughts, feelings, comments – into a number of categories. These categories seem to incorporate most of the ideas being put forward. Of the categories (namely, organisational differences; lack of role clarity; status concerns; communication difficulties; inter-personal factors; perception of threat) all but one represent a blaming of the person (dispositional attribution). Even in the isolation of organis-ational differences, these differences seem almost to be bound to the 'organising personality' or organisational *ability* of the other person. In that sense, these organisational differences are taken to be examples of such dispositional attribution. Only one of these categories – lack of role clarity – could be said to constitute blaming of the situation: a situational attribution.

The discussion that follows therefore concentrates on the place of these dispositional attributions in the process of role-making. Situational attributions will be examined at the close of this discussion and in the next two chapters.

TEAM PARTICIPANTS' VIEWS ABOUT THEIR PROBLEMS

Chapter 9 elicited a number of bipolar constructs which classroom team participants appeared to be employing in making sense of these teams. At that time the distinction was drawn between personal constructs and the construals of others' constructs, the latter being an important facet of role-making in personal construct theory. Prior to examining in closer detail my own role-making during the participant observation, I shall examine and categorise the set of personal constructs elicited in chapter 9, for (1) personal constructs (self) and (2) construals about the constructs of others (other). These were:

1 *self* (i.e. personal constructs)

attacked	v	accepted
low self-esteem	v	high self-esteem
low self-regard	v	high self-regard
low status	v	high status
alienated	v	included
marginality	v	teamness
unskilled	v	professional
redundant	v	professional
restorative teacher status	v	teacher status

2 *other* (i.e. construals about the constructs of others)

tight organiser	v	loose organiser
formal	v	informal
formal	v	mixed ability
rigid	v	flexible
difficult	v	easy (to get on with)
threatened	v	accepting
threatened	v	open
poor relationship	v	good relationship
restorative	v	preventative
poor communicator	v	good communicator

If these sets of constructs are examined, certain of the constructs can be shown to be similar and they can be grouped together. If these similar constructs are grouped in this way they can be seen to comprise three broad schemata. The first subset, relating to self, comprises professional concerns, acceptance and status. The second, relating to the other person or people, comprises organisation, security and interpersonal skills. Thus:

1 subset 1 – schemata relating to 'self'

professional/	unskilled	–	professional
ideological	redundant	–	professional
	restorative teacher	–	teacher
acceptance	marginality	–	teamness
	attacked	–	accepted
	alienated	–	included

status	low status	–	high status
	low self-esteem	–	high-self esteem
	low self-regard	–	high-self regard

2 subset 2 – schemata relating to 'other'

flexibility	formal	–	informal
	formal	–	mixed ability
	tight	–	loose
	restorative	–	preventative
security	threatened	–	accepting
	threatened	–	open
interpersonal skills	poor communicator	–	good communicator
	poor relationship	–	good relationship

These generalised schemata may now be used to define the parameters of a model which can be used to predict a constellation of different kinds of classroom team. The model can be drawn as a 3D graph, rather like a cube. Each dimension of the cube (height, breadth or depth) represents one of the generalised schema.

Individual points within each three-dimensional block can then be used to describe particular kinds of conceptual position out of which roles might be made. Relationships between the blocks, in which points might be plotted, will imply particular kinds of team dynamics. The particular kinds of relationships implied by the model will be tested against the observations already drawn upon above.

The graphical representation of the model is given in figure 11.1. The relationship of this model to the current study will be discussed shortly. Before that, though, it may be worth discussing some ideas generated from the model.

From the 'SELF' block, it can be seen that the ideal self would occur in the region of A, where status is high, and where professional skills are valued and appropriately used, and where the supporter feels accepted and included. The antithesis of this would be at B, where status and acceptance are low, and where professional skills are interpreted as inappropriate by the colleague.

On the evidence of the interview responses in chapter 9 and on the evidence of the diary notes in the participant observation, it would be expected that the values of these dimensions would tend to co-vary. In other words, a single, higher-order factor, which might exist as *valuedness* would be predominantly and uniformly shaping these schemata of status, acceptance and professional integrity. This is not to deny, however, the existence of idiosyncratic variations in the values of these dimensions. For instance, at D there might be an individual who sees herself as accepted

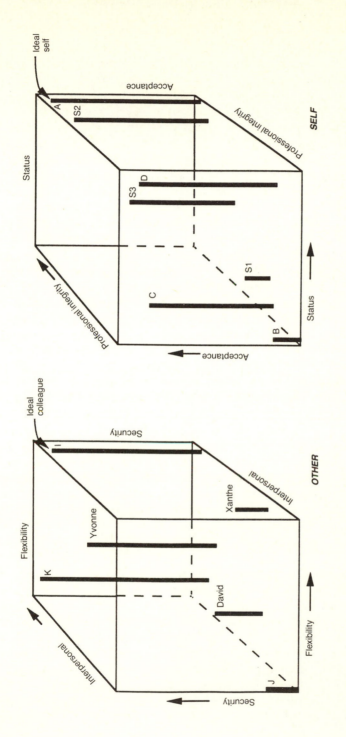

Figure 11.1 Model of self and other in classroom teams

and with high status, but who simultaneously sees herself as a supporter adopting an inappropriate professional role. At C there might be someone who feels that she is accepted (perhaps due to fraternity) but has low status and poor professional integrity. In general, though, it might be postulated on the basis of the evidence in these studies that supporters will view their professional selves falling somewhere near to a line drawn between A and B.

On the 'OTHER' block, the ideal colleague occurs at I. Here, the colleague has good interpersonal skills, is secure and flexible. By contrast, the antithesis occurs at J, where the colleague is inflexible, insecure and has poor interpersonal skills. At first glance it would appear less likely that these dimensions will co-vary (i.e. there is, for instance, no reason for believing that one's interpersonal skills should be related with one's professional flexibility). However, reflection indicates that these might indeed co-vary, if a higher-order factor, such as *confidence*, is seen to be at least in part responsible for the way that these dimensions are actualised.

This integration of professional and personal schemata might here be explicable in Kellyan terms: *threat* according to Bannister and Fransella (1986) is the awareness of an imminent comprehensive change in one's core structures. They say that we are threatened when our major beliefs about the nature of our personal, social and practical situation are invalidated and the world around us appears to become chaotic. On the basis of this research, *professional* has to be added to *personal, social and practical*. Our confidence to act spontaneously, to accept change and to be willing to communicate will be predicated on the integrity of these core structures.

It might follow, then, that most colleagues will be viewed on the 'OTHER' block falling somewhere near to a line drawn between I and J. A possible avenue for further research would be to test this assumption empirically. However, again, exceptions can be postulated. For instance, at K might be seen an individual who is secure, and with good interpersonal skills, but who is formal in her teaching and not open to change.

THE PLACING OF INDIVIDUALS IN THE MODEL

By using the model we can see how individuals' roles might be constructed in classroom teams. This construction, or role-making, can be viewed as an interactive process depending on the position of the individuals on each of the dimensions in the blocks. In other words, one's own position on the block – one's own feelings about status, acceptance and professional integrity – will depend crucially on the characteristics of the other person. One's own position will likewise affect that of the other person: high status, for instance, (as externally defined by a position of authority, perhaps) may affect the perception of threat in the host, and push the host teacher towards the J position.

The individuals in the previous chapter can be placed on this model. Xanthe, the inexperienced science teacher, would fall in the lower front foreground of the model (as shown in figure 11.1). She was flexible, to the point of lack of direction or cohesion; her interpersonal skills were unremarkable, and she is insecure. Yvonne is less flexible, her organisation and goals being tighter, but her interpersonal skills are stronger and she appears secure in her role. David is less flexible than either Xanthe or Yvonne, and is insecure about his ability with lower-achieving children. Though his interpersonal skills are not generally taken to be good by his colleagues, he is communicative and reasonably open with a colleague whom he perceives to be high status.

The interactive nature of the role-making process can be seen by the way that I view my own position on the 'SELF' block, depending on the colleague with whom I was working.

In Xanthe's class I place myself at S1 on the SELF block. Although I assumed my status was high in Xanthe's mind (which contributed to her perception of threat) this was in no way made clear in class, where the activity gave me a feeling of low status. Perhaps because of the perception of threat, I perceived little sign of any overt acceptance of my position in the class. I felt little recognition of my professional skills or that I had any special part to play in the class.

In Yvonne's class, I place myself at S2 on the block. I felt accepted and that my status was high and that I had a professional contribution to make. In practice, the contribution that was made did not match up to this perception of self – near to the ideal self. This mismatch of personal perception and actual contribution seems to lie in the lack of an explicit definition of role. The need for such explicit definition is therefore made clear here, as it has been in the interviews, and it will be followed up in the next chapter.

In David's class, I place myself at S3. Though David's view of lower-achieving children is at variance with mine, he appeared genuinely to value my opinion and sought it on several occasions. However, this optimistic view of the ability of our ideological positions to coincide has to be tempered with his view that I was useful as an extra competent adult, and 'not for any high falutin' academic reasons'. He accepted me and accepted my views but did little or nothing in the lessons to demonstrate his acceptance of me or to increase my status in the eyes of the children.

My positioning of myself on the 'SELF' block is somewhat confounded by my peculiar position in the school. Perhaps it was because of my special position as a visitor that status figured little in my own account, in relation to the accounts of those in the interviews in the previous studies. I was outside the political system of the school, unconcerned with rivalries over status. Where I was concerned with status, it was the children's rather than the adult's view of me which was my concern.

Clearly the use of the blocks is a heuristic device which blurs much of the fine detail of the accounts. However, it enables a clearer perception of the major ways in which the process of role construction occurs in the classroom.

Both of these blocks have focused on the place of dispositional attributions in the role-making process. There is, as noted in the commentary on the diary, the suggestion in making such attributions that indefinable qualities mysteriously inhere in people and that these qualities are beyond explication. The subsequent analysis has, it is to be hoped, done something to confound this view.

It is still clear, though, that in understanding the nature of the dispositional attributions there is no *necessary* improvement in the team situation. However, some insights may be provided by such an analysis: simply realising that one is attributing success or failure to individuals rather than to the situation may in itself help one to move into a different kind of mind-set.

Aside from these insights, the model is capable of another extension. One can think of the blocks as determinants of an *overall team personality*. Each team personality is dependent upon the *individual team personalities* comprising it. These are framed by the personal constructs and belief systems of individuals, by the assumptions they make about their co-members, by the attributions they make about the behaviour of those members, and by their own constructs about the construing system of the other.

The metaphor of the team as a personality reinforces further the interactive nature of the emerging team process and the fact that role, in the absence of explicit definition about tasks, can take place in a multitude of ways.

While focusing on dispositional attributions neglects the place of situational attribution in the diary, it also emphasises the discreteness of that set of ideas (i.e. situational attributions) as an explanatory feature of the working of classroom teams. Role clarity is identified in the last chapter quite clearly as problematic. Its separation from the other schemata is as clear there as it was in the cognitive maps of the interviews. In both studies, both situational and dispositional attributions are employed and, thus, both definitional solutions and status solutions emerge. From the emergence of the importance of definitional solutions comes the realisation that clarity of role is an essential ingredient in the success of the team. This is true as much in the classroom as anywhere else.

As shown in chapter 9, the situational attributions are related to relatively simple routine matters. Simply being told what to do, even if it conflicts with views about one's status and 'appropriate' activities, assuages the tension of uncertainty. This chapter confirms the need for such simply given definitions and reassurances. The question of whether further refinements in role clarity can be made which can be logically located in analysis of the teacher's role will be put in the next two chapters.

Lack of role clarity may also exist because of the teacher's lack of organisation, or, paradoxically, by virtue of tight organisation. Either can leave the other person without a clear role.

A perhaps unpalatable conclusion to emerge from all of this is that a set of tasks to be done on the basis of any logical subdivision of the teacher's task (i.e. any definitional solution) might more easily be done by an ancillary helper than by a teacher. Indeed, even without such a subdivision, the suggestion arose more than once in my participant observation that one's presence *as a teacher* may have inhibited or threatened the host in a way that the presence of a welfare assistant or ancillary helper would not have done. The rationale for the support teacher's presence rests in large part on the contribution that he or she is able to make to planning in the curriculum. If day-to-day pressures make such planning impossible (as the interviews and my own participant observation seem to indicate), alternative ways of inputting the support personnel's expertise need urgently to be sought.

The last point that needs to be made about role clarity (situational attributions; definitional solutions) is that its enhancement is possible if it is framed within a wider context. Thus, the existence of a whole-school policy on special needs specifies the commitment of the school to a particular kind of delivery of support. Such a commitment makes role definition simpler and neutralises many tensions that may arise out of misunderstanding. This would be just as true if it were applied to parental involvement: a whole-school policy on parental involvement could do much to clarify the role of parents.

Given the importance of role clarity as a discrete schema in determining the success of classroom teams, its possible parameters are explored in the next two chapters.

12

A KEY TO THE PROBLEMS?

Tasks to be fulfilled by the team

The previous three chapters have shown that members of classroom teams are likely to experience little definition of what has to be done by the team. Moreover, the team is unlikely even to be thought of as a team; there are important ideals – such as parental involvement or mainstreaming – behind people working together in the classroom and the manifest importance of these ideals means that attention is not explicitly focused on the dynamics of the team enterprise. Rather, individuals are likely to see themselves fulfilling important functions individually and perhaps autonomously. If interpersonal dynamics raises its ugly head, this is viewed as an unwelcome irritant, making the tasks to be done by the individuals more difficult.

In the absence of role definition or even of the recognition of the existence of a team the ground is open for people to develop their own ideas about what ought to be done in these shared classrooms. But while the team is not recognised as a team, these ideas develop in isolation; there is no structure for enabling communication between team members. Without this recognition and without this structure there is ample opportunity for misunderstandings to arise among team members. In such an atmosphere the team will not work as effectively as it might.

As the evidence in chapters 2, 3 and 4 showed, when tasks have to be shared things have a habit of going wrong. Good teams are more than the sum of their parts, but most teams are unfortunately not good. To enable them to be effective, teams have to be helped. We cannot realistically expect people to share a work environment and continue to work as effectively in this new shared environment without help. All kinds of ambiguities, misunderstandings and mismatches now enter into this new environment. If these are not recognised the situation will deteriorate. People start blaming each other for the difficulties of the team: in the jargon of social psychology, they make dispositional attributions about these difficulties. By contrast, they are less likely to blame the situation or the system – less likely to make situational attributions.

The lesson learned from groupwork research is that we ignore the dynamics of the team at our peril. Likewise, it is as well to acknowledge the findings of attribution theory research, which show that a more productive way forward when faced with the difficulties of the team is to make situational rather than dispositional attributions. In other words, it is better to look for solutions to the team's difficulties in the problems of the system within which you are operating, rather than in the colleagues with whom you are working.

What, then, is this 'system' to which we should encourage people to look when considering the team? The familiar concepts of team dynamics – role definition and role clarity – are helpful as a start: ambiguities and mismatches have to be minimised. People need to have a clear idea about what they are doing, and they need to have shared goals in mind. But the culture of schools actively seems to eschew this role-giving process and team participants often have to fall back on their own ideas about what they ought to be doing. Communication (if it occurs at all) is often strained. If we are to give practical help in these circumstances we therefore need to sharpen the clarity of already-existing notions about roles. As we have seen, these notions are built around team members' (i.e. teachers, parents, ancillaries) ideals about pedagogy, professionalism and organisation. Chapter 9 showed that support teachers were able to identify situations in which the team had succeeded. These had involved clear definition of what each team member had to be doing, and within that an appreciation of the professional integrity of each of the team participants.

If the success of the team hinges in large part on the ability of its members to define the tasks to be done, it is important at the outset to ascertain what these tasks might be. This is one of the main aims of this chapter.

A SUMMARY OF PROBLEMS AND OPPORTUNITIES IN CLASS TEAMWORK

Problems

Much of the work reviewed in the earlier chapters of this book related to the problems involved in expecting people to work in team situations which are in some way discordant with what is known about the conditions necessary for successful teaming. I shall briefly review those problems and the features of the situations which conspire against the success of teaming in the classroom.

There appear to be a range of mismatches in terms of ideologies and personal or interpersonal styles among adult participants. Those mismatches create stress. There are also simple definitional misunderstandings or ambiguities: people getting in each other's way; people becoming distracted by the activities of the other adults rather than focusing on the demands and the needs of the children; people duplicating the effort of others, or conversely, not doing something on the assumption that someone else has done it.

It appears that this cluster of factors is responsible for the phenomenon of diminishing returns (noted in chapter 1), wherein the allocation of additional staff to a project results in each person's effectiveness actually falling. The extra people may detract from rather than enhance the effectiveness of the project.

Stress engendered by teaming problems may be ameliorated by the participants' use of strategies – such as fraternity – to relieve that stress. (However, the working of the group may or may not be improved, depending on the ultimate nature of those strategies.) In other words, the process will lead – in an unplanned, almost *ad hoc* way – either to the development of teamwork skills, or to the increased isolation of the various participants.

In practical terms, a new set of problems may emerge out of attempts to reduce stress; these are linked with the *autonomy solutions* to the stress of teamwork identified in chapter 2. Such solutions include increases in

1 *territoriality*, wherein team members seek to maintain their autonomy through establishing or reinforcing territory and minimising communication with their 'partners';
2 *professionalism*, where the issues are based on status – through crystallising or reinforcing one's own higher status or the lower status of others; and
3 *fraternity*, where politeness and pleasantry take the place of discussion and negotiation. Fraternity is a simpler option than these more complex processes. It serves to mask tension and relieves the need to tackle sensitive issues about mismatches in teaching style, curriculum or class management.

If strategies are to be employed to facilitate teamwork they need to break into this cycle at the stage where participants are seeking to attenuate the effects of stress. The lesson from the work so far reported is that participants will aim to reduce stress for themselves in one of two main ways. They will reduce stress either by facilitating teamwork processes, or alternatively by actively (if tacitly) working to minimise team processes. The latter in effect involves participants working to maintain their own autonomy and make the set of adults into simply a set of individuals working in the same environment.

Opportunities

Alongside the problems reviewed so far, it is possible to contrast the opportunities that arise from the presence of additional people if appropriate processes (i.e. role solutions) in teamwork can be facilitated. These include the four outlined below.

Differentiation

A centrally important opportunity arises out of the differentiation of the teacher's role. Thus, participants may be able to fulfil elements of the teacher's role which it is difficult for her to fulfil on her own given that she has to undertake a number of tasks and functions simultaneously – for example, they may be able to provide far more individual help than is possible for the teacher on her own.

Communication

Communication is (in theory at least) facilitated between classteachers, parents, ancillaries, specialist teachers and/or support service personnel when they work together collaboratively, rather than in separate settings.

Integration

The work that specialists do is more easily integrated with the curriculum of the classroom and the school than if they worked on a withdrawal basis.

Involvement

Team members (such as parents and support teachers) are more fully involved in the work and life of the school than if they work entirely on extracurricular activities or activity which places them outside the classroom.

FACTORS MEDIATING SUCCESSFUL TEAMWORK

The leader, or 'host', in the situation (usually the classteacher) is, then, confronted with problems and opportunities. Whether she is able to minimise the forces arrayed against the successful cohesion of teams, and thus facilitate teamwork and take advantage of the opportunities, depends upon a number of factors. It appears to depend on the attributions she makes about the situation, which in turn rest upon her personality, her ability to communicate and the time available to negotiate workable solutions. The strategies ultimately adopted may or may not be appropriate in terms of, for instance, improving role definition.

As noted earlier (p. 45), in certain educational environments the question of improving role definition has been addressed through the allocation of specific roles and procedures to the class team members. A focus of this kind – on the system rather than on the individuals who comprise it – is crucial for the success of any attempt to improve the working of the team. The aim of the following is to determine the parameters of classroom organisation that have been identified by researchers in mainstream classrooms in order that these may be used to frame the basis of similar operational strategies in the mainstream class. It is possible to construe this, following the model proposed in chapter 5, as a framework for making the most of situational attributions. If participants make situational attributions, then to capitalise on these it is necessary to have some mechanism for analysing the team process and making specific its various components.

CLASSROOM MANAGEMENT

Any quest for such operational strategies is destined to meet obstacles, particularly if it rests upon a framework of existing classroom management research. Many have noted that in the 'ecosystem' of the classroom any transposition of the constructs and parameters determined by research is difficult, if not impossible. Smyth (1981), for instance, in reviewing research on classroom management, concludes that much teaching research has resulted in the issuing of 'teacher should' statements which may have little validity for individual teachers.

None the less, a large body of literature confronts the issue of classroom management and it seems appropriate to explore this in order to meet the objective of investigating operational strategies for the team. Bennett (1978) agrees with Smyth that much observational research has provided little empirical knowledge of practical value, but he goes on to suggest that a model that draws from this research and uses a small number of 'simplifying concepts' would be of value. If such simplifying concepts can be isolated as far as the roles which the teacher is fulfilling in the classroom are concerned it may assist the subsequent analysis.

Much of the literature that will be reviewed here therefore delineates features of the teacher's role as important to success in classroom management. In so doing, it differentiates aspects of the teacher's activity. It therefore enables a matching to take place between the various tasks of the teacher, thus delineated, and the contributions of any additional available personnel. A delineation of these tasks stresses the complexity and diversity of the roles in which teachers are cast; as Trendall (1989) notes, stress in teachers is centrally related to role conflict and role overload and teachers are often uncertain about an appropriate course of action because of the many roles in which they are cast.

Such delineation may offer opportunities in the deployment of additional people in the classroom, if, as has been noted, many of the difficulties of teamwork in classrooms rest upon poor (or poorly understood) role definitions.

THE TWO CENTRAL ROLES OF THE TEACHER

In his 'small number of simplifying concepts', Bennett (1978) ties together research from different methodological stables in an attempt to demonstrate the generality of some findings. Drawing together research from Brophy, Good and Doyle he stresses the importance in classroom management of feedback and circulating. He quotes Doyle's ethnographic work, which emphasises the need for timing and 'overlap' (i.e. the ability to cope with two activities at once) and relates this to Kounin's constructs of smoothness and momentum. These key elements of feedback, circulating, overlap and flow form a useful framework in determining role responsibilities of additional adult participants and are worthy of further examination.

Brophy (1982) and Kounin (1970) point to similar conclusions about the complexity of the teacher's task and the diversity of functions comprising it. Kounin used videotaped recordings of normal elementary school classrooms to come to the conclusion that it was

> for any one teacher, neither the degree of clarity, firmness, and intensity of her desist effort; nor whether she focuses on the misbehaviour, or on the legal activity or both; nor whether she treats the child positively, negatively or neutrally; makes any difference for how readily a child stops his deviancy or gets on with the prescribed task.
>
> (Kounin 1970: 70)

More important than these ways of approaching individuals for the success of the class (in terms of children's time on task and rates of deviant behaviour) were the classteacher's methods of classroom management. These he summarised according to a number of main dimensions:

1 'withitness' and overlapping, i.e. the ability to maintain smoothness in activity flow by, for instance, dealing with misbehaviour while not interrupting the flow of learning activity;
2 initiating and maintaining activity flow – keeping the session moving along smoothly without, for instance, 'overdwelling' on a particular behaviour or learning point;
3 maintaining group focus by keeping the children alert to the presence of the teacher and accountable for their work; and
4 avoiding satiation through showing enthusiasm and through maintaining variety in the content of the subject matter.

Running through Kounin's work is the notion of 'flow'. While experienced teachers acquire strategies for enabling them to maintain flow in a session, that is nevertheless an extremely difficult task. Many of the kinds of events which Kounin identifies as important for the teacher to respond to, involve her attending to two things at once or require her being in two places at once. In the understanding of classroom processes that Kounin's work facilitates is the realisation that a multitude of events – to which the teacher may or may not have to respond – are *simultaneously* taking place in the classroom. As such, what emerges is the notion that the various elements comprising the teacher's role are characterised not by synchrony but rather by exclusivity: doing one more effectively inhibits the effective execution of the others.

If this is the case then there is a clear opportunity for the effectively organised use of additional help to reduce in size and scope some of these diverse demands.

Further evidence as to the complexity of the classroom environment (and thus as to the importance of the teacher's organisation and management) comes from the work of Brophy:

> Effective teachers know how to maintain and organise a classroom learning environment that maximises the time spent engaged in productive activities and minimises the time lost during transitions, periods of confusion, or disruptions that require disciplinary action.
>
> (Brophy 1979: 2)

Brophy goes on to say that group instruction (i.e. classteaching) survives because it is relatively easy to plan and manage. Alternatives to group instruction multiply rather than diminish the kind of management problems identified by Kounin. In supporting the work of Kounin he says that 'good organisation and management *is* good instruction'. Here, good organisation is identified with minimising time lost, whether that is through transition, confusion or disruption. Employing extra people may therefore be directed toward such a goal.

In further research, Brophy (1982) made a meta-analysis of recent research on classroom management. Among the features which are identified as important by this analysis are attention to individual differences and techniques for group management during active instruction. Thus, there seems to be a tension in the teacher's role between providing for the needs of individuals and maintaining contact with the class as a whole. Indeed, these two facets of the teacher's task could be said to comprise essentially different roles.

From this analysis an additional dimension emerges for an understanding of the working of the classroom; it is of use to us in trying to work out how teams may operate successfully. It becomes clear that there are at least two necessary elements in the successful management of the classroom (with success in these terms generally assessed on outcome measures such as time on task and children's attainment) whose integrated provision it is very difficult to provide. Those two elements are individual teaching and maintenance of class engagement. It would appear that at the core of many of the 'flow' characteristics outlined by Kounin is the development by the teacher of strategies to reconcile the problems which arise out of the need to be attending to the individual while simultaneously attending to the needs of the rest of the class.

Alongside these findings about group management are findings about the most effective frameworks for children's learning. The work of De Vault *et al.* (1977) has already been reviewed. In its complex analysis of Project Follow-Through's findings it noted that curricula which were more successful were associated with more small group and individual teaching.

Likewise, Monk (1982) goes beyond the simple associations of higher engaged time/higher achievement findings to seek the structural arrangements in classes which underpin such findings. He notes, following observation in 13 classrooms, that although higher achievement is associated with lower teacher–child contact, the contact that children do have in these classes tends to take the form of small group or individualised instruction. Thus, the importance of individual teaching seems clear, but in providing it teachers seem to need to implement organisational procedures which remove them from the larger demands of the class.

Reinforcing the notion that one of the most crucial yet also one of the most difficult features of classroom management is the ability to reconcile individual teaching with group engagement is the research undertaken in the ORACLE study (Galton, Simon and Croll 1980). Here, the identification of teaching styles and pupil groups (from a total of 58 primary school classes), enabled the interactions among these categories to be explored. The research identified four main groups of teaching styles and four pupil groups. As far as an extension of the insights which may be drawn from Brophy's work goes, it is useful to concentrate on one of these pupil groups and two of the teacher groups.

The group of 'intermittent workers', comprising about one-third of the total sample of children, showed the lowest levels of contact with the teacher while showing the highest levels of contact with other pupils. They are described by the authors as 'adept at carrying on their private exchanges with other pupils without drawing attention to themselves'. They spent 20 per cent of their time in activities coded as 'distraction' and, the authors go on, 'Most teachers while not expecting children to work continuously would probably agree that 20 per cent is too high a level'. Teachers who were 'individual monitors' (that is teachers who characteristically engage in a large number of brief contacts with individual children) generated the highest proportions of intermittent workers, with on average nearly 50 per cent of the children in their classes being so classified. 'Class enquirers', however, had the lowest proportion of intermittent workers. Central to this strategy, though, is a high proportion of classteaching with little individual or group teaching.

The dilemma that emerged from Brophy's work is again evident in the ORACLE research. In the chosen teaching strategy teachers appear to be choosing to sacrifice one important ingredient of classroom activity for another. Choosing to give relatively large amounts of individual help has its consequence in the relatively low engagement of the class as a whole; on the other hand, those teachers who choose a strategy which enables high engagement among the class generally do not provide as much individual teaching. In other words, *one person* cannot effectively provide individual help while simultaneously keeping engagement among the group high.

In similar findings, Bloom (1984), in an overview of research into individual versus group instruction, suggests that different skills are needed in teaching individuals and in teaching large groups; the integration of these skills is complex and difficult to achieve.

If Bennett's simplifying concepts are used in this context it seems that at least two distinct sets of difficult-to-reconcile tasks emerge: the need to teach individuals, and the need to teach the main body of the class.

It is here interesting to note that in situations which have traditionally had more than one adult available to work in the classroom, breakdown of responsibilities (where, indeed, attention has been paid to the question of role definition) roughly parallels that which would be suggested by these analyses. As already noted, in those situations, such as the day nursery or the school for children with severe learning difficulties, analysis has started from the assumption that roles need to be more clearly defined and has moved on to determine *what* needs to be done, and *how* it should be done before deciding *who* ought to be doing it.

ROOM MANAGEMENT

Research has been undertaken in special settings and in nursery schools into the way in which the teacher's role might be 'fractured' in order that additional people can take on elements of the role. That research employs constructs which are remarkably similar to those, just examined above, drawn from research into mainstream classroom management. McBrien and Weightman (1980), in refining *room management* procedures, delineate three separate sets of activities which classroom adults fulfil interdependently: the 'individual helper' works exclusively with individuals; the 'activity manager' works entirely with the larger group or groups (depending on the organisation of the class); the 'mover' attends to activity that might impede the smooth running of the class.

Such a system of organisation (and others such as that developed by Bush, Williams and Morris 1980) is consistent with notions about the irreconcilability of individual and group management activities, which can be drawn from the work of Brophy and from the ORACLE research, and it finds consonance in Kounin's work on the importance of flow. Thus, the main system of organisation developed to date – and developed in the context of environments outside mainstream education and drawing entirely on a research body independent of mainstream education – suggests a way of working for additional personnel which would also be recommended from the mainstream research. This way of working calls for the maintenance of flow (embodied in the notion of a mover) and the separation of two sets of activities (individual work and classroom work) which are mutually exclusive.

The system also draws on the importance of circulating and giving feedback to children, other facets of the simplifying concepts noted above. Spangler and Marshall (1983, see also p. 46) in a variant of room management, delineate activities along similar continua to those already noted – providing feedback, circulating, prompting – which in turn are grouped or 'chunked' into individual or group activities.

Disappointingly, however, none of these studies (which have the merit of attempting to seek a solution, rather than simply reflecting on the difficulties) examines in any very great detail the interpersonal antecedents to the success or otherwise of the team. None takes the discussion forward qualitatively by, for instance, asking for participants' interpretations of the team process in the classroom.

CONCLUSION

A number of possible avenues are open in looking for operational strategies to improve the functioning of classroom teams. Both the literature and the research reported in previous chapters have shown that teams' difficulties can be attributed (by the team participants) either to dispositional factors or to situational factors. An examination of the latter (potentially, as I have tried to show, the more useful examination) focuses research interest on the structural features of the teaching situation and in particular the teacher's role.

A number of elements can be shown to comprise the teacher's role in the classroom. There appear to be grounds, on the basis of the evidence reviewed here, for believing that this role can be 'broken' into these elements. Research in special education has shown that if these elements are allocated to extra people in the class, there are clear benefits in terms of the working of the team.

On the basis of this logic and the research that gave rise to it, the following chapter will examine the hypothesis that clarifying the role definitions of extra individuals in the class will assist in the functioning of the team.

13

THE EFFECT OF DEFINING ROLES

This chapter constitutes a marked departure from the methodology of the previous chapters, with their interviews and participant observation. In those, it was possible to enter the world of the team member in the classroom and examine the processes by which roles were established. In so doing it was possible to shed light on the constructs and attributions employed by those team members in making sense of the team process. A model was tested by these studies and validated by them. In short, it was found that team members, through the use of particular personal constructs and attributions based on these, generate either *status* or *definitional* solutions to the tensions they inevitably face in the team. The latter, definitional solutions, are judged to be the more productive strategy, being more likely to result in the kind of synergy which is usually taken to constitute the essential value of a team, over simply a collection of individuals.

This chapter therefore tests the hypothesis that structuring these definitional solutions will be productive. It aims to do this experimentally, following an analysis of what such role definitions might comprise in a classroom.

THE DELINEATION OF ROLES IN CLASSROOM TEAMS

With the importance being assigned to role clarity in the definitional solutions already discussed, it follows that there is a need to establish the parameters of those roles in the classroom. An attempt at this was made in the last chapter. It was suggested that there are two elements to the teacher's role which it is difficult to fulfil at the same time. These are the need to work with individuals and the need to work with the whole class.

In situations where traditionally more than one adult has been present in the classroom, for example, in schools for children with severe learning difficulties, the division of the teacher's role for the purpose of allocating roles to others has occurred on broadly the lines that this mainstream analysis would suggest. Indeed, where three people are present, as

186

they are in some such classrooms, the rationale behind methods for organising such personnel closely parallels the rationale outlined in the previous chapter. 'Room management' procedures, arising out of the work of Hart and Risley (1976), have now been assessed in a variety of settings for severely handicapped adults and children (Porterfield, Blunden and Blewitt 1977; Coles and Blunden 1979; McBrien and Weightman 1980). As discussed in chapter 2, results from these studies indicate that use of room management procedures can more than double mean engagement levels and substantially increase time for individual teaching. In other words, it has proved to be an effective way of structuring teamwork. Its interest for us in the current chapter is that it does this structuring through defining and specifying roles for the team participants.

Room management essentially involves clear setting of roles with account being taken in that definition of the need for very widely differing functions to be operating in a group setting. Thus, returning for a moment to the interpretation made of the findings of the ORACLE research, there is a need for a teacher of individual children, represented in the room management scheme by an 'individual helper'; there is a need for someone to maintain the engagement of children who are not being taught individually, a role fulfilled in room management by an 'activity manager'; and there is a need for someone to maintain flow, for which in room management the duties of a 'mover' are suggested.

At the core of room management lies a period of time known as the 'activity period', when classroom team participants – teachers, ancillary helpers or parents – take on specific roles. Different roles will be assumed by the people involved; the exact arrangement of those roles will depend on the needs of the class and the number of people available to help. The definitions of those roles are as follows:

1 *Individual helper*: the individual helper concentrates on working with an individual on a teaching activity for 5–15 minutes. So, in an hour it should be possible to arrange between four and twelve individual teaching sessions.
2 *Activity manager*: the activity manager concentrates on the rest of the class, who will normally be arranged in groups of between four and eight. She will quickly move around keeping them busy and occupied.
3 *Mover*: the mover may fetch and move equipment, etc.; supervise emptying paintpots, sharpening of pencils, etc.; deal with all interruptions to routine, e.g. spillages, visitors, in order to keep the activity manager and individual helper free from distraction.

As the system has been described in the research noted earlier, the staff might plan to switch roles during the hour. In line with the importance of situational attribution, the emphasis is on roles and definition rather than the professional status of particular groups of people. The person who occupied the role of individual helper during the first half-hour may become the activity manager in the second. There is no suggestion that the teacher should always take on one role while the ancillary helper always takes on another. The roles of activity manager, individual helper and mover may be allocated in a number of ways depending on the preferences of the personnel involved, the organisation of the classroom or the needs of the children. For example, in one class there may be one individual helper, one activity manager and one mover while in another there may be one individual helper and two activity managers.

Given the positive results that have been obtained using room management in settings for adults and children with learning difficulties, it was felt appropriate, in the context of the importance of definitional solutions to the teamwork problems noted, to test the system in a mainstream class for the limited period when an ancillary helper and parents were helping.

HOW THE STUDY WAS UNDERTAKEN

The school and the children

The school at which the study took place is a rural primary school. The class was one of 10–11 year-olds. Twenty-one children were available for observation. No child was excluded from the observation but numbers for observation were reduced as children were eliminated from the observation if they were absent on any one of three video-recordings made. The children were accustomed in their formal work to a pattern of working independently from books, workcards and other materials, making their own way to the teacher for clarification or marking. For these formal sessions an ancillary helper was also sometimes available in the classroom. She normally devoted her time to one or two children who found difficulty working independently. A practice of parents also being involved in the classroom had also evolved. The normal pattern had been for these parents to work almost exclusively with their own children.

Procedure for room management

Clearly, the dynamics of a class of children with severe learning difficulties differ extensively from those of a class of year 6 primary children. Given, however, the validity of the general principles of room management, the question arose as to how to extract its relevant features for the primary classroom setting. It was felt that the role of mover would be underused and that it would be more profitable, with less opportunity for role ambiguity, to specify the activities of a third or fourth person in terms of individual helper or activity manager. The only other major feature of change was in the way that the individual helper worked. Rather than taking a succession of children from a rota she limited her work to involvement with two children. The overall pattern was therefore three activity managers (two parents and one ancillary helper) responsible between them for four groups of six children each, and one individual helper. In preparation for the room management session the classteacher read the outline of the roles (below) and discussed these with me. She then discussed them with each of the individuals working within her class. The individuals kept to the same roles throughout the room management session.

Detailed description of roles

The following description of roles is adapted from M. Thomas (1985).

What an activity manager does

Before the activity period:

1 organises a variety of tasks/activities for each group;
2 informs the individual helper when she is ready to begin.

During the activity period:

1 ensures that each group member has appropriate materials/books/ equipment;
2 prompts children to start working if necessary;
3 supervises use of shared materials;
4 moves around the group to praise and reward group members who are busy;
5 gives minimum attention to children who are not busy.

Thus, activity managers move from one group member to the next, commenting on activities, giving help and praising those who are busy. They also very briefly prompt group members who are not busy. These prompts should as far as possible be gestural or physical (e.g. pointing or placing the child's hand onto the materials) rather than verbal prompts. Apart from a brief gestural or physical prompt, group members should be given attention only when they are busy.

What an individual helper does

Before the activity period:

1 has available a list or rota of children for individual help and the activities and materials required for each;

189

2 helps the activity manager to organise the classroom for the activity period;
3 assembles materials needed for each child's work in the area to be used for individual work. For example, if it is to be a one-hour session with 15 minutes for each child, four children will be seen in the hour and four sets of activities should have been prepared ready for each child to start straightaway when s/he is called.

During the activity period:

1 asks the first child on the list to come and work. Fifteen minutes should be the maximum for an intensive individual activity. In order to minimise the possibility of the session becoming frustrating and failure-laden it should be stressed to the individual helper that the emphasis should be on praise and gentle encouragement;
2 asks subsequent children on the list to come and work at the end of each session.

The design of the study

Many difficulties confront those who are brave or foolhardy enough to try and measure what goes on in classrooms. The dangers of over-simplifying the richness of classroom life are manifest and certain of the more crude systematic classroom observation measures indeed invite much criticism. An excellent discussion of systematic classroom observation is given by Croll (1986).

Despite all the problems, the *engagement* of the children was chosen as the measure of what was going on in the class: a simple on-task/off-task measure was used to determine the effects of classroom management. This was done for a number of reasons. First, economy: it was a simple, if crude, measure of whether room management was having an effect. Second, precedent: it was the measure which had been used in other research into room management and comparisons would be possible between this and that research. Third, though insensitive, it is a reliable and robust measure of classroom activity: two decades after the heyday of engaged-rate research, Stallings *et al.* (1986) are still able to claim that engaged rates relate solidly to achievement.

Videotape recordings were made of the group under three conditions:

A with the classroom functioning normally with one teacher without a support team;
B with the same classroom functioning with two parents and one ancillary;
C with the classroom functioning under room management with the same team as in B.

190

An hour's recording was made of each condition, with each child in the class being observed for 6 minutes in each condition. Results are therefore based on a total of 6 hours, 18 minutes of observation. Identical days (Fridays) were used for recording and identical times (9.15 am–10.15 am). As far as it was possible to control for this, the children were undertaking the same kind of task on each recording. Unit sampling was undertaken on a 10-second basis. Categories for on-task/off-task were devised on the basis of the Becker, Madsen, Arnold and Thomas (1967) categories for behaviour incompatible with learning (off-task), and relevant behaviour (on-task). Criteria for time on-task were however not as strict as those set by Becker *et al.*: time samples were rated on the basis of which category was a better fit for the sample. Time when a child was not in sight on video was not scored.

Results were handled in terms of mean engagement levels for each child and a repeated measures design was used, comparing each child with him/herself across the conditions.

RESULTS

Mean engagement levels over the different conditions are shown in table 13.1.

Table 13.1   Mean engagement levels across the room management conditions

Condition	A	B	C
mean engagement %	58.57	69.14	90.19
SD	27.1	25.3	11.0

Predicting that engagement would rise over the conditions, a Pages L trend test was conducted to detect whether such a trend indeed existed. In fact, on the basis of the work of McBrien and Weightman (1980), who found that the number of staff present either did not affect or was inversely related with engagement, such a prediction is at best optimistic. However, in this setting such a trend was found to exist (L/Kn = 4.31, p <0.05). This trend is shown in figure 13.1.

Results were further subjected to a one way analysis of variance, with the results analysed as shown in table 13.2.

Table 13.2   Analysis of variance

	D.F.	M.S.	F ratio	p
Among conditions	2	5440.82	54.22	<0.01

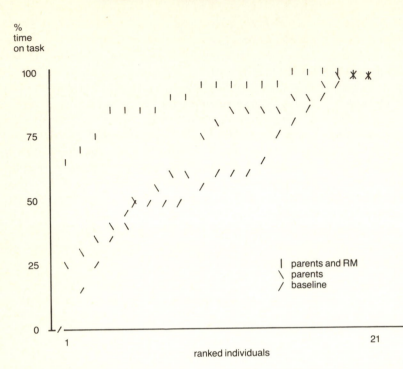

Figure 13.1 Individuals ranked by engagement under the three conditions

Comparison of the conditions using post-hoc tests (Newman–Keuls) revealed the results summarised in table 13.3.

Table 13.3 Comparison of the conditions using Newman–Keuls test

Compare Conditions	Mean 1	Mean 2	diff.	q(calc)	r	p
A v C	58.57	90.19	31.61	14.464	3	<0.01
A v B	58.57	69.14	10.57	4.836	2	<0.01
B v C	69.14	90.19	21.04	9.628	2	<0.01

Notes:
A = Teacher on her own
B = Teacher plus team
C = Teacher plus team using room management

Analysis therefore shows clear differences existing (at p <0.01) between baseline (no team) and the two conditions where the team was in support. The greatest difference existed between A (baseline) and C (the team working with room management). Significant differences were also found

192

to exist between baseline and the team working in the classroom without room management, and between the condition where the team was in support without room management (B) and that in which room management was used (C).

DISCUSSION

Room management is shown to have an effect on the team that influences positively the engagement of the children in class. In other words, structuring the team's work by defining the roles of the team members appears, as predicted, to be a successful solution to the problems that are likely to be experienced by teams. However, before proceeding to discuss the substantive matters in relation to the aims of the chapter, a number of limitations in the design and conduct of the study have to be stated.

The shortcomings of the current chapter as an assessment of room management may be listed as follows.

1 Given the importance which is being assigned to role definition and role clarity it is clear in retrospect that there was a need for more structured training in the procedure – for even more definition and even more clarity. It would have been valuable to give feedback to staff and parents on the way in which they were fulfilling their various room management roles. It was apparent in viewing the tapes that quite idiosyncratic interpretations were being made of the role definitions. That being stated, it was nevertheless clear that between conditions B and C parents and staff responded positively to having such definition explicitly articulated, however interpreted.

2 Given that this was a short study, it is possible that a Hawthorne effect (Roethlisberger and Dickson 1939) was responsible for the results obtained. A longer term assessment might indicate how far this is the case. Alternatively, adding a further series of the treatment conditions, following their withdrawal, would enable stronger conclusions to be drawn. The other main weaknesses of the repeated measures design, according to Cook and Campbell (1976: 260–1) are in (1) threats to internal validity, and (2) threats to construct validity. The former, relating to results due to maturation, seems unlikely over such a short time-scale and with such significant results. The latter relates to respondents' sensitivity to the hypothesis being tested and their consequent differential response. The respondents on whom the dependent variable is measured – i.e. the children – are unlikely to be this sensitive. However, the possible effect on the personnel is acknowledged.

3 No account was taken of adult behaviour, nor of the nature of the interactions among adults and children. Given the needs of children

who are experiencing difficulty as elaborated above, it would have been valuable to tap the quantity and quality of adult–child interactions under a system such as room management. It would be valuable to explore the differential influence of a system such as this on the behaviour and language of parents, ancillaries and teachers operating in the classroom. Of particular interest here would be the amount and nature of individual teaching sessions conducted under room management.

4 Although quality of learning would be difficult to assess, it would be useful to note on what sort of activities the increase in on-task behaviour noted under room management had the most beneficial effects.

5 It would be useful to assess the effects of room management in terms of individual teaching sessions and time on-task when in a group specifically for children with learning difficulties in mainstream classes, given the findings noted above (Galton *et al.* 1980) that in general such children receive little or no extra individual attention when compared with higher-achieving peers. A high SD was obtained on the first and second set of scores, i.e. without room management (in other words mean engagement scores disguise wide variation in on-task behaviour); it is expected therefore that room management would have a differential effect in favour of those with low engagement levels.

Another avenue for further research would be to explore with the team participants their reactions to operating a system such as this which clarifies role definition. This study rested on the assumption that *role* [or definitional] *solutions* to team-working problems hold out greater promise than those that aim to explore and disentangle problems emanating from participants' use of dispositional attributions (such as Wilson's [1989] attempts to devolve consultation skills to support teachers – see chapter 3). Thus, the primary concern was to measure the outcome of the organisation on one of the tasks of the team, namely managing the class. However, the long-term success of a system such as this is surely predicated on participants' reactions to it and it would therefore be valuable to gauge these.

It seems reasonable to suggest that the results obtained in this study are attributable mainly to the enhanced definition of role which room management provides. It may be that greater gains in terms of on-task behaviour and number and quality of individual teaching sessions would be obtained if more attention were to be paid to the specific features of room management – perhaps through a greater investment of time in terms of training staff and parents.

One of the most important findings made here for subsequent research is the effect of additional personnel *per se*. As noted earlier, an assumption that additional people will have positive effects in terms of time on task is not necessarily justified. However, it is clear from this chapter that additional personnel in the numbers used and in the setting studied did have a positive effect which was measurable and significant.

If the specific effects of the room management procedures are taken to be attenuated through (in retrospect) a shorter than appropriate training programme, a valid conclusion from this chapter might be that definition of role *per se* is a potent influence on team behaviour. Such a conclusion is certainly consistent with the findings of the research into teamwork which have been reviewed and it is also consistent with the interviews and the participant observation reported in chapters 8–10. In this sense the general emerging thesis about the significance of role definition in classroom teams is validated.

14

OVERVIEW AND CONCLUSION

THE NEW TEAMS

Over the last decade a new kind of team teaching has crept up on us. Because there has been no fanfare, no top-down initiative, it has emerged almost unnoticed among the many upheavals in education over the decade 1980–90. Indeed in many senses, the new teaming could be said to have arisen because of these upheavals. The 1981 Education (Special Educational Needs) Act has been at the root of many of the integration, outreach and support developments concerned with the 20 per cent of children who, the Warnock Committee (Department of Education and Science 1978) calculate, have special educational needs. The involvement of parents in their children's education has received a stimulus from legislation such as the 1986 Education Act (which gave parents an enhanced role in schools' governing bodies), the 1988 Education Act and the government of the time's emphasis on 'parent power'. The already-existing trends to parental involvement and various kinds of integration initiative were augmented by these policy and legislative frameworks.

The work reported in this book affirms that the effects of these trends are emerging in primary schools: additional adults from varied backgrounds are moving into the classroom to work alongside the classteacher. The new teams, at least in the temporal snapshots taken, are commonplace and varied. In the main they comprise, as would be expected on the basis of the trends that underpin them, two main categories of people: (1) parents and (2) personnel associated with children with special educational needs. The surveys undertaken here clearly indicate the nature of the activities these individuals are undertaking in classes, and the form in which they do those activities. Some crude features of the nature of the new teams are therefore provided by these surveys and the broad shape of the teams has been determined. These have provided the basis for determining the likely nature of the tensions and stresses that might be experienced therein.

These tensions are by no means insignificant. At times they seem insoluble. People with sometimes fundamentally different ideas on what has to be done in class, on what education is all about, find themselves rubbing shoulders with one another and, more than this, having to cooperate. People who had no expectation that they would have to share their working environment in this way suddenly find themselves having to work in teams. People whose training has included nothing on people-management, negotiation or working in groups find themselves having to manage people, negotiate and work in groups.

It has been assumed that people would slide effortlessly into the classroom. The principles bringing them there were so conspicuously merit-worthy that few could argue that the new teams weren't for the best. But a decade of experience has shown us what we should have appreciated at the outset: groups and teams are fragile, fickle creatures. Bringing people together to work on a project – especially if they aren't prepared for it – can do more harm than good. To work well they need a lot of help.

ROLE IN THE NEW TEAMS: UNDERSTANDING IN PLACE OF DEFINITION

Perhaps because these new teams have emerged largely unnoticed (or at least undocumented), few attempts have been made to assess or analyse the problems or opportunities that are their organisational accompaniments. The central aim of this book was therefore to research and document the nature of these teams and their dynamics.

The second chapter examined the nature of role as it had been discussed in the literature on teams generally, and in particular on classroom teams. The Krech model was used as a framework for conceptualising the dynamics of teams, the place of *role* in those teams and the dynamics which may emerge in classroom teams. It was noted that notions such as 'role conflict' which had been taken from the literature on management of groups in other settings were being used to interpret the dynamics of classroom teams. For example, Hargreaves (1972) outlined a range of different ways in which role conflict may exist in schools. Such an analysis is viewed on the basis of the research undertaken here to be simplistic. Rather, on the basis particularly of the research in chapter 8, it can be seen that role exists too loosely for such conflict to exist in the classroom. 'Conflict' is altogether too active a word to describe the process of negotiation and developing of understandings and misunderstandings that exists in its place.

While the Krech model correctly posits the emergence of understanding about roles (the *emergent process*), it nevertheless (in the light of the evidence here) is too clear in its expectation that there will be some formulation of role definition at the outset. Role definitions do not exist in that sense in classroom teams. What appears to exist in the place of those definitions is a set of consensual understandings about broad ranges of activities which various participants should or should not undertake in the classroom. These tacit *understandings* are framed and constrained by a number of professional and affective concerns, such as the personality of the participants, their experience and status, and the ways in which each of these factors is *viewed* by the other participants. There is thus a constant flux in which this assortment of variables interplay.

TEAM COPING STRATEGIES

In order to achieve some equilibrium in this situation, in which there is ample room for misunderstanding and friction, two processes moderate the possible ensuing stress. One of these is the selection of the participants (in heterogeneous teams, at least) in such a way that personality or other mismatches will be minimised. Possible threats to status or professional autonomy may be screened in such selection procedures. The other is the process by which participants 'get along' with one another, which has been called fraternity in this book.

Much of this is consistent with the observations of others who have examined the group process, particularly those who have adopted a qualitative methodology in their studies. Bate (1984), for example, talked of a root construct of 'unemotionality' by which participants protected themselves from the stresses of team life. Goffman (1961) talked of 'role distancing' in much the same context. From a different vantage point, others, such as Hackman and Oldham (1980), talked of appropriate ingredients for team success, which included appropriate degrees of heterogeneity among the team. This strikes a chord in the research findings here, where it has been noted that heterogeneous teams may be more successful than homogeneous teams.

The research here certainly confirms Cohen's (1976, 1979) findings that successful teaming rests not so much on top–down decisions as upon informal negotiations among team members. The success of these negotiations will depend upon the random admixture of personality features, views, thoughts and feelings held by the various participants. It will also depend upon the protective features – fraternity, role distancing or status solutions developed by teams. It may be that particular kinds of teams develop particular kinds of defence. It is, for instance, easy to see how unemotionality develops on the shop-floor. It is as easy, in the light of the interviews reported and analysed here, to see how fraternity develops in the classroom.

One of the clearest indications of the first part of this research is that classroom teams cannot simply be 'left to get on with it'. Strains may develop which may be camouflaged by a variety of devices. Guidance may be needed on the appropriate structuring of teams – in other words, who should comprise a team. Enabling some degree of choice and self-selection seems to be an implication of the research: people will, unsurprisingly, work better with those with whom they feel comfortable than with those with whom they feel ill-at-ease. A more counter-intuitive conclusion is that heterogeneous teams will, in general, 'work better' than homogeneous teams: the team process will be more straightforward with fewer ambiguities where there is a mix of participants from different backgrounds.

In general, coping strategies – such as fraternity, reinforcing territory, highlighting status differences – may evolve out of stresses engendered because of ideological or personal mismatches or misunderstandings.

THE NEW TEAMS AND OTHER TEAMS

Many of these notions have already been taken up in the research on different kinds of classroom teams, although the issues have nowhere been identified as a discrete set applying to various kinds of adult co-working practices in the classroom. The various kinds of existing arrangements – involving team teaching, classroom assistants, special education teams and so forth, as discussed in chapters 3 and 4 – show nevertheless a remarkable degree of uniformity in the stresses and strains that are experienced therein.

Throughout accounts of research into classroom co-working a number of themes arise repeatedly which are mirrored in the research undertaken for this book. There is – in accounts of team teaching – the reluctance to teach before colleagues, the need for autonomy and the implicit differences in ideology which impede the teaming process. Hargreaves (1980) makes the point that these are all the more difficult to reconcile *because* the differences are implicit; in being implicit they are unspoken and therefore incontrovertible. One might add that the lack of ventilation about these differences or about this discomfiture is actually a process entered into by the participants. Learned helplessness or fraternity – in the absence of the structures which would enable a resolution of these difficulties – is preferable to the stresses that exist by virtue of them.

The findings are quite consistent for team teaching, even in the different educational environments of the USA and UK. Bennett *et al.*'s (1980) findings are echoed in those of Miskel *et al.* (1983) who find that co-working typically occurs on an informal and low-frequency basis. The findings in the current research confirm the inference made in chapter 5 that the reasons for this lack of effective joint endeavour are located in the micro-climate of the classroom – in the perceptions of interpersonal difference; in clarity of managerial and task responsibilities; in perception of philosophical or pedagogical mismatch.

ATTRIBUTIONS AND ROLE-MAKING

Attribution theory suggests that people will 'blame' the failure (or success) of the team either on the others in the team (dispositional attribution) or on the system or the general situation (situational attribution). It further suggests that in the absence of guidance, people will tend to the former of these explanations for success or failure: they will tend to blame *people* – their team-mates, or indeed themselves.

If people are unsupported in these new teams – if indeed they even recognise themselves as being in teams – they will tend to this person-blaming, this dispositional attribution. If no one helps them to define what roles ought to be, for instance by developing whole-school policies on special needs or parental involvement, then working practices will emerge which may not be altogether beneficial. If this happens, and if team-mates are in some way held to be responsible for the conspicuous breakdown of the team enterprise, the result is that what I have called 'status solutions' may be developed by participants: participants will reinforce status or territorial demarcation lines.

However, all is not doom and gloom. There were also clear articulations of system-related solutions to the problems teams faced. Role definition existed as a fairly discrete construct in interviewees' minds, unrelated to those dispositional attributions. The different kinds of attributions made can be related to the solutions team participants propose for themselves, which are viewed here as means of attenuating stress.

The dichotomy that I draw here has a correspondence in the literature. There, it can be seen on one side that there are suggestions for team members to become skilled in understanding the roles which they are to fulfil in the classroom. These exist in techniques such as room management, and can be related to those definitional solutions. On the other side are solutions which rest in ameliorating stress arising from the dispositional attributions which exist by virtue of mismatches in ideology, personality and so forth. Those latter solutions have most comprehensively been explored by Wilson (1989) who has sought to equip team members with a set of consultation, counselling and negotiation skills with which they will be able to alleviate some of the tensions and misunderstandings which occur in the shared classroom.

Although this would appear to be a worthwhile endeavour, it would seem destined to meet with many of the practical problems (such as lack of time) which create the conditions in which communication will be absent and misunderstandings thereby occur. In other words, it seeks to improve communication in conditions where such improvement, due to the exigencies of school life, is unlikely to be possible. Were there unlimited time for discussion and planning, it may be that few of the difficulties noted would exist in the first place. The search for solutions based around these dispositional attributions, then, is somewhat circular. It is asserting that tensions exist in teams because of personal deficits which can be remedied by a kind of skill training. The alternative position, based in a set of situational attributions, would posit that individuals had the skills and the will to communicate, but simply lacked the 'setting conditions' for this to happen.

ROLE DEPENDING ON 'TEAM PERSONALITY'

The process of role-making is shown to be yet more problematic in chapter 10, where participant observation revealed that the way in which one's role develops is highly variable, and in terms of one's position as a team member, dependent very largely on the team 'leader' – in this case, the classteacher. One's own role, in terms of status, feelings of acceptance and professional integrity, was shown to be constructed very largely out of the professional flexibility, security and interpersonal skills of one's colleague. The enormous variability possible in the nature of the role thereby constructed is highlighted by this research and further suggests that to attempt to construct a role nearer to the 'ideal self' through counselling or negotiation skills is unlikely to be successful.

Perhaps the most important finding to emerge from chapter 10 is that the process of role-making is an interactive one, depending on the *team personalities* of the participants. The constructs of each and their interlocking constructs about the construing processes of the other(s) will determine the nature of the relationship that emerges.

HOMOGENEOUS AND HETEROGENEOUS TEAMS

No attempt has been made to distinguish between different kinds of team in different kinds of school. An assumption throughout this book is that the dynamics of classroom teams are characterised by generic problems; I have looked for generic features of these dynamics without actively seeking out differences between different kinds of team. However, arising out of the research, pointers to methods of categorising teams have emerged and these might form the basis for a typology and for differences, for instance, between the composition or personality of teams in secondary schools, as against those in primary schools.

An assumption throughout has been that when people get together in a team, alterations occur in the nature of the task to be undertaken. These alterations will occur irrespective of the nature of the participants. A further assumption was that although classroom teams are developing for a variety of reasons, all of those teams thus constituted confront these alterations, and that the climate or 'ecology' of the classroom is changed in important respects due to the interpersonal dynamics of the team members.

The aim throughout has been to examine these changes in dynamic, and not to examine the specific problems or features of particular groups of people in the classroom. However, I recognise that important differences do exist in different kinds of team and I have noted these for discussion where they have arisen. Indeed, these differences have provided important pointers for an analysis of the kinds of dynamics that may exist in the classroom when extra people are present. In particular, it is possible to elicit significant distinctions in personal constructions about *status* and *threat* from participants' accounts about teamwork with different kinds of team member, and these distinctions have formed an important element of the analysis and findings.

If differences between different kinds of team are focused upon, the broadest and perhaps most useful dichotomy which can be drawn is between heterogeneous and homogeneous teams. It has to be remembered that while chapter 8 was about the heterogeneous team, chapters 9 and 10 were both about the homogeneous team. The research shows that although important differences exist between these different kinds of team, they do nevertheless appear to share dynamics. Among the participants of both, situational and dispositional attributions occur, and definitional and status solutions are tacitly arrived at. A direct comparison of these differences was not attempted here since it was assumed at the outset that the classroom team, in itself, possessed consistent features irrespective of its structure. Throughout though, differences have been noted, in passing, and these would form a worthwhile topic for further research. The differences as they have been found and the implications of these differences are discussed in the following paragraphs.

Homogeneous teams exist where all the members are similar – in this case, all of the same professional status. Since all classroom teams must have at least one teacher, this means that a homogeneous team must be a team comprising only teachers.

The homogeneous team is characterised by certain kinds of difficulty that do not afflict the heterogeneous team. The fear of being watched or judged is accentuated when the co-member is of one's own profession. Furthermore, attribution theory would predict that the failure of a team to operate completely successfully is less likely to be attributed to parents or to ancillary helpers, since they are unlikely to be perceived by the host as foreseeing events with which they are associated. Teacher colleagues, on the other hand, are less likely to be given the benefit of the doubt.

These various kinds of team are being introduced into classrooms with neither a discussion of the problems general to teaming nor any consideration of the needs of team members in different kinds of team. It seems appropriate to note here that at least some kind of superstructure is necessary to support the team process. This is necessary at Bronfenbrenner's (1979) exo-system level, in the provision of appropriate guidelines within a school on why teams are existing (for example, to give effect to integration or to parental involvement) and how they might operate in terms of the specific activities which individuals might undertake. It is also necessary at the micro-system level, where it has been shown that focusing on the routine activities of team members is probably a more fruitful (if less juicy) path to follow in helping to promote successful teamwork than that of examining the interpersonal dynamics of a team.

THE TEACHER'S TASK AND ITS SUBDIVISION FOR THE PURPOSES OF ROLE DEFINITION

Chapter 13 took as a starting point the idea that focusing on and enhancing role definition is a productive way of structuring the work of the team and obviating some of the problems noted in teamwork. It suggested that the delineation of the tasks which had to be performed by the teacher in her management of the classroom constituted an important starting point in enabling a set of role definitions to be allocated to other team members in the classroom. It took as its basis the analysis undertaken in chapter 12 and linked this analysis to a particular system of role definition in personnel organisation which has been used in nursery education and in special education. Room management, in the specific allocation of tasks to individuals and in the nature of the task to be done, was seen to be broadly congruent with the analysis in chapter 12, and was therefore viewed as an appropriate model for testing the notion that formally structuring the work of the team around a definitional solution would be beneficial. The benefits were measured in terms of improvements in children's engagement, showing substantial and significant gains when the team was so organised.

Further research in this last area might measure benefits in terms not only of the 'quality' of children's work but also in terms of perceptions of the team process by the team members. Such research might thereby link the imposition of such a system with notions such as 'team personality' advanced in chapter 11, and with the inclination of team members under such a system of organisation to attribute team problems to individuals in the team.

RECOMMENDATIONS

How might the classroom team operate most effectively given that a major conclusion from this research is that clear role definition is a crucial ingredient of team success? How can teams be encouraged to devise for themselves *role solutions* rather than *autonomy solutions* when faced with the inevitable pressures and stresses of teamwork? A number of recommendations emerge from the research:

1 The shared classroom should be seen in the context of developments which are worthwhile and worthy of promotion by the school. The formulation of whole-school policies on parental involvement, community participation and special educational needs will be beneficial, if the whole-school community, including ancillaries, visiting teachers and parents, is genuinely involved in the process of developing such policies.

2 Opportunity should exist from the outset for discussion about the pedagogic, professional and affective concerns and expectations of team members. Tension that arises out of a mismatch between participants' concerns and expectations appears to be at the root of *team defences* which inhibit teams' effective working.

3 However, mismatches in the team should not assume an unwarranted significance. Teamwork stresses are likely to be handled more successfully through clear task and role definition than through strenuous attempts to resolve mismatches through improved communication among participants. Strategies directing attention to the task are more likely to meet with success than those directing attention to the participants.

4 Planning for teaming will ideally be a joint exercise involving all classroom participants. People need to be able to discuss the roles they will be fulfilling and whether they would feel comfortable undertaking a particular set of tasks. The opportunity of exchanging and interchanging roles needs to be discussed.

5 Individuals' strengths and weaknesses need to be identified during planning.

6 Clear definition of classroom tasks and activities needs to be made during planning.

7 The composition of the team needs to be considered carefully. On the basis of this research there are grounds for believing that heterogeneous teams will experience fewer stresses than homogeneous teams.

8 The team needs to meet regularly to discuss and evaluate the way that they have been working. The openness of a 'quality circle' (see chapter 2) has to be the hallmark of such meetings; the atmosphere should be informal with individuals encouraged to suggest ideas.

Of these recommendations, the suggestion that mixed teams will form more harmonious, more effective units than teacher-only teams is probably the most controversial. The move to integration resulted in many committed, hard-working special needs teachers changing their style of work, so that they worked in the mainstream class instead of withdrawing pupils. Experience has taught, though, that this experiment has revealed a number of serious problems. The experience of a decade of support teaching perhaps leads us to look again at the role of the support teacher and to make a further reappraisal. Does this support have to take place in the classroom in the shape of team teaching, with all the questions and problems that entails? Or is it possible to view the support that the teacher gives (i.e. the teacher as distinct from a welfare assistant or ancillary helper) in a much more flexible way, as Sewell (1988) has suggested?

The new classroom teams, as I have attempted to indicate, constitute an important, but neglected feature of school life. It was necessary to document features of their nature and to examine the problems which confronted them. The idiosyncratic nature of the classroom team (as a *team* rather than simply a collection of individuals) has been emphasised, with its unclear boundaries and its loosely defined tasks. The particular stresses that emerge in such teams have been identified, as have the kinds of strategies employed by participants in ameliorating the effects of those stresses. The formulation of role in such a situation is seen to be largely a developmental process depending on a number of factors including the nature of the attributions made by team participants. On the basis of the foregoing, guidelines to the ways in which these teams might work better have been advanced and tested.

APPENDIX
Extracts from the diary

26 April Shown into chemistry class, where a third year class of children are working with their young and inexperienced teacher, Xanthe. They are the 7th of 8 sets, and because of their notorious boisterousness, have an ancillary helper with them to provide support. I, as the temporary member of support staff, am asked to provide additional support. I ask the teacher at the start how she would like me to provide support: to individuals, generally, or in some other way. She's not sure – as they seem to need it. Discussion with Pauline, the ancillary, has already revealed that she is very unsure about what she should be doing. She doesn't have a specific group of children to help.

The class is having a lesson on photosynthesis. The explanation which leads into the practical activity is having little impact on most of the children. Comments from the children pepper the explanation from the teacher, which is faltering and almost impossible to follow. The subject of the lesson isn't really apparent; all that we know from following the teacher's account is that there are four test tubes, two with green plants in, and all with an indicator fluid. The pupils realise that something has to be done with the four test tubes, but beyond that little is clear; I am unclear about the purpose of the lesson, or what the children have to do. The children call out quite frivolously: 'She's got AIDS – yeugh'; 'She's sitting too close to me', to which the teacher replies 'Well tell her to move away a bit then'. She responds to most interjections of this kind which is probably encouraging them to continue. Questions to the class are met with the inconsequential first responses shouted out:

T: Two of the test tubes have got plants in and two . . .?
C: Are dead! (laughter)

There is some extremely unclear instruction to get test tubes and undertake the experiment. I feel redundant while the explanation is going on; more than redundant – embarrassed both for myself, and for my colleague. Anxious to be providing 'support' now that the explanation has finished I look around to see if anyone seems to be unsure about what to do. There is a general air of disorganisation – pupils are wandering around, shouting in a fairly good-natured way to one another, spraying water at one another. There is no obvious way to provide support to any of these groups; they all patently need support since the lesson was taken so badly, the instruction so inadequate. Eventually, and surprisingly, most pupils seem to become part of a group which has obtained a set of test tubes for the experiment, and they seem to set these up appropriately, two with plants in, two without and two with black paper around them. I ask some of the pupils if they know why they are doing this – no, but they have a diagram which tells them what to do. I wander around looking for pupils who look as though they need help, but on doing this, all seem to need some kind of help. None understands what they are doing or why they are doing it:

GT: Why have you put the plant in that red liquid?
C: It's carbon dioxide.

Where do I begin to explain? Two degrees in the social sciences don't equip me to provide a good explanation, and I suspect that even if I had a Nobel prize in chemistry I couldn't begin to get through the pupils' confusions. Help is limited to procedural advice: Put the card round this one; draw this here; now do this. But the confusion in the lesson generally is such that my presence merely acts as an aid to attention for the pupils for as long as I am present. They more or less know what they have to do – they need help staying on the task in hand. When I move on to someone else, they lose attention from the task in hand. I'm merely someone who is helping the pupils to focus on the task in hand, since there are few if any constraints on behaviour imposed by the teacher. Messing around, turning on gas taps, splashing water, calling to mates on the other side of the room are all more attractive propositions than writing about fluid in test tubes. The teacher leaves the room to get some textbooks and in the three or four minutes that she is gone the atmosphere remains much the same. When she comes back with the books, the children are told to put their test tubes on the window-ledge to be in the light – no other explanation is forthcoming. There is no real opportunity for me to provide an explanation in the way that I am providing support; to approach a child (which child?) and start to explain about the effects of the sunlight would be injurious to the self-esteem of the child I approached (peers would wonder what was going on) and would break into any little flow that existed in what the teacher was doing. The textbooks are handed out – with the customary messing about. The teacher tells them to read from a certain page, mentioning a couple of paragraphs. There is much negotiation about who should read – when finally names are decided upon, other children are not happy and intervene while the nominated children are reading. The reading is seemingly completely without meaning for the children, but again my presence is superfluous, as it seems to be with all 'central' activity i.e. activity focused upon a central focus, whether that be child or teacher. To break into such activity would be intrusive and counter-productive.

Throughout all this is the question, should I intervene by raising my voice and taking a higher profile, rather than merely supporting. To do so would undermine rather than support and would be de-skilling for this young teacher. Such team teaching would have to have been well planned in advance, with agreed aims and methods.

Following the reading out loud, the children have to copy a paragraph of the book and then explain it in their own words, then answer some questions on the same page. This is done with the usual disorganisation and messing around. I go round asking the pupils to explain in their own words, but they can't. What they write is merely a reorganisation of the words in the textbook, if indeed they have written anything at all. They are unable to answer the accompanying questions e.g. what four things are necessary for plants to photosynthesise – answer from one girl: 'black card and fluid'. Again, I wonder what I can be doing in this situation to support these children; they have no understanding at all of what they are supposed to be doing. They know that they merely have to go through certain processes, produce an answer, have something written in their books. My 'support' is merely a means to those simple ends – helping them get the right answer.

Subsequent discussion with the teacher is a rather hurried exchange before the next class comes in. She is embarrassed by the clear failure of the lesson to achieve any aims which could be called educational, and I spend most of my energy trying to convince her that I am not being judgemental, but that I am interested in how support can best work. I can sympathise with teachers who dread this kind of hurried exchange: the defensiveness, the lack of understanding, the perceived intrusion. To explain what one really wants to do would take hours and only minutes are available.

Talking subsequently with the head of support and (coincidentally) the head of chemistry, we decide that the only meaningful kind of support in this situation is one of shared teaching, and that next week's session will begin with planning for shared teaching in a subsequent session.

After this session I go to help support a group of slower first-year children taking French. French is taught in 'non-random mixed ability' with a group of slower children in their own class. These children, though, follow the same work as the others in the year group, i.e. they have the same textbooks, not completing all of the exercises. There is one classroom assistant helping already.

There are about fifteen children in the class and I sit (randomly – again, the teacher doesn't have any specific preferences about whom I should support) next to John. It's oral French at a very simple level, but even at this level (I have 'O' level French!) I find it difficult to keep up with the conversation. Some of the children are coping, some clearly are not. The atmosphere in this class is much calmer and more workmanlike, though. The teacher is more experienced and more confident, the children more docile. The differentiation of the secondary curriculum must create considerable problems for the support teacher. They cannot hope to be sufficiently knowledgeable to cope with even first-year work in specialist subjects where syllabuses will reflect very different content from their own schooldays.

Here again I find it difficult to know what to do in this 'centrally' organised activity. The teacher is working with the whole class, asking them questions in French. How do I help the boy I'm sitting next to without seriously disturbing the flow and the sequence of the teacher's work. I'm also having difficulty in keeping up with it. As with the previous session, my support is limited to simply helping with the mechanics of the session – in this case giving the child the correct answer, when the class is asked a question. This oral French continues for fifteen minutes or so and I feel redundant. The teacher then moves on to working from a textbook, again with the whole class and the same problems occur for me, mainly because of the whole-class, centrally directed nature of things. This continues for another 20 minutes or so, and then the children move onto working in their exercise books, doing an exercise based on the previous class activity. There is more opportunity for support truly to operate in this situation, and I wander around looking for children who appear to need help. Again the nature of the curriculum and the nature of the tasks being undertaken is problematic. 'Support' in this situation, where the children have a limited time to complete a task (filling the appropriate word in the blank space in sentences) essentially means telling the children the answer, or, hardly better, giving them such gross clues that they cannot fail. The task seems meaningless and my support equally so.

My relationship with this teacher is rather easier as she is more confident. She spontaneously comes over to me to explain in more detail what she is doing, the aims of this session, and how this class and activity fit in with this year group and the wider curriculum.

Discussion with the classroom assistant as we are going out reveals the same problems as I have been sensing: not knowing who to help, how to help them, when to intervene, whether one might be intruding. Differences between staff are seen to be all important. She finds it extremely difficult supporting some staff: one teacher simply asks children to copy from books, and here her support, she feels, is totally wasted.

3 May   I make my way to Xanthe's class again, a little late, having been talking to the head of support. I haven't spoken in detail to Xanthe yet about the team teaching idea. Last week's meeting with her was too tense to broach the topic. It was taken with establishing confidence. When I come in this week the situation seems rather similar. Xanthe is taking the class from the front and the children are messing around as they were last week. Xanthe holds up a small glass tank with a funnel upside down over something (a small plant, I think) and compares it with another similar set of objects. The children have to compare the two sets and say how they are different:

C: There's more water in that one.
C: One's all dirty – yeugh.

The session is to show that carbon dioxide is taken up by plants:

C: That dirt's carbon dioxide!

Explanations are again punctuated with inconsequential intrusions:

C: Anyone got a rubber!

These become so intrusive that Xanthe eventually loses her temper and raises her voice. This has some effect on the children, who temporarily quieten down. She capitalises on this by saying

T: Right we'll have two minutes of complete silence – not a word.

The children respond to this: it's the first clear instruction they have had; they are clear about the rules and what is expected of them. Again I feel redundant – not only redundant, but worse that I am compounding the situation by my presence, and perhaps that Pauline the ancillary is in a similar position. She must feel some degree of inhibition about doing what comes naturally to her to quell the sorts of problems that she is experiencing. Again, there is no way that I feel I can intervene in the immediate situation without making things worse. I am also slightly concerned that if we ultimately move to team teaching I am losing credibility by being associated with this degree of control.

Eventually the explanation is complete and the children are told what they have to do with their own glass containers. A few begin to do it. Some conspicuously, or not so conspicuously, do not. I make my way to a boy who has not associated himself with any group, and has begun no work. He is drawing pictures of cars. He says that he cannot start as he hasn't got his book. 'Miss' is engaged elsewhere and ought not to be disturbed to get the book. Would she have it anyway? This boy seems quite happy in the knowledge that he will not have to do, nor will he be pestered to do the work in hand. His answers about the experiment are monosyllabic. The explanation wasn't sufficient, clearly, and I am left wondering, again, where I should begin given the nature of the work and the children's difficulties understanding it.

The noise level rises and children generally seem to be only very peripherally concerned with the task in hand. They have to draw the two sets of apparatus, and say how they look different. The task seems meaningless. About 50 per cent of the children have drawn something; the others are making no attempt to start, are chatting, walking round the class or occasionally shouting something out. There doesn't seem to be anyone particularly in need of help, though certain of the children clearly are demanding more of the teacher's attention, and they are getting it. Asking them what they understand of the task in hand, the answers are very similar to last week's, limited to procedural comments, or a rehashing of the answers made earlier: the water's dirty; there's more water in this one. My responses can also only be procedural, given the inappropriateness of the task for this group. They are nowhere near understanding what is going on, neither do they care. My comments are of the variety: do you know what to do? How are they different? Have you drawn anything yet? The children's responses last for only as long as I am present. I feel more acutely the inappropriateness of this kind of support and the support which the ancillary is providing. It can only be meaningful if I can share with the teacher some ideas about what tasks are useful and meaningful for these children, if we have joint planning about the teaching objectives and content.

The children are drawn together for an unsatisfactory account of what they have been doing. There is then, out of sequence, a reminder of what they had been doing last week (photosynthesis) and an instruction to go and get their test tubes from the window-ledge. This a few of the groups manage to do. They are asked what colour the tubes have gone. A variety of answers is proffered. Again no rules for answering; kids shout out and are attended to almost irrespective of the nature of the contribution. It is unclear at the end of the explanation why some of the jars should have changed colour. They are told to draw the jars and say why they have changed colour. I go to help the group of four children who are nearest to me; this seems to be as good a criterion as any for identifying children who need help. In fact one or two of them seem to be coping at the 'process' level: one girl has in fact drawn quite a neat diagram of the jars. Questioning them, though, reveals that they have no idea at all of why there has been a change of colour. Even the single words – photosynthesis, carbon dioxide, etc. – have disappeared from last week.

The children are stopped again and drawn together. Most have done very little. My support has been peripheral, and procedural, only serving very transitorily to focus the children's attention as I talk to them. The focus is now the teacher again, though the inconsequential intrusions are if anything worse than before and begin to be slightly personal about the teacher. She shouts at them again and demands five minutes' silence. They comply for about a minute but then following 'operant coughs' and sighs one or two of them begin to make comments, ostensibly directed to the teacher at this stage. She responds in a fairly good-humoured way, eventually establishing a quiet dialogue with a few children. While this is happening the others gradually begin their banter again and before long the situation is as before. This time, though, they have no direction at all, since this is supposed to be a period of five minutes' silence; it has slid into being nothing. Pauline (the ancillary) and I realise what the original instruction was and keep to this by not intervening at all in the emerging interactions among the children. I feel frustrated at the inability to intervene in this confusion. Again, to do so would only undermine the teacher.

I agree to see Xanthe after school and when I do see her I again emphasise the nature of my interest. I am acting as a support teacher, and am not in any way in any inspectorial capacity. My feelings are that I am not being any meaningful support in the way that I have been operating and that I can only help meaningfully if I talk with her about the nature of the lesson and if we jointly talk about its content and presentation. She is happy with this and we agree to meet before the lesson next week to plan some team teaching.

French. The children are working from the same books. I ask whether the teacher wants me to do anything different from last week. She says no, just help as it seems to be necessary. I sit beside a different boy this week and similar issues arise to those that arose last week: why am I helping this particular child? Why not another? The ancillary is supporting a statemented child, who doesn't appear to be the butt of any teasing because of this from the other children. The lesson goes on mainly in a chalk and talk vein, in French. My help is again limited to merely repeating to the child what the teacher has said; it would be pointless to give the answer, and prompting or more elaborated help seems unproductive for the same reasons as last week – it would interrupt the flow of the teacher's work or her explanations, and I'm not sure in any case whether I can elaborate helpfully even at this simple level of French.

The chalk and talk ends and the children are asked to pair up so that they can ask each other questions, as outlined in the textbook. One child doesn't have a 'pair', so I work with him. The children don't seem to think it odd that there are extra teachers in the classroom and accept this kind of arrangement quite happily. On doing the questions with this boy, who seems to suffer from quite severe eczema, it becomes apparent how difficult this work is for the children in this class. He clearly has very little understanding of what is going on or what is required, as is the case with the previous boy I was helping and indeed seems to be the case with all of the children. Their apparent facility with oral French seems to have come from constant repetition, week after week. The oral French done in chalk and talk at the beginning of this lesson is almost exactly the same as the oral French at the beginning of last week's lesson. We finish this exercise very quickly and then have to find other supplementary activities for the rest of this session while the other pairs are working.

My reflection on this does not suggest to me that team teaching is the obvious and necessary answer to support in this situation. The children are doing the same work as the other children in this year group and it appears to me as a non-specialist that it is being well taught. It is not for me to suggest that the children are achieving very little from these exercises, especially as the national curriculum will demand that all children (Sec 17–19 allowing) do the full curriculum.

I reflect also that some research I have read indicates that the most productive class size (in terms of attainments of children and their engagement) is around 20, which is the size of this class. There appears to be a delicate balance between different factors – teaching style, content, expectations, children – which teachers establish taking into account all these factors; each is dependent on the other and the result is the best possible result with the given constraints. To inject a new factor – such as a support teacher does not necessarily improve the situation – one can only dabble at the edges. The children's understanding of what they are doing in the lesson I'm supporting in at the moment isn't improved, neither is their understanding of why they are doing it. I merely help them through the itinerary, which is perhaps a valid thing to do, but even where I am doing this I have to ask whether this is of benefit. Are they thinking as much if they are helped in this way? Is it stopping them from working more appropriately with a group or with their teacher?

We end the session by lamenting how long it takes children even to learn that *s'il vous plait* means 'please'. Not one of them knew this when asked the question in an unfamiliar format at the end of the lesson.

I finish (after having seen Xanthe after school) by talking to the head of support. He is pleased by the help I am giving and says that it has the most enormous spin-offs for him in terms of the understanding of staff of what he is doing.

10 May Go straight to the lesson and talk to Xanthe before it starts. Clarify that we shall be planning my team teaching this week and I shall be beginning next week. She had assumed that I would be starting this week but I am unhappy with this idea since I feel I need to have a good preparation in hand to establish my authority with the class. I feel that this is crucial given the current situation. While they have no respect for the authority of the teacher they will not take anything else of the lesson in. The content of the lesson is also in need of attention but this can be dealt with relatively simply.

Into the lesson and it starts in much the same way as usual; the kids are relatively ordered (after lunch) when they come in. As soon as there is a full complement though, the banter and noise level begins to start rising.

Xanthe makes no clear signal of the beginning of the lesson, nor does she expect any behaviour (e.g. sitting in seats) before the lesson begins. She engages in quiet informal discussion with a few of the children, encouraging the others to do likewise among themselves. This kind of error is so clear yet it is the kind of point which it is extremely difficult to put over to a colleague, especially when one is ostensibly at least trying to help those *children* who have particular difficulties. I suppose that the only real way is through example and team teaching – again. Team teaching in this situation has a lot of pluses to it.

The session this time is on ecology and the children have been promised that they will go outside, though there is no indication when this will be. The teacher begins by giving an instruction to the class about food chains, which they follow, again by recipe. Most do not realise what they are doing when I talk to them – most are not even following the 'recipe' about the work from the book. They are far more interested in the sexual politics of the class; there is a lot of loud banter between the children. Only one or two of the class do not take part in this. The tasks they are being asked to do are meaningless and they have no framework or system of rules or controls for their own behaviour in the classroom.

Subsequent discussion with Xanthe shows her to be rather embarrassed again, but we agree to proceed with the team teaching.

French and the same problems arise again: who do I sit next to, whom do I help? The lesson follows much the same format, with repeated questions to which they reply in French. As I've said before there is no real way in which one can provide support in this kind of situation. I realise here why I thought the children were so good at French at the beginning of the term: they have identical questions week after week. Of its kind the lesson is good – its just that there is nothing for me to do in the actual lesson, partly because these children are setted already and this teacher has effectively addressed the question of how she will make the curriculum accessible to all children.

There is some activity in the lesson; the children are asked to find a way to a certain place in the town and we have to tell them in French. I take the role of a 'native' like the other children; I realise in doing this how much of a spare part I feel and how out of control I am of my own impression (in the kids' minds), and my own autonomy.

17 May I arrive having prepared material to work with the science class. It is the lunch hour still and I have 20 minutes to talk to Xanthe about the lesson ahead. I show her the materials and she approves. We agree roughly on a running order for the lesson, who will talk first and how we will take over from one another. The plans for this action are not very clearly drawn, yet this must always be the case with support since time for this kind of preparation will always be in the squeezed lunch hour or after school. We take 10 minutes or so discussing this and the rest of the time is taken up in talking with the other members of the science department, in whose area we are sitting. We then go and spend some time looking for appropriate books and jamjars for the lesson. We finally arrive at the classroom and the children begin to come in.

I place myself at the front of the class this week to signal to the children that I am actually sharing the teaching with Xanthe. However, this does not appear to have much effect on their behaviour, probably because I have had little or no chance to establish my credibility over the previous three weeks; I have simply been an adjunct to the teacher – and one that seemed to the children to be insignificant and powerless – because of the in-between situation in which I placed myself, not wanting to undermine or usurp Xanthe's authority. I realise that I need to establish my authority fairly firmly if I am to retain any credibility at all. However, hopes of this are not helped by Xanthe failing to introduce me effectively, and handing out my worksheets at the beginning rather than leaving me to do this, as we had agreed. Not only does she do this, a boring and distracting task, but she accompanies it with the line 'Mr Thomas has done these nice worksheets for us on his computer'. There is laughter, ooohs and then clapping. I smile, but realise that establishing authority now will be an even more difficult task.

As she finishes giving out the worksheets I feel I have to seize the initiative and clear with her that I will say a few words about the sheets. This is in any case necessary since they have been inadequately explained. My main purpose, though, is in making clear to the class who I am and what I intend them to do, and also the fashion in which I intend them to behave. I first say to them that they must put up their hands when they wish to talk to me and a few other rules of classroom conduct. There is some banter, but I make it clear that I will expect these rules to be followed. To my surprise, order is established relatively quickly, though there are a lot of questions about who I am – 'Are you the new head-master?' 'Are you a student?' When I tell them that I am a teacher who is helping and that I am with the support department and Mr Fairfax, there is a telling question: 'Does that mean that you can't control the class?' I make it clear that it doesn't. I give them a task to do before we go outside to look in a wall, and they complete this relatively quickly and without any com-plaints about the work being too easy. The work I would put at third year junior level and these are third year secondary. Clearly they don't mind *how* easy the work is. Far better to err on the easy side than the difficult.

The centre of control moves back to Xanthe as I finish my talk and the fragile nature of control and sharing of control becomes more clear as the carefully established rules of conduct I have established are immediately neglected and violated by Xanthe. It is surprising how quickly the children perceive this and how quickly the control collapses as she takes over. This is quite dispiriting. The children are broken into two groups and we go outside with them, each group to look at a different hedge. My group is a nice group of children, who become even nicer when in a small group such as this. We look for animals in the hedge, though they are unpractised in this kind of task and find the interpersonal mechanics of the group far more interesting than the mini-creatures on the wall.

We make our way back to the class and Pauline (the ancillary) is there. She joins us as they haphazardly come back into the class. Control is again my main concern as this happens. It is going to be even more difficult to communicate with them as a group, Xanthe's group seeming rather high having come back from the field. I try to reestablish the rules set earlier, and manage this with rather more difficulty this time. The kids are milling and find some group support in this. Eventually they settle. There are only a few minutes left and the lesson ends rather scrappily, probably mainly because of the lack of clear authority or chain of command between Xanthe and me. She is in command, in theory, so I leave her to finish the lesson – to mark its end – though I would have been happier doing it myself. This kind of event – getting them in and getting them out – will have to be made clearer next time.

I go to the next session; this week I can't go to French (or at least it will not be very useful if I do) because they are doing a test. Mr Fairfax tells me that it will be useful if I go to geography with the 4th years instead but when I find my way there the teacher does not arrive for reasons that are not understood (by anyone). After five or ten minutes another teacher stems the breach and takes the class as a holding operation. I decide that it will be more fruitful if I use this time to discuss the session previously with Xanthe. On arriving she is discussing something else with a local policeman and with Pauline. After some polite chit-chat we get to talking about the session. She clearly feels it went well, though the impression she is giving is that the session has enabled her to split into groups and management is easier from this point of view. My feeling, though I do not say this, is that the session has gone rather better because I have established at least some authority in the session and the children are at least doing tasks of which they are capable and they know what they are supposed to be doing. We decide to continue with similar work next week and that I will continue to produce worksheets.

Subsequent discussion with Mr Fairfax indicates that he has been in similar situations to me. He has felt that impotence when a teacher is struggling and you know that to intervene will undermine. He describes a situation with a young teacher who was having problems with a class, and with whom he is providing support. He notes exactly the same situation as I have: that in which to assume a degree of authority with the class will take away from the confidence of the teacher – he describes it as a vicious rather than a virtuous circle.

26 May   First I talk to Mr Fairfax (head of support) who tells me about the teacher he wants me to go in with this week after science. He is an experienced teacher with a bottom set of 4th years doing geography.

I then go to talk to Xanthe about this week's work. She tells me, before the lesson starts, that she has been having trouble with one of the girls in the class, Jane. She had been asserting her authority with the children and had sent two of them to the year tutor; after that they had been fine. However, at the end of the last lesson, Jane had spilt a jar of water and had been told by Xanthe to wipe it up. She told her to get her a cloth. When she refused and there was a clash of wills, she went over to her and repeated her request. Jane then hit Xanthe in the arm; she was now excluded from science. Xanthe was clearly upset about this and wanted to talk about it. I tried to make it clear that I thought that she was correct in what she did. She needed to make it clear to Jane that she was in charge; I said that I thought it would be tantamount to blackmail if she gave in because of any implied threat, violent or not, against her. She seemed reassured by this.

The children started to come in, in a rather more orderly way than in previous weeks. This may have been a reflection of my presence (though I doubt it since my status has clearly been established) or possibly a reflection of Xanthe's stance against miscreant children over the last week. On reflection though, they often do come in fairly quietly. It is only over the lesson that the disorder builds. I again position myself at the front and try in a way not to associate myself with Xanthe's rather ineffectual attempts at establishing control. I look into the distance and try to keep a straight face at the banter which is going on. Xanthe switches from an authority voice to engage in pleasant, mild banter with one or two children, losing any control which she had with the whole class. Is this appropriate support from me – to look into the distance? Surely I should be coming in with banter with Xanthe to show that we can support and work with one another. Again I feel ambiguity about how to support. Will this undermine her? Probably not – we now have a clear enough relationship for me to be able to do this kind of thing. However, there is still uncertainty about who is to be doing what. We've only had a short time to prepare this session together and in any case the lessons don't reflect the preparation, if last week's was anything to go by. After some rather loud, and ineffective commands from Xanthe she passes over to me and I again try to make it clear that I expect that rules will be followed when I am talking to the class. I suspect that I shall need to do this each week. Even with this fairly simple exercise, though, I wonder about the effect this will have on Xanthe. The fact that I am asserting that there shall be no shouting out and that they shall always put up their hands if they have anything to say to me contrast sharply with Xanthe's method of management. Will she learn by example, or will she feel that she cannot use methods such as this?

I talk to them about their worksheets and they listen attentively, eventually. I wonder here whether the support teacher can achieve any status with the group, given that s/he is always an adjunct to the status of the existing classteacher. This is in addition to the problems noted last week (Support teacher – that means you can't control the class, doesn't it). The answer is that you probably can achieve status, but at a cost – in terms of your own energy, and the time you have to devote each session to establishing the rules and also in terms of the cost of the possible injury done to the ego of the person you are teaching with.

I hand over to Xanthe to make the arrangements for going out to the pond, this week's exercise. I have again prepared worksheets and I have discussed these briefly with the children. Rather haphazardly we go out to the pond and the children make notes while we are there. The exercise seems a little pointless once we are there; they have seen all they are going to see within a few minutes.

We go back to class (my group, for they are split into two groups, Xanthe's and mine) and get on with the worksheets that I have given them. They do it well, though I realise that I have gone over the top in making things easy for them. While one or two cannot do the sheet, most can do it easily and for one or two of the brighter ones it seems a bit of an insult. Xanthe's group then come back, straggling in and disturbing whatever continuity already existed in my group. Order goes, and there are only three or four minutes before the lesson change. I can't begin the worksheet with the new group. Xanthe notionally takes over, but doesn't make it clear to the kids that she is doing so. The last few minutes are a little straggly.

At the end, we have to part fairly rapidly since I am to go to geography. We exchange a few words and I say that I will be in touch before my next visit since I will not now be in for two weeks.

I go to the geography class and talk to David, an experienced teacher – seems rather tense; who can blame him? He has one of the most difficult classes in the school to take, and here am I, an unfamiliar colleague, going to be in the classroom with him. He briefly tells me something about the lesson and the children before the lesson starts. He asks me to simply help as and where it appears to be necessary, but signals to me where the help is most necessary.

The kids come in, looking fed up. They are not disruptive; they just look bored. Their movements indicate weariness and resentment – sullen. They do not overtly do anything outwardly naughty, but bang into furniture and loudly drag out and position their chairs. They call to one another.

David's voice of control is rather shrill and forced. The kids are presumably not relaxed by it. It is more of a shout than anything else. I sit and again try to appear fairly stern – I want to maintain some kind of distance at this stage. David introduces me as a member of the support department, and the mention of support invokes a snort from at least one child.

David begins the lesson, which is about the development of towns along different lines of communication over the last one or two hundred years. I am surprised by how attentive many of the children are. There is only one group of girls who are being a nuisance, talking over the teacher. He deals with this by loudly and shrilly drawing attention to them – the impression is that it is almost manic. He is far from being relaxed and my presence probably is not helping. Most of the opening session is from the front and here again the problems of how to support from the front are replicated. Eventually, the kids are expected to do things on their own in their books. Here I walk around and help them with their work. It is in fact much easier in this lesson since the work is correctly pitched for most of them and they know what they are supposed to be doing and why they are supposed to be doing it. Every so often the individual work is punctuated by the teacher's instructions and here I have to stop and listen. I try to park myself near the girls' group when this happens so that I can focus their attention on the work in hand. This is less effective than it might be, since I have had no opportunity to establish my authority with them and my mere presence does not help them to focus.

The kids are kept working fairly hard in this way (mixture of classteaching followed by individual assignments and copying from the OHP), though there is not much for me to do when this happens. I help those who David flagged to me as in most need of help, though to me it is not that obvious that it is this group who is most in need of support. They seem to be getting on OK, or at least no worse than anyone else. Those who need most support (of whatever kind) are the three girls, who are not concentrating at all, are talking and shouting at one another, and doodling in their books. Raises questions about the nature of what is 'special': here, where the work is fairly appropriate, the most special needs are those of the girls, even though they are among the brightest. The three girls are kept back at the end and an admonition given to them, but the threat of having to stay behind and do more work is not kept to.

Afterwards I talk to David about what we will do next session and feel that there is some genuine attempt to include me in the discussion; but even though I am more competent in geography I wonder about the value of my contribution to this debate. The talk is about the content of the lesson, not the way in which I provide support. While the content is important, I feel that our working relationship together should be higher up the agenda. At least we have more time to talk here since the school day has now finished – David is very keen and doesn't seem rushed to be on his way home. There is time to talk.

14 June I get to science and find that Xanthe has produced some quite nice worksheets for the kids to work from. I wonder whether this has been my influence. Pauline is also there. First Xanthe asks Pauline and me to sort the worksheets into three piles for the kids to work from. Although the task is mundane, I'm glad Xanthe has had the confidence to ask me to do it. The kids drift in as usual, with the usual loud banter among them. I have a quick word with Xanthe about returning some work that I've marked and say that it's probably best if I leave it until the end. She quickly explains to the kids what they have to be doing. She very cursorily explains the terms 'habitat' and 'species', almost as though she were reminding a group of Masters degree students of some very simple terms. These kids need this sort of terminology explained in several different ways; and they need to do something to understand these words. She explains that they have to go to a habitat (same theme as in recent weeks) and count the number of species they find there. They also have to estimate the total number of animals/plants in that particular habitat. Although Xanthe is clearer in her instructions (about behaviour – e.g. waiting for them to be quiet) this week (and I again wonder if this has been my influence – perhaps there has been a modelling effect from my teaching the class) the instructions are quite perfunctorily given and the kids are unsure about what they are supposed to be doing. She then asks me if I want to give feedback on the children's marked work; I'd said earlier that I thought this would be best left till the end, rather than break into the flow of what she was doing. This again points to a problem of sharing the teaching: if there is any kind of differentiation in tasks, coordination needs to be good to prevent this kind of break in flow occurring. I repeat that it's better left until the end. Xanthe then gets the kids into groups by pointing numbers at them. They aren't attending when she does this; she tells them to get up to go out and tells them to get into their groups. After having been told, they don't know which groups to go into. There is much milling around and much of 'Miss, which group am I in?' A minute or so of chaos convince Xanthe that she'll have to start again and get the kids into new groups; even this she does very superficially.

We eventually move outside and my group follows me down to the field. They deliberately confuse me when I ask for advice on which field we should go to, but we eventually get to the field we were supposed to be going to (I think). We sit down and start to work on the questions on the worksheet. Problems immediately become evident; the task is rather difficult for the children, though it is a good one for the time allotted (finding species and estimating the total number in the habitat); they need total help with it though – they can't manage on their own. We (I) work out that there are 250 million grass plants in the field, something I find amazing, but the kids don't even pass comment. Are they so switched off by school that they affect boredom at *everything*? We go back and the problems of interweaving with another teacher (and ancillary) again come into play: since we've been in groups this time the new groups as they are coming in disrupt everything that's going on with the other groups (though I can't pretend there was very much 'flow' going with mine).

21 June I begin today by attending a meeting with the staff and myself which Mr Fairfax has arranged. Sixteen or so people are present to talk about support. Mr Fairfax has billed this as me sharing my thoughts with the rest of the staff on my experiences at this school and a seminar has been arranged during lunchtime for the benefit of any staff who want to come. It's a good turnout.

I first of all talk about my experiences at the school and we then go on to a freer discussion about how support should operate. I make a number of points which are based on my diary and invite questions and discussion about them. I start by talking about how to target those in need of help – particularly if the organisation of the year groups is by setting and there is therefore a fairly homogeneous group of children in each set – and there are assenting nods from those who provide support in the school, notably Mr Fairfax and his colleague and from the two ancillary helpers. I talk about knowing *what* to do when the classteacher is giving the formal part of the lesson. I then go on to talk about how to provide the help and the problems of achieving status among the children when you are a support member. I talk about the difficulties in being primarily a supporter of children and moving to a situation in which one is a supporter of the teacher, collaborating in achieving targets, observing, changing roles, etc. I talk about the difficulties in finding time for this change in role. This all provokes a wide-ranging discussion.

The first point that is made is about the person who is giving the support; the point is made that in this school support is principally given by the ancillary helpers. They say that for the ancillary it is not possible to be more of a support to the teacher, although it clearly depends on personalities. This develops into a more wide-ranging discussion about LMS and the possible effects on special needs.

The point I made about the difficulty in knowing who to help is taken up by one or two members of staff who make the point that there is in fact quite a bit of difference between the children in the class. To them it is quite evident who should be helped. I say that this is not my experience, though it does seem to be the case that there are some children in each of the lowest sets who are capable of a great deal more than the others.

On the more interesting point of the way in which people interact next to one another the consensus seems to be that this is very much a matter of personalities and teaching styles. In some classes those who are supporting find it easy to team teach and work alongside colleagues; in others it is merely a matter of giving procedural advice to the children.

After some additional exchanges about the value of mixed ability teaching/GCSE for all/NC for all, Mr Fairfax brings the subject back to support and I suggest that there are considerable difficulties keeping up with the lesson, albeit at a very simple level. The teachers say that they had not appreciated that this would be the case, precisely because the lessons were so simple. They hadn't noticed any look of puzzlement or discomfiture from me. Perhaps this is testament to the ten school years of learned strategies in coping with confusion and puzzlement in lessons which were too hard or badly explained; all of us perhaps learn to look inconspicuous – or develop more disruptive strategies for coping. Whatever, one of the support ancillary staff comes up to me after the talk and says how much she appreciates what I was saying – that teachers don't realise that you (as support staff) don't know or understand the lesson, and that if this is the case, how much worse is it for the kids.

The Deputy Head also catches me after the meeting and continues with a theme I had begun to develop in the meeting: the need for team teaching as an appropriate solution to the tensions that I had been talking about and the need for it to be based in adequate time for preparation and evaluation. She says that with LMS it is unlikely or impossible that such time will be available and points to the likely scenario of support teachers increasingly being replaced by ancillaries. There isn't time now to develop this with her.

I then go down to science, where Xanthe is already with the kids. The start of the lesson is characteristically straggly. She has decided that the lesson will continue to be on habitats and gives them a brief, unsatisfactory talk on what they are to be doing in this session. There is no clear guidance; I am confused and the kids certainly are. This added confusion between us is perhaps compounded by the fact that we missed our preparation time because I was giving my talk to the staff. Pauline (ancillary helper) is also confused, though she says nothing. Kids are put into groups, and then have to be reallocated because none of them got the message first time round. We go out, me with my small group of five kids. They are very boisterous and it is more difficult to control them (for me) in this situation than in the classroom. The problems of status again come through louder than ever here outside on the field and some of the points made in the meeting are echoed for me. The kids are in the set of messing around for this session; a support member of staff has no status which enables him or her to intervene in this.

On return to the class (from the field) the kids come in aimlessly. The feeling is of aimlessness for me also. What will the kids be doing next; there is only about five minutes left to the lesson. Xanthe arrives with some kids and then Pauline with hers; there's a great deal of loud banter among the kids which is ineffectually dealt with by Xanthe. She raises her voice and doesn't follow through with any of her threats. She doesn't wait for the kids' attention before moving on.

On to geography. I see David who catches me at the beginning to go over some of the points I raised at the meeting. Again he raises the point that there are children in his class who are significantly below the level of the others in literacy and that they need extra help. He also makes the point that it is extremely valuable having someone else competent in the classroom, not for any "high falutin' academic reasons" but simply to assist with simple routine matters because the teacher can't be in two places at once. What he is saying seems to reinforce the point made by the Dep Head at the end of the meeting: the support that one offers is appreciated more as an extra pair of hands than as a skilled teacher; and I suppose reflecting on this it makes sense and is also in keeping with the ethos of Warnock and the 1981 Act – in a specialist lesson, one isn't being a skilled subject specialist, one is providing procedural help to children and as often as not administrative and procedural help to the teacher. As such a competent ancillary is as effective as a trained support teacher; indeed may be more effective. It may mean that there are fewer tensions in the class, less ambiguity about who should be doing what. And if the point I made in the meeting is indeed correct – that team teaching is impossible without adequate preparation time, this may indeed be the appropriate solution for support.

The kids come in and the class as usual has to be rearranged into groups from rows. The kids do this characteristically noisily, making as much scraping noise and banging as possible. Not the best way to start a lesson. However I'm in a supporting role – not an inspectorial one – so how can I mention this kind of simple management point? With another teacher it may be possible, but not with David, who is fairly highly strung and rather defensive. It would take quite a time to build trust and teamwork before this kind of point could be made. One would need to negotiate a working arrangement whereby the two teachers agreed to monitor each other's work and provide feedback for instance on management methods.

The lesson starts, and kids come in rather in dribs and drabs, and affecting total boredom. David gives instructions to the lesson but although he is crisper than Xanthe and far better prepared, he is perhaps too much so and expects too much of the children. He is perhaps affected here by GCSE expectations on these children and wants to push them on too much. He is perhaps too conscientious. He repeats that he came from work in a 6th form college, and makes it clear that he is unused to this kind of work. He talks to them for a short while and I listen. They then move to working on their own on mapwork of the local district, incorporating questionnaire data from schoolfriends about where they live. There are indeed, as David had suggested, vast differences in their ability to cope with this material. Most of the class can manage and a few, perhaps four or five who are finding the concepts associated with the instructions very difficult, e.g. the number of degrees in a circle, using a protractor, etc. For these, almost total help is necessary and I'm surprised to find that when total help is provided some of the most difficult kids in the class become easy to manage. These kids seem to have a respect for me which I haven't noticed them expressing or showing to David, maybe because when he was out last week I managed to talk to them in a fairly matter of fact way without raising my voice, by treating them as adults and talking to them as though they commanded the respect that adults would command. Whatever the reason, they respond well when I help them today. I note some interesting strategies when I go round to them to help. Those kids who have most difficulty (in this case in drawing a pie graph) survive by making up the answer (and why not!) or simply by copying. Their estimates of the pie graph size seem to be almost as accurate as those that have been calculated.

I'm left in charge of the class for a while and have a strange feeling of freedom. Immediately I'm able to address the whole class as well as addressing individuals; again the question of establishing working rules from the outset with the person you're working with is highlighted; once other rules are got into, it must be very difficult to get out of them; they become an established norm. This perhaps also brings into play the whole question of a whole-school policy for special needs and whether it should be stated at the outset that the support teacher is there to support the teacher as well as the children. This would put on the agenda at the outset the issue of establishing ground rules for collaborative work. My (our) rules in this situation are rapidly developing into teacher up-front, me as the assistant, only taking the up-front role when the teacher is out of the classroom. But this leads me onto another reflection: is it possible to go into a whole set of classrooms, each with a different subject being studied, and be knowledgeable enough in each to enable one to team teach effectively in each situation. I doubt it.

The lesson ends in the usual way – rather scrappily and with much shouting from David to those who haven't finished their work. The kids go out sulkily and noisily. We talk about next week, when we will be taking them out to do a survey of shop use in the town. I ask whether the kids will be able to do as he is suggesting or whether it will be too much; David is confident that they will be able to cope. He reaffirms how useful it is having me around and we talk about some of the kids. He remarks on how well behaved some of them have been this week and I comment on one particular girl who I have helped and comment on the contrast between this girl's demeanour when she is left to her own devices, and when she is helped. When she had undivided attention from me she was pleasant and well mannered and receptive to suggestions; if left to her own devices (partly because she couldn't cope with the work) she was the most loud-mouthed and disruptive member of the class. David confirms this. I feel here, though I don't say it to David, that my input may have had some influence on how receptive the kids have been today – and not just in being an extra pair of hands but also in having treated the kids more like adults.

20 June   Arrive at school late this week because I'm caught up with some American visitors; I've told Xanthe that I'll probably miss most of her lesson – in fact miss all of it.

Arrive for David's lesson, a couple of minutes late, with the kids. David isn't there when I arrive but comes in half a minute after me, looking a little harassed and carrying the equipment for the field trip. He gives out the materials, maps and clip boards, and gives the kids some instructions on what to do. This is rather perfunctory and is peppered with loud rebukes to children for either not listening or for interrupting. The kids aren't being attentive. Half are told to walk down one side of the street and half down the other then to cross over at the bottom of the road and come back marking the uses of the shops. Again this seems ambitious to me, even with a group of totally compliant children. I'm not even sure if I could do it, let alone the kids. Too late to change now though. They get sent out and I follow with David. He wonders whether he should have sent them in a crocodile, but decides that with fourth years that would be absurd. On crossing the road, all of the kids have cut a corner across a field and he calls them back to walk across the road so they won't miss any of the shops – this in fact seems unimportant to me since there aren't many shops at the top of the High St (it turns out later that in fact there aren't any). This highlights for me another problem of team teaching and support – that of the personality clash. In our case it's not so much of a clash as a mismatch, though if I pushed it it would be a clash. In this situation, I'd be far more laid back about what the kids were doing, especially in view of the time constraints, which I seem to feel more acutely than David. Can I say to him 'Oh it doesn't matter' (which is what I want to say) if the kids are cutting this corner. I don't think he'd react to it well. I'm supposed to be supporting him, not directing him. It's up to him to set the direction and for me to support him in having taken it. This aspect of management could, I suppose, be shared if colleagues knew each other well enough and if they trusted each other enough. In this situation, though, I feel unable to intervene. Perhaps I should have done. We walk around the corner and half way down the hill without coming across any children. David is giving me his philosophy on education for lower-achieving children. He thinks it is unrealistic to expect these children to do the GCSE course that they are doing, given that they have to undertake the same work as the other children. I suggest that we walk down on different sides of the road to help kids as we are going along, but David thinks we ought to go down together and meet them at the end. It's almost as though he himself wants the support; this would seem to be an ideal chance to use an extra person effectively, where there is perhaps more opportunity for the kids to get lost or confused.

We come across two of the more docile girls who are actually trying to do the task in hand, but have no idea what they are supposed to be doing. David begins to help them. I feel rather redundant and indicate to David that I will go off and find kids who are having difficulty. There are two boys (again two of the more docile ones) who are confused about what to do and I put them straight. Time is getting short and I move on down the hill without coming across any other kids. Then at the bottom where they have been told to wait there is a cluster of children. I go up to them and ask them what they have done; almost without exception (there are seven or eight children there) they have done nothing. They protest that they didn't know what to do, and one has in fact done something but not as directed, indicating that perhaps the directions weren't as clear as they might have been. I tell them to set off again, having given some additional directions to them. They set off up the hill and meet David coming down, who stops them again and gives them a new set of directions. One of the boys in fact says 'It's too difficult to do in 20 minutes – we'd need all day to do this properly!' My sentiments also. However, David protests that if they had listened to the instructions and had concentrated on their trip down the hill, they could have done it in the allotted time. I doubt it very much. He sends some of the slower boys across the road with a totally new set of directions: to count the cars in the car parks. I follow them for a while to make sure they're on the right track and then set off up the hill after David who is now sans kids and following them up. Time is very short; there's only five minutes or so to get back to school. More ideas from David on how difficult it is to achieve anything with these kids. Asks me for my advice on how to work with them. I say that it is very difficult when you're following a syllabus to tailor-make the work for the kids, though I must confess I feel out of my depth here – would a GCSE board allow different kinds of work from these kids? It might well be possible, I feel, though clearly a simpler piece of work wouldn't be graded as highly. I say to him that in retrospect (though in fact I had said it before) a simpler task would have been more appropriate and that the task should have been much shorter (i.e. a much smaller section of the map) for the time allowed. There is clearly a role here for the support teacher to negotiate on curricular issues with the mainstream teacher, but the lesson seems to be that the mainstream teacher has to initiate it. When we get back to the classroom we find that all of the children bar three have arrived back already, left their work and gone – they have to catch the bus at 10 past and it's already 5 past. Three haven't arrived back, however. We go to look at the work which has been left and it is fairly uniformly of very poor quality: they haven't followed instructions; many of them have nothing at all marked on the map, and those that have only have an indecipherable scrawl. I can't blame the kids entirely. David is looking dejected by this and I try to offer some support. The most constructive thing I can think of to say to him is 'You try too hard, David', and there is some truth in this. Materially and in terms of preparation this lesson was fine; the problems came in unrealistic expectations in terms of speed of work and intellectual grasp on the topic in hand.

I offer to go and look for the missing kids but David feels he ought to; I say that I'll hang on here in case they turn up. After 10 minutes or so they haven't. I go down to see whether there are any other developments and meet Mr Fairfax.

I tell Mr Fairfax that this lesson was something of a washout, and seeing that I'm looking less than totally happy and somewhat dispirited and disillusioned, he is extremely supportive of me. We talk over some of the irreconcilable issues to do with support and talk again over the seminar which I gave last week, which he said had been extremely valuable in opening up staff to new ideas. I recount this afternoon's experiences and he sympathises, saying that David's commitment was undoubted but that his feelings about the lower-achieving pupils were of long standing and that it was clearly an attitude transformation which was necessary if there were to be any development here.

I go back to the geography room with Mr Fairfax and see David on the way. The kids took themselves straight to the bus and got on without reporting back. David less than amused.

GLOSSARY

Attribution In short, attribution theory suggests that we attribute events either to personal causes (dispositional attributions) or situational causes. If a man falls off a scaffold, is this attributed to the fact that he's a silly fool (dispositional attribution) or to inadequate safety procedures (situational attribution)?

Construct A way of viewing the world. The construct is rather like a template that we put in front of our eyes: it cuts off bits that we don't want to see and it forces us to see a new experience in terms of a 'shape' we have established on the basis of our past experience. Kelly suggests that constructs are bi-polar (i.e. they have two ends). We might, for instance, have a construct by which we view teachers; such a construct might be 'good teacher versus bad teacher'. When we meet teachers we will fit them somewhere onto this continuum.

Emergent process The idea that things emerge out of teams rather than being laid out clearly and once-and-for-all at the outset. Thus, role *emerges* from the understandings of the team participants.

Heterogeneous team A team comprising people from more than one group. Thus, a team comprising a teacher and an ancillary is a heterogeneous team.

Homogeneous team A team comprising people from one professional group only. In classroom teams this means a team of two or more teachers.

Meta-analysis An analysis of many other pieces of research all relating to the same issue. Thus, someone may look at 100 pieces of research into the effectiveness of parental involvement to see what conclusions can be drawn.

Schema Defined by Deaux and Wrightsman as 'an organised configuration of knowledge derived from past experience which we use to interpret our current experience' (1988: 105). In other words, it's a way of 'chunking' or categorising our experience. When we come across new

228

experiences in the shape of people, events or whatever, for convenience we put them into a category which we already have created on the basis of other experiences. We may, for instance, say that a person is 'friendly'. As we get to know a person better, we may say that he or she is 'territorial', 'neurotic' or 'helpful'. In short, a schema is a means of organising experience.

Schemata   Plural of schema.

Synergy   The idea that a good team creates an energy in and of itself. The set of people working as a team is able to do more than the set of people working individually could do. The whole is more than the sum of its parts.

Transformation   The idea that even if someone does prescribe what a role should be at the outset, this will inevitably be transformed by the team participants. The way in which the transformation occurs will depend on the views and experiences of the participants.

REFERENCES

Adair, J. (1986) *Effective Team Building*, Aldershot: Gower.

Arikado, M.S. and Musella, D.F. (1973) 'Status variables related to team teacher satisfaction in the open plan school', paper presented at the American Educational Research Association, New Orleans, USA (ERIC, ED 076 562).

Atkin, J. and Bastiani, J. (1985) *Preparing Teachers to Work with Parents: A Survey of Initial Training*, Nottingham: Nottingham University School of Education.

Bannister, D. and Fransella, F. (1986) *Inquiring Man: The Psychology of Personal Constructs* (3rd edn), Beckenham: Croom Helm.

Bate, P. (1984) 'The impact of organizational culture on approaches to organizational problem solving', *Organization Studies* 5, 1: 43–66.

Beardsley, B., Bricker, K. and Murray, J. (1973) 'Hints for survival in open plan schools', *Curriculum Theory Network* 11: 47–64.

Becker, H.S. (1970) 'Problems of inference and proof in participant observations', in N.K. Denzin *Sociological Methods*, London: Butterworth.

Becker, W.C., Madsen, C.H., Arnold, C.R. and Thomas, D.R. (1967) 'The contingent use of teacher attention and praise in reducing classroom behaviour problems', *Journal of Special Education* 1: 287–307.

Bennett, S.N. (1978) 'Recent research on teaching: a dream, a belief, a model', *British Journal of Educational Psychology* 48: 127–47.

Bennett, S.N., Andrae, J., Hegarty, P. and Wade, P. (1980) *Open Plan Schools*, Slough: NFER.

Bines, H. (1986) *Redefining Remedial Education*, Beckenham: Croom Helm.

Bliss, J., Monk, M. and Ogborn, J. (1983) *Qualitative Data Analysis for Educational Research*, London: Croom Helm.

Bloom, B.S. (1984) 'The search for methods of group instruction as effective as one to one tutoring', *Educational Leadership* May: 4–17.

Borg, W.R. and Gall, M.D. (1983) *Educational Research* (4th edn), New York: Longman.

Brighouse, T.R.P. (1985) 'Parents and the local education authority', in C. Cullingford (ed.) *Parents, Teachers and Schools*, London: Robert Royce.

Bronfenbrenner, U. (1979) *The Ecology of Human Development*, Cambridge, MA: Harvard University Press.

Brophy, J. (1979) 'Advances in teacher research', *Journal of Classroom Interaction* 15, 1: 1–7.

—— (1982) 'Classroom organisation and management', unpublished paper, Michigan State University (ERIC, ED 218257).

Bucklow, M. (1972) 'A new role for the work group', in L.E. Davis and J.C. Taylor (eds) *Design of Jobs*, Harmondsworth: Penguin.

Burgess, R.G. (1984) *In the Field*, London: George Allen and Unwin.

Bush, A., Williams, J. and Morris, S. (1980) 'An activity period for the mentally handicapped', *Occupational Therapy* Sept.: 297–300.

Caudrey, A. (1985) 'Volunteer army steps into the firing line', *Times Educational Supplement* 12 April: 8.

Clift, P., Cleave, S. and Griffin, M. (1980) *The Aims, Role and Deployment of Staff in the Nursery*, Windsor: NFER.

Clifton, R.A. and Rambaran, R. (1987) 'Substitute teaching: survival in a marginal situation', *Urban Education* 22, 3: 310–27.

Cohen, E.G. (1976) 'Problems and prospects of teaming', *Educational Research Quarterly* 1, 2: 49–63.

Cohen, E.G., Meyer, J.W., Scott, W.R. and Deal, T.R. (1979) 'Technology and teaming in the elementary school', *Sociology of Education* 52, Jan.: 20–3.

Cohen, L. and Manion, L. (1985) *Research Methods in Education* (2nd edn), Beckenham: Croom Helm.

Coles, E. and Blunden, R. (1979) *The Establishment and Maintenance of a Ward-based Activity Period within a Mental Handicap Hospital*, Research Report No. 8, Mental Handicap in Wales Applied Research Unit, University College Wales, Cardiff.

Cook, D.T. and Campbell, D.T. (1976) 'The design and conduct of quasi experiments and true experiments in field settings', in M.D. Dunnette *Handbook of Industrial and Organisational Psychology*, Chicago: Rand McNally.

Croll, P. (1986) *Systematic Classroom Observation*, Lewes: Falmer.

Cronbach, L.J. (1982) *Designing Evaluations of Educational and Social Programmes*, San Francisco: Jossey Bass.

—— (1987) 'Issues in planning evaluations', in R. Murphy and H. Torrance (eds) *Evaluating Education: Issues and Methods*, London: Harper and Row.

Cullingford, C. (1984) 'The battle for the schools: attitudes of parents and teachers towards education', *Educational Studies* 10, 2: 113–19.

Cummings, T.G. (1978) 'Self-regulating work groups: a socio-technical synthesis', *Academy of Management Review* 3: 625–34.

Cyster, R., Clift, P. and Battle, S. (1979) *Parental Involvement in Primary Schools*, Windsor: NFER Publishing Co.

Deaux, K. and Wrightsman, L.S. (1988) *Social Psychology*, Pacific Grove, CA.: Brooks Cole.

Denzin, N.K. (1970) *The Research Act in Sociology*, London: Butterworth.

—— (1970a) *Sociological Methods*, London: Butterworth.

Department of Education and Science (1975) *A Language for Life* (The Bullock Report), London: HMSO.

—— (1978) *Special Educational Needs*, Report of the Committee of Enquiry into the Education of Handicapped Children and Young People, Cmnd 7212, London: HMSO

DeVault, M.L., Harnischfeger, A. and Wiley, D.E. (1977) *Curricula, Personnel Resources and Grouping Strategies*. St. Ann, MO.: ML-Group for Policy Studies in Education, Central Midwestern Regional Lab.

Doyle, W. (1977) 'The uses of non-verbal behaviours: toward an ecological view of classrooms', *Merrill-Palmer Quarterly* 23, 3: 179–92.

Drucker, P.F. (1985) 'Getting things done: how to make people decisions', *Harvard Business Review* 63, 4: 22–6.

Eiser, J.R. (1978) 'Interpersonal attributions', in H. Tajfel and C. Fraser (eds) *Introducing Social Psychology*, Harmondsworth: Penguin.

Epstein, J.L. (1985) 'Home and school connections in schools of the future', *Peabody Journal of Education* 62, Winter: 18–41.

—— (1986) "Parents' reactions to teacher practices of parent involvement", *The Elementary School Journal* 86, 3: 277–94.

Escudero, G.R. and Sears, J. (1982) "Teachers' and teacher aides' perceptions of their responsibilities when teaching severely and profoundly handicapped students", *Education and Training of the Mentally Retarded* 17, 3: 190–5.

Ferguson, N. and Adams, M. (1982) 'Assessing the advantages of team teaching in remedial education: the remedial teacher's role', *Remedial Education* 17, 1: 24–30.

Firth, J. (1983) 'Experiencing uncertainty: organisational lessons from the clinic', *Personnel Review* 12, 2: 11–15.

Galton, M.J., Simon, B. and Croll, P. (1980) *Inside the Primary Classroom*, London: Routledge and Kegan Paul.

Gartner, A. and Lipsky, D.K. (1987) 'Beyond special education: toward a quality system for all students', *Harvard Educational Review* 57, 4: 367–395.

Geen, A.G. (1985) 'Team teaching in the secondary schools of England and Wales', *Educational Review* 37, 1: 29–38.

Gill, S.J., Menlo, A. and Keel, L.P. (1984) 'Antecedents to member participation in small groups: a review of theory and research', *Journal of Specialists in Group Work*, 9, 2: 68–76.

Glaser, B.G. and Strauss, A.L. (1967) *The Discovery of Grounded Theory: Strategies for Qualitative Research*, New York: Aldine.

Glowinkowski, S.P. and Cooper, C.L. (1985) 'Current issues in organisational stress research', *Bulletin of the British Psychological Society* 38: 212–16.

Goffman, E. (1961) *Asylums*, Harmondsworth: Penguin.

Goode, J. (1982) 'The development of effective home school programmes – a study of parental perspectives in the process of schooling', unpublished MPhil thesis. University of Nottingham.

Hackman, J.R. and Oldham, G.R. (1980) *Work Redesign*, Reading, MA.: Addison-Wesley.

Hargreaves, D.H. (1972) *Interpersonal Relations and Education*, London: Routledge and Kegan Paul.

—— (1980) 'The occupational culture of teachers', in P. Woods (ed.) *Teacher Strategies: Explorations in the Sociology of the School*, London: Croom Helm.

Hart, B. and Risley, T.R. (1976) 'Environmental reprogramming: implications for the severely handicapped', unpublished paper, Kansas: Center for Applied Behavior Analysis.

Hatton, E.J. (1985) 'Team teaching and teacher orientation to work: implications for the preservice and inservice education of teachers', *Journal of Education for Teaching* 11, 3: 228–44.

Heider, F. (1944) 'Social perception and phenomenal causality', *Psychological Review* 51: 358–74.

—— (1958) *The Psychology of Interpersonal Relations*, New York: Wiley.

HMI (1988) *A Survey of the Teaching of English as a Second Language in Six LEAs*, London: HMSO.

Hodgson, A., Clunies-Ross, L. and Hegarty, S. (1984) *Learning Together: Teaching Pupils with Special Educational Needs in the Ordinary School*, Windsor: NFER–Nelson.

Jackson, A. and Hannon, P. (1981) *The Belfield Reading Project*, Rochdale: Belfield Community Council.

Johnston, J.M. (1984) 'Problems of prekindergarten teachers: a basis for re-examining teacher education practices', *Journal of Teacher Education* 35, 2: 33–7.

Jones, E.E. and Davies, K.E. (1965) 'From acts to disposition: the attribution process in person perception', in L. Berkowitz (ed.) *Advances in Experimental Social Psychology* (Vol. 2), New York: Academic Press.

Jones, S. (1985) 'The analysis of depth interviews', in R. Walker (ed.) *Applied Qualitative Research*, Aldershot: Gower

Jowett, S. and Baginsky, M. (1988) 'Parents and education: a survey of their involvement and a discussion of some issues', *Educational Research* 30, 1: 36–45.

Kahn, R.L., Wolfe, D., Quinn, R., Snoeck, J. and Rosenthal, R. (1964) *Organizational Stress: Studies in Role Conflict and Ambiguity*, New York: Wiley.

Katzan, H. (1985) *A Manager's Guide to Productivity, Quality Circles and Industrial Robots*, New York: Van Nostrand Reinhold.

Kelly, G.A. (1955) *The Psychology of Personal Constructs*, Vols I and II, New York: Norton.

Knight, K. (1983) 'The case for DIY in organisation design', *Personnel Management* 15: 38–40.

Kounin, J.S. (1967) 'An analysis of teachers' managerial techniques', *Psychology in the Schools* 4: 221–7.

—— (1970) *Discipline and Group Management in Classrooms*, New York: Holt, Rinehart and Winston.

Krech, D., Crutchfield, R.S. and Ballachey, E.L. (1962) *Individual in Society*, New York: McGraw-Hill.

Kuhn, T. (1970) *The Structure of Scientific Revolutions* (2nd edn), Chicago: University of Chicago Press.

LeLaurin, K. and Risley, T.R. (1972) 'The organisation of day care environments: "zone" versus "man to man" staff assignments', *Journal of Applied Behaviour Analysis* 5, 3: 225–32.

Leyser, Y. (1985) 'Parent involvement in school: a survey of parents of handicapped students', *Contemporary Education* 57, 1: 38–43.

Likert, R. (1961) *New Patterns of Management*, New York: McGraw-Hill.

Linton, R. (1945) *The Cultural Background of Personality*, New York: Appleton-Century.

Lippitt, R., Watson, J. and Westley, B. (1958) *The Planning of Change*, New York: Harcourt Brace.

Macleod, F. (1985) 'Parental involvement in education: the Coventry experience', *Early Child Development and Care* 21: 83–90.

Magee, B. (1982) *Men of Ideas*, Oxford: Oxford University Press.

Malinowski, B. (1922) *Argonauts of the Western Pacific*, London: Routledge and Kegan Paul.

—— (1982) 'The diary of an anthropologist', in R.G. Burgess *Field Research: A Sourcebook and Field Manual*, London: George Allen and Unwin.

McBrien, J. and Weightman, J. (1980) 'The effect of room management procedures on the engagement of profoundly retarded children', *British Journal of Mental Subnormality* 26, 1: 38–46.

McCracken, G.D. (1988) *The Long Interview*, Beverly Hills: Sage.

McGregor, D. (1960) *The Human Side of Enterprise*, New York: McGraw-Hill.

Meighan, R. (1981) 'A new teaching force? Some issues raised by seeing parents as educators and the implications for teacher education', *Educational Review* 33, 2: 133–42.

Miskel, C., McDonald, D. and Bloom, S. (1983) 'Structural and expectancy linkages within schools and organisational effectiveness', *Educational Administration Quarterly* 19, 1: 49–82.

Monk, D.H. (1982) 'Resource allocation in classrooms: an economic analysis', *Journal of Curriculum Studies* 14, 2: 167–81.

Mortimore, J. and Mortimore, P. (1984) 'Parents and school', *Education* 164, 14: i–iv.

Newton, H. (1988) 'Deployment of support staff', unpublished MEd dissertation, University of Birmingham.

Nolan, R. (1977) 'Preparing teachers for collaboration: team teaching and open space', unpublished PhD dissertation, Stanford University.

Olesen, V.L. and Whittaker, E.W. (1970) 'Role making in participant observation: processes in the researcher–actor relationship', in N.K. Denzin *Sociological Methods*, London: Butterworth.

Olmstead, P.P. and Rubin, R.I. (1983) 'Linking parent behaviours to child achievement: four evaluation studies from the parent education follow through programme', *Studies in Educational Evaluation* 8: 317–25.

O'Hanlon, C. (1988) 'Alienation within the profession: special needs or watered down teachers? Insights into the tension between the ideal and the real through action research', *Cambridge Journal of Education* 18, 3: 297–311.

Paisey, A. (1981) *Small Organisations: The Management of Primary and Middle Schools*, Slough: NFER-Nelson.

Parlett, M. and Hamilton, D. (1987) 'Evaluation as illumination', in R. Murphy and H. Torrance (eds) *Evaluating Education: Issues and Methods*, London: Harper and Row.

Paul, W.J., Robertson, K.B. and Herzberg, F. (1969) 'Job enrichment pays off', *Harvard Business Review* 47: 61–79.

Popkewitz, T.S. (1984) *Paradigm and Ideology in Educational Research*, Lewes: Falmer.

Porterfield, J., Blunden, R. and Blewitt, E. (1977) *Improving environments for profoundly handicapped adults: establishing staff routines for high client engagement*, Cardiff: Mental Handicap in Wales Applied Research Unit, University College Wales, Cardiff.

Riches, C.R. (1982) 'The micropolitics of the management of non-teaching staff', *Educational Management and Administration* 10, 2: 151–6.

Robson, M. (1982) *Quality Circles: A Practical Guide*, Aldershot: Gower.

Roethlisberger, F.J. and Dixon, W.J. (1939) *Management and the Worker*, Cambridge, MA: Harvard University Press.

Sadler, D.R. (1984) 'Follow-up evaluation of an inservice programme based on action research: some methodological issues', *Journal of Education for Teaching* 10, 3: 209–18.

Scott, W.R. (1983) 'From technology to environment', in J.W. Meyer and W.R. Scott, *Organizational Environments*, Beverly Hills: Sage.

Secord, P.F. (1986) 'Social psychology as a science', in J. Margolis, P.T. Manicas, R. Harre and P.F. Secord *Psychology: Designing the Discipline*, Oxford: Blackwell.

Sewell, G. (1988) 'Free flow and the secondary school', in G. Thomas and A. Feiler *Planning for Special Needs*, Oxford: Blackwell.

Shaw, M.L. (ed.) (1981) *Recent Advances in Personal Construct Technology*, London: Academic Press.

Shulman, L.S. and Carey, N.B. (1984) 'Psychology and the limitations of individual rationality: implications for the study of reasoning and civility', *Review of Educational Research* 54, 4: 501–24.

Smyth, W.J. (1981) 'Research on classroom management: studies of pupil engaged learning time as a special but instructive case', *Journal of Education for Teaching* 7, 2: 127–48.

Spangler, P.F. and Marshall, A.M. (1983) 'The unit play manager as a facilitator of purposeful activities among institutionalised profoundly and severely retarded boys', *Journal of Applied Behaviour Analysis* 16, 3: 345–9.

Stainback, W. and Stainback, S. (1990) *Support Networks for Inclusive Schooling: Interdependent Integrated Education*. Baltimore: Paul H. Brookes.

Stallings, J.A. (1976) 'How instructional processes relate to child outcomes in a national study of Follow-Through', *Journal of Teacher Education* 27, 1: 43–7.

Stallings, J., Robbins, P., Presbrey, L. and Scott, J. (1986) 'Effects of instruction based on the Madeline Hunter model on students' achievement: findings from a Follow-Through project', *Elementary School Journal* 86, 5: 571–87.

Steiner, I.D. (1972) *Group Process and Productivity*, New York: Academic Press.

Stephenson, G. (1978) 'Social behaviour in organisations', in H. Tajfel and C. Fraser (eds) *Introducing Social Psychology*, Harmondsworth: Penguin.

Stewart, I. (1990) *Does God Play Dice?*, Harmondsworth: Penguin.

Stierer, B. (1985) 'School reading volunteers: results of a postal survey of primary school headteachers in England', *Journal of Research in Reading* 8, 1: 21–31.

Strain, P.S. and Kerr, M.M. (1981) *Mainstreaming of Children in Schools: Research and Programmatic Issues*, London: Academic Press.

Tajfel, H. and Fraser, C. (eds) (1978) *Introducing Social Psychology*, Harmondsworth: Penguin.

Thomas, G. (1985) 'What psychology had to offer education – then', *Bulletin of the British Psychological Society* 38: 322–6.

Thomas, M. (1985) 'Introduction to classroom management', in P.T. Farrell (ed.) *Proceedings of the 1983 EDY Users Conference*, Manchester: MUP.

Thousand, J.S. and Villa, R.A. (1990) 'Sharing expertise and responsibilities through teaching teams', in W. Stainback and S. Stainback *Support Networks for Inclusive Schooling: Interdependent Integrated Education*, Baltimore: Paul H. Brookes.

Tizard, B. (1981) 'Clift, P., Cleave, S. and Griffin, M. (1980) *The Aims, Role and Deployment of Staff in the Nursery* (Book review), *British Journal of Educational Psychology* 51: 128.

Tizard, B., Mortimore, J. and Burchell, B. (1981) *Involving Parents in Nursery and Infant Schools*, London: Grant McIntyre.

Tizard, J., Schofield, W.N. and Hewison, J. (1982) 'Collaboration between teachers and parents in assisting children's reading', *British Journal of Educational Psychology* 52: 1–15.

Toffler, A. (1985) *The Adaptive Corporation*, Aldershot: Gower.

Trendall, C. (1989) 'Stress in teaching and teacher effectiveness: a study of teachers across mainstream and special education', *Educational Research* 31, 1: 52–8.

Turner, R. (1952) 'Role taking: process versus conformity', in A. Rose (ed.) *Human Behavior and Social Processes*, Boston: Houghton-Mifflin.

Van Sell, M., Brief, A.P. and Schuler, R.S. (1981) 'Role conflict and role ambiguity: integration of the literature and directions for future research', *Human Relations* 34, 1: 43–71.

Ward, B.A. and Tikunoff, W.J. (1979) 'Utilizing nonteachers in the instructional process', in D.L. Duke (ed.) *Classroom Management*, Chicago: National Society for the Study of Education.

Ware, J. and Evans, P. (1987) 'Room management is not enough?', *British Journal of Special Education* 14, 2: 78–80.

Weiner, B. (ed.) (1974) *Achievement Motivation and Attribution Theory*, Morristown, NJ: General Learning Press.

Widlake, P. (1985) 'How should we respond to change', *British Journal of Special Education* 12, 2: 50–2.

Williamson, J. (1989) 'An extra radiator? Teachers' views of support teaching and withdrawal in developing the English of bilingual pupils', *Educational Studies* 15, 3: 315–26.

Wilson, A.J. (1988) 'Teachers' assumptions and beliefs about exceptionality',

paper presented at the fourth conference of the International Study Association on Teacher Thinking, University of Nottingham, September 1988.
—— (1989) 'Teacher development and colleague consultation: the case of the school based resource teacher', paper presented at the conference 'Teacher Development: Policies, Practices and Research', Ontario Institute for Studies in Education, Toronto, February 1989.
Woods, P.A. and Cullen, C. (1983) 'Determinants of staff behaviour in long term care', *Behavioural Psychotherapy* 11: 4–17.

NAME INDEX

SUBJECT INDEX